D1566440

The
Greatest
U.S. Army Stories
Ever Told

Thanks for your help with the story.

The
Greatest
U.S. Army Stories
Ever Told

**UNFORGETTABLE STORIES OF COURAGE,
HONOR, AND SACRIFICE**

IAIN C. MARTIN

THE LYONS PRESS
An imprint of The Globe Pequot Press
Guilford, Connecticut

"Washington's Crossing" from *Washington's Crossing* by David Hackett Fischer, copyright © 2004 by David Hackett Fischer. Used by permission of Oxford University Press, Inc.

"Dispatches from the Mexican War" from *Dispatches from the Mexican War* by George Wilkins Kendall, © 1999 by the University of Oklahoma Press, Norman, Publishing Division of the University. All Rights Reserved.

Selection from "Old Hickory's Finest Hour" copyright © by Thomas Fleming. Reprinted by permission of Military History Quarterly. All rights reserved.

Selection from *Yanks: The Epic Story of the American Army in World War I* by John S. D. Eisenhower with Joanne T. Eisenhower, reprinted with the permission of The Free Press, a Division of Simon & Schuster Adult Publishing Group. Copyright © 2001 by John S. D. Eisenhower. All rights reserved.

"My War-Normandy" from *My War* by Andy Rooney. Copyright © 1995 by Essay Productions, Inc. Reprinted by permission. Reprinted with the permission of Simon & Schuster Adult Publishing Group

"And Yet We Got On" used by permission, © 2000 Scripps Howard News Service. All Rights Reserved.

"The Longest Day" from *The Longest Day* by Cornelius Ryan. Copyright © 1959 by Cornelius Ryan; copyright © renewed 1987 by Kathryn Mrgan Ryan, Victoria Ryan Bida and Geoffrey J. M. Ryan.

"Dachau" Copyright © 1945 by The New York Times Co. Reprinted with permission.

"The Story of the Bulge" from *Battle: The Story of the Bulge* by John Toland. Copyright © 1959, 1987 by John Toland. Reprinted by permission of Brandt and Hochman Literary Agents, Inc.

Selection from "Lovely Americans" by Robert Shaplen, originally published in *The New Yorker Magazine*, Copyright © 1945 by Robert Shaplen. Reprinted by permission of the Estate of Robert Shaplen.

"Inchon" from *The Korean War* by Matthew B. Ridgway, copyright © 1967 by Matthew B. Ridgway. Used by permission of Doubleday, a division of Random House, Inc.

Selection from *A Reporter's Journal from Hell* (www.digitaljournalist.org). Copyright © 2002 by Joe Galloway. Reprinted by permission.

Selection from *If I Die in a Combat Zone* by Tim O'Brien, copyright © 1973 by Tim O'Brien. Used by permission of Dell Publishing, a division of Random House, Inc.

Selection from *Crusade: The Untold Story of the Persian Gulf War* by Rick Atkinson. Copyright © 1993 by Rick Atkinson. Reprinted by permission of Houghton Mifflin Company. All rights reserved.

Selection from *Black Hawk Down* by Mark Bowden. Copyright © 1999 by Mark Bowden. Used by permission of Grove/Atlantic, Inc.

Selection from *Among Warriors in Iraq* by Mike Tucker copyright © 2005 by Mike Tucker. Used by permission of The Lyons Press.

The Lyons Press is an imprint of The Globe Pequot Press.

10 8 6 4 2 1 3 5 7 9

Printed in the United States of America

ISBN-13: 978-1-59228-858-8
ISBN-10: 1-59228-858-8

Design by Compset, Inc.

The Library of Congress Cataloging-in-Publication Data is available on file.

Contents

Introduction

Duty, Honor, Country

The greatest army of the modern era began with the most humble of origins. Colonial townships, in need of organizing their own defenses, established local militia forces. These men volunteered to assemble and train periodically under leaders elected by each company. Each man would supply his own weapon, ammunition, clothing, and food. In a time of crisis they would be expected to rally and protect the lives and well-being of their fellow citizens. In times of war they may have been sent to regions unknown in support of British regulars under the command of English officers. Militia units had served the British well in the French and Indian War, yet they were never accorded the respect held only for European regular soldiers.

It was these same citizen soldiers who defied the British as they stood in the path of the advancing redcoats at Lexington green on the morning of April 19, 1775. In the "shot heard around the world" their stand against tyranny ended in bloodshed. Eight men where killed and ten wounded—an unthinkable price for a small township. As the British moved on to Concord the word spread, and the militia formed along the flanks of the British column. Their attacks forced the British to fall back to Boston, suffering over 270 casualties. The war for independence had begun. Militia from all over the colonies marched toward Boston where they put the British effectively under siege.

The Continental Army was born of necessity on June 14, 1775, to meet the threat of all-out war. Congress undertook to raise ten companies of expert riflemen, and appointed a committee that included George Washington to draft rules and regulations for the government of the army. The riflemen authorized on June 14 were the first units raised directly as Continentals, a standing force under the direct supervision of Congress and military authority. Congress intended to have the ten companies serve as a light infantry force for the Boston siege. At the same time it symbolically extended military participation beyond New England by allocating six of the companies to

Pennsylvania, two to Maryland, and two to Virginia. Each company would have a captain, three lieutenants, four sergeants, four corporals, a drummer, and sixty-eight privates. The following day Congress unanimously elected George Washington to lead the Continentals, granting him the rank of General and Commander-in-Chief.

Washington was the natural choice for the job. He was one of the most experienced colonials, having fought bravely in the French and Indian War, where he commanded militia forces. Congress hoped that Washington's appointment to command would help win support from the southern colonies. For what he lacked in experience he made up for with personal qualities of determination, a belief in the American cause for independence, and a sense of honor and dignity that inspired respect and confidence in all around him. In the habit of wearing his old uniform to the military committee meetings at Congress, the six-foot-tall Washington cut an impressive figure. In a time of great confusion, chaos, and uncertainty, the formation of the Continental Army and the appointment of Washington to command was one of the greatest achievements of the Continental Congress.

It is entirely appropriate the origins of the United States Army began with citizen soldiers. Unlike the European armies with traditions of inherited privileges, purchased titles, servitude soldiers, and mercenary allies, the Americans were bound by an understanding that to live as free men they must first work together to overcome all challenges. This sense of individualism and spirit has never left the American soldier. It also validates the concept of volunteer service. A soldier from a free society, who volunteers to serve in a cause deemed righteous, is a force to be reckoned with. As an instrument of force, the United States Army was founded with the mission to protect American freedoms, a role that it has served from 1775 to the present day.

Collected in this volume are twenty-three true stories selected for their narrative and historical merits. The authors range from professional soldiers to draftees, from journalists to historians. They are presented in chronological order and cover all the major conflicts from the American Revolution to the current war in Iraq. The intent of this work is not a glorification of war, but a tribute to those who served and continue to serve, a means of reflection and remembrance, and above all, to provide an engaging read by some of the greatest authors to write about the United States Army.

—IAIN C. MARTIN
CLINTON, CONNECTICUT
JANUARY 27, 2006

Washington's Crossing

DAVID HACKETT FISCHER

Here succeeded a scene of war, which I had often conceived but never saw before. The hurry, fright, and confusion of the enemy was [not] unlike that which will be when the last trump shall sound.
—Colonel Henry Knox, December 28, 1776

There are few moments in American history that rival the importance of events in December of 1776. The euphoria of declaring independence from England that July had been tempered by a major defeat of General Washington's Continental Army at the battle of Long Island in August. Washington avoided catastrophe with cunning and luck on the night of August 27, when his army crossed the East River at night leaving their campfires burning as they escaped. The British Army under Maj. General William Howe routed Washington's army from New York and across New Jersey, defeating them again at White Plains and securing Fort Washington and Fort Lee, taking thousands of rebel prisoners along the way.

In early December, Washington moved his army across the Delaware river into Pennsylvania as a new force of 6,000 men under British Lt. General Charles Cornwallis approached Trenton. The American position was dire. Washington's army was greatly reduced at the end of November when many of the enlistments in his army ran out. Only 4,700 men remained fit for duty. A second round of enlistments would run out on December 31, reducing his force to a mere 1,500 men. Food and supplies were critically short, and many soldiers lacked winter clothing. His loss of New York and retreat from New Jersey left the Continentals and militia without a victory over British regulars. Morale among the ranks was low. Members of the Continental Congress, which had fled from Philadelphia to Baltimore, were beginning to question his ability to lead. As the weather grew colder, Washington knew the British would continue to move against him after the river had frozen. The time had come for decisive action to secure a victory over the enemy or the revolution could fail with the onset of winter.

A Hessian garrison under Col. Johann Rall had taken winter quarters in Trenton across the river. Washington planned a surprise attack for the morning after Christmas with two divisions under Nathaniel Greene and John Sullivan. Twenty-four hundred Continentals and militia would cross the river under the cover of darkness to attack the Hessians at dawn. The poor weather conditions and effects of Christmas celebrations in the enemy camp would work in their favor, yet it was a daring mission fraught with danger. Washington ordered the watchword for the mission to be 'Victory or Death.'

At 11:00 PM a heavy snowstorm began, which soon became freezing rain. The river was choked with ice. An officer would write in his journal, "It is fearfully cold and raw and a snow-storm is setting in. The wind is northeast and beats in the faces of the men. It will be a terrible night for the soldiers who have no shoes. Some of them have tied old rags around their feet; others are barefoot, but I have not heard a man complain. They are ready to suffer any hardship and die rather than give up their liberty." As the men entered the boats to cross the river, their officers read to them the words of Thomas Paine's *The Crisis*, written only days earlier in Philadelphia, "These are the times that try men's souls. The summer soldier and the sunshine patriot will, in this crisis, shrink from the service of their country; but he that stands by it now, deserves the love and thanks of man and woman. Tyranny, like hell, is not easily conquered; yet we have this consolation with us, that the harder the conflict, the more glorious the triumph."

By 4:00 AM Washington's force had navigated the river crossing and prepared for the ten-mile march to Trenton. Author David Hackett Fischer describes the battle from his acclaimed *Washington's Crossing*.

★   ★   ★   ★   ★

The American columns were now about two miles from Trenton, and the time was about 7:30 in the morning. George Washington urged his men forward, hoping to salvage something from his ruined plan. They had already passed the hour of sunrise, which was 7:20 local time, but no sun was in sight that day. The nor'easter was raging more violently than ever, and the clouds were very thick. One American remembered that the weather was "dark and stormy so that we could not see very far ahead." Sleet and snow were falling heavily again, with intervals of heavy rain. The men struggled to keep their flints and powder dry. Some wrapped their weapons in the blankets that Robert Morris had brought them.

As the Americans moved closer to the town, scouts came up to Washington and reported the location of Hessian outposts. The German commanders had established a ring of forward positions about a mile outside the center of Trenton. One large outpost (in company strength) was on the River Road to the west. Another with twenty-four men was near the intersection of the Scotch Road and the Pennington Road to the northwest. A third guarded the Princeton Road to the northeast, and others protected the bridge over Assunpink Creek south of the town, and the ferry landing. Many "night sentries" were posted in between, five or seven from each outpost. At first light they were replaced by "day pickets."

Colonel Rall had been thorough in his precautions. German outguards covered every major approach by land into Trenton, and other men were in place along the Delaware river. Behind the outposts were duty companies that could offer support. In the center of town, one Hessian regiment was always on alert in "alarm houses," and the others were ready to muster quickly.

George Washington was well informed about the German dispositions in Trenton. His tactical intelligence was excellent this day. After hearing from his scouts, Washington halted the American left wing on the Pennington Road, behind a screen of woods. They were about eight hundred yards from the Hessian guardhouse, a small wood-frame cooper shop that belonged to Richard and Arthur Howell, a mile from the town center. Senior American officers deployed their brigades in three attacking columns: Mercer's New Englanders and Maryland men on the right; Stephen's Virginians with Stirling's Delaware men in the center; and Fermoy's Pennsylvanians on the American left. The vanguard were Virginia infantry, led by Captain William Washington and Lieutenant James Monroe.

On command the three columns started forward in a thick flurry of snow. George Washington himself led the attack in the center. As the men emerged from the woods into open fields on both sides of the road, Washington picked up the pace. One soldier remembered that he led them forward at a "long trot" across the fields. Peering ahead through dense clouds of swirling snow, they saw a door open at the cooper shop, and a Hessian emerged. An American raised his weapon, fired at long range, and missed. Other Hessians ran out of the cooper shop, pulling on their coats and equipment. The Americans managed to get off a ragged volley in the storm, then a second and a third. The Hessians formed and fired back.

The time was a little past eight o'clock. Three minutes later, the heavy boom of American artillery was heard from the lower River Road. In the center of the town, German kettledrums suddenly began to beat the urgent call to arms. George Washington could scarcely believe it. Both American wings attacked at nearly the same moment, through a heavy squall of snow that masked their approach. Against all expectation, they had taken the Hessians by surprise.

The Hessian who appeared in the door of the cooper shop on the upper road was Lieutenant Andreas von Wiederholdt. He had been sent to take command of the outpost after the raid on Christmas night. The strength of the outpost was doubled, and Wiederholdt's orders were very clear. With his twenty-four men he was told to put out night sentries beyond the cooper shop to give warning of a surprise attack, to send out a dawn patrol before first light, and to put day pickets in position from sunrise to sunset.

Weiderholdt had followed his instructions, and even exceeded them. Later he wrote that he "sent out seven posts, as well as I could during the night, and sent out one patrol after another to prevent being surprised." His night sentries made a chain that stretched from Wiederholdt's position in the cooper shop to the outguards from the River Road to his left and to the outpost on the Princeton Road to his right. Other outpost commanders did the same thing on that Christmas night.

Then came the storm. Wiederholdt remembered that "the night passed quietly." At first light he recalled his sentries and sent out a dawn patrol. By now the weather was very bad, and the patrol appears not to have ventured far beyond the cooper shop. Wiederholdt remembered that before eight o'clock "my day patrol was already back for a while, reporting that everything was silent and quiet."

After a week of constant alarms, and the American raid on Christmas evening, Weiderholdt's men were very tired. Many had been on sentry duty or patrol through the night, and again at dawn. In the morning, as the storm grew more violent than ever, they relaxed their vigilance a little. Weiderholdt testified that his seven day pickets were all in place, but he complained that they were not very alert, and they saw nothing in the storm. The lieutenant allowed his seventeen men who were not on picket to get warm and dry in the cooper shop, as any good officer would have done.

Inside the building the air must have grown very stale, with so many men who bathed so seldom in so small a space. At about eight o'clock Weiderholdt decided to step outside. He stood for a moment by the door and looked across the frozen fields toward the woods along the Pennington Road. As he peered through the storm, he dimly saw something moving in the distance. Weiderholdt looked again through a white veil of snow and made out the shapes of men coming toward him. He first thought that they were the patrol of Captain Johann Brubach, the inspector of the guard, who made his rounds every morning, checking each outpost and sentry outside the town. Brubach sometimes approached from that direction.

As Weiderholdt studied the distant figures in the storm, they began to multiply. He counted sixty, too many to be Captain Brubach's small party. Then one of the figures stopped and raised a weapon. Weiderholdt saw the muzzle flash, then another, and a third. He turned to his men and shouted, "*Der Feind!* The Enemy!"

The Hessians came running out of the cooper shop, tugging on their equipment. "We were quickly under arms," Weiderholdt remembered, "and we waited to give the enemy a firm challenge, thinking they were merely a roaming party. They fired three volleys at me and my seventeen men, who held their fire. After the third volley I gave the order to fire." They were at extreme range; nobody on either side appears to have been hit in the first exchange.

Wiederholdt began to see the full size of the American attack. This was no raiding party. Hundreds of men were now visible, advancing through the fields on both sides of the road. He was seeing Mercer's brigade southwest of the Pennington Road, Stephen and Stirling in the middle, and Fermoy to the east. Together they threatened a double envelopment of the small Hessian outpost. Weiderholdt later wrote, "We fought with them until we were almost surrounded by several battalions. I therefore retreated, under constant fire."

The American brigades pressed forward. Washington ordered Fermoy's troops to move east across the country to block the Princeton Road. That task went to Edward Hand's veteran regiment of Pennsylvania Riflemen and Haussegger's battalion of German-speaking infantry from Pennsylvania and western Maryland. They responded quickly and attacked the Hessian outguard on the Princeton Road. Weiderholdt looked to the right, and saw the Hessians fall back. His men were doing the same thing.

The two Hessian detachments withdrew in good order toward the town in a fighting retreat. They converged on the high ground at the north end of Trenton where the main streets came together. There a duty company of Lossberg troops under Captain Ernst von Altenbockum came forward to help them. Weiderholdt remembered, "While we had been engaging the enemy this company formed a line in the street in front of the captain's quarters. I took a position on their right wing and together we fired at the enemy. But soon we were forced to retire in the same manner as before so that we would not be cut off from the garrison."

The American infantry were closer now, and some were able to fire their muskets in the storm. Weiderholdt remembered that Hessians began to fall. Captain Altenbockum's company fought stubbornly against heavy odds, with the outguards at their side. The Hessians fell back slowly toward the village, using houses and outbuildings for cover. The fighting retreat of these small Hessian detachments, against heavy pressure from half the American army, was done with courage and skill. George Washington observed them with a keen professional eye and admired their performance. After the battle he went out of his way to mention that the Hessian outguards "behaved very well, keeping up a constant retreating fire from behind houses."

On the River Road, the other wing of the American army advanced toward the lower end of the town at the same time. General Sullivan led from the front, with Captain John Flahaven's New Jersey troops in the van and Colonel John Stark's New Hampshire brigade close behind. Just ahead of the Americans was a small house close to the road where the Hessians had posted a day picket. Beyond it was the Hermitage, General Philemon Dickinson's home. The Hessians made it their main outpost on the River Road and held it with a company of Jägers under Lieutenant Friedrich von Gröthausen.

As the Americans came forward along the River Road, a Hessian picket fired at them. Lieutenant von Gröthausen heard the shot, mustered his Jägers at the Hermitage, and led them forward to support his picket. The Americans moved into the fields on both sides of the road and brought their artillery into action. Major James Wilkinson remembered, "It was now broad day, and the storm beat violently in our faces. The attack had commenced on the left, and was immediately answered by Colonel Stark in our front, who forced the enemy's picket."

John Stark had a reputation as a fighter. He was devoted to the Revolutionary cause and wrote to his wife that he was determined to "live free or die," a phrase that his state later made its motto. Stark had trained his New Hampshiremen to use the bayonet, and he led them forward through the fields along the River Road. The Hessians were astonished to see the despised American rebels running toward them through the storm with "fixed bayonets." Lieutenant von Gröthausen retrieved his pickets and ordered his men to fall back.

As the Hessian Jägers retreated toward Trenton, the Americans launched yet another part of their attack. Massed artillery on the Pennsylvania side of the Delaware began firing into the town. That part of the battle does not appear in most American accounts, but Hessians remembered it well and testified that they came under heavy fire from seven batteries across the river. Solid shot smashed the ice along the waterfront, and shells "from the Howitzers on the other side of the Delaware" exploded around the Hessian positions. German troops near the water's edge were forced to leave their posts "on account of the cannonade." Trenton was now under heavy attack from three sides.

In the center of town, the three Hessian regiments came running out of their quarters at the first sound of firing at the Hessian outposts. They were alert and responded quickly to the attack. Boston fifer John Greenwood was there and wrote later in his memoir, "I am willing to go upon oath, that I did not see even a solitary drunken soldier belonging to the enemy,—and you will find, as I shall show, that I had an opportunity to be as good a judge as any person there."

The German responses to the American attack were not those of intoxicated revelers. When the alarm sounded, the three Hessian regiments in the center of town formed rapidly near their quarters. There was no single alarm post for the entire garrison, but every unit had its own place and went to it, as they had done the day before. The Rall regiment was the "*regiment du jour*" and had been on full alert in their alarm houses all that night, ready to march at a minute's warning. They assembled in a few moments on lower King Street and moved up the street to pick up their colors at Colonel Rall's headquarters. The other two regiments had been sleeping in full uniform, with cartridge boxes strapped on. They also assembled very quickly. The Regiment von Lossberg formed on King Street, and the Regiment von Knyphausen gathered near the lower Queen Street, by the Quaker meetinghouse.

When the first shots rang out, the Hessian brigade adjutant, Lieutenant Jakob Piel, sprinted to Colonel Rall's headquarters on King Street and shouted, "*Der Feind! Der Feind! Heraus! Heraus!* The enemy! Turn out!" Piel ran to alert others, then returned to find Rall standing at a window in his nightshirt.

"*Was ist los?*" Rall shouted. "What's the matter?"

"Do you not hear the firing?" Piel asked.

"I will be there immediately!" Rall answered. He dressed quickly, ran out of his headquarters, and mounted his horse.

As the Hessian regiments began to form, the American infantry converged on Trenton from two directions. On the River Road, John Stark and his New Hampshiremen continued their attack from the west and "pressed it into the town." Wilkinson remembered that "the enemy made a momentary shew of resistance by a wild and undirected fire from the windows of their quarters which they abandoned as we advanced, and made an attempt to form in the main street, which might have succeeded."

Greene's division approached the upper part of the town from the north, with Washington in the lead. The American troops were running forward in open order through the snow. Colonel Clement Biddle wrote, "Indeed I never could conceive that one spirit should so universally animate both officers and men to rush forward into action." They occupied the high ground at the head of King and Queen streets and could see the entire town below.

Lieutenant Wiederholdt's retreating Hessian outguards and Captain Altenbockum's company of Lossbergers resisted bravely, but the larger American force flowed around them on both flanks. To avoid being cut off, the Hessians retreated to another position "in the town at the first houses and fired at the enemy, who were forming for battle on the heights above." The Hessian outpost troops were very tired. They also felt very much alone. Wiederholdt wrote that "no one came to see what was happening, or to reinforce and assist us. But they did their duty."

A few moments later Colonel Rall rode up and asked for a report. It was a fateful conversation. Weiderholdt told him that this was not another small raid, that "the enemy was strong, that they were not only above the town but were already around it on both the left and the right." Rall inquired about numbers. Wiederholdt answered that he did not know but had seen four or five battalions "moving out of the woods."

Wiederholdt was accurate in most ways, but he was mistaken in one vital fact. The American troops were not yet around the town "on both the left and the right." They were attacking from the west and north of Trenton. The Hessians still held the stone bridge across Assunpink Creek, which led to good defensive ground southeast of the city. Had Colonel Rall made a fighting retreat across the bridge, he could have put his brigade in a strong position on rising land behind the creek, with his front and flanks protected. In that position his three regiments would not have been easy to defeat. They would also have had an open line of communication with Donop's Hessians at Mount Holly, Stirling's Highlanders at Blackhorse, and Leslie's troops at Princeton, by way of Crosswicks, which was guarded by a Hessian detachment.

That response might have caused major trouble for George Washington, who knew the desperate risk that he was running. If the initial American assault did not succeed quickly, the small Continental army would be in grave danger. Even a drawn battle at Trenton would put it in a perilous situation, surrounded by four British and Hessian brigades, which greatly outnumbered the Americans. An awakened enemy who moved with energy and decision could trap them against an ice-choked river. The result could be another heavy defeat for Washington's army, even its destruction.

And what if the Continental army were destroyed? After so many defeats around New York, another disaster could end Washington's command. The recruitment of another American army would become difficult, perhaps impossible. Without an army, the American Revolution could become yet another failed rebellion, much like the Scottish rising of 1745, or the Irish insurrection of 1798. American independence could have been lost on the banks of the Delaware.

In that multitude of might-have-beens, several facts are clear enough. Lieutenant Wiederholdt reported erroneously that the Americans had enveloped the town, nearly an hour before they succeeded in doing so. Colonel Rall responded with a decision not to retreat across the creek, but to counterattack the Americans in the town. The Hessian commander seemed not to know that a line of retreat was still open to good ground just beyond the creek. Later in the battle, Colonel Rall discovered what had happened. A Hessian officer remembered that Rall "sent Lieutenant Piel to the Bridge in order to see if they could still get through." By then it was too late.

Colonel Rall was also misled in another way, by his own contempt for the American attackers. His attitude was not unreasonable, given the conduct of American troops in the battles around New York. In Trenton, Rall often remarked that a ragtag force of rebels could never stand against German Regulars. He also had a habit of responding to an attack with a strong counterattack, which was German tactical doctrine in many wars. For all of these reasons, Colonel Rall decided to fight the Americans by attacking directly against their main strength inside the town of Trenton. It was a mistake of historic consequence.

While Wiederholdt and Rall discussed the situation, the American artillery unlimbered on the heights that commanded the town, and the infantry deployed into line. With them on the high ground (very near the present battle monument) was George Washington. He had a clear view of the town below, the river beyond, and Assunpink Creek to his left. To his right he could see Sullivan's division marching toward the town along the River Road. Just below him to the right, Mercer's brigade was moving down the hill along the west side of the town and entering the village through house lots and alleys. Some American troops were getting into the houses and outbuildings and taking positions that commanded the street.

Inside the town, Washington could see the Rall regiment as it formed by the alarm house, marched up King Street to Rall's headquarters, and brought out its regimental colors. He saw the Lossberg Regiment join them and the Knyphausen Regiment form in the lower part of Queen Street below the Friends meetinghouse and move to the right into an open field east of the meetinghouse. Washington remembered, "we presently saw their main body formed, but from their motions they seemed undetermined how to act."

Colonel Rall observed the Americans on the heights and called to his men, "Artillery Forward!" The German artillerymen ran to their guns by the Hessian headquarters on King Street and brought out their heavy horses, which had been kept permanently in harness for such an emergency. Rall ordered his artillery officers to take two guns up King Street and to go into action against the Americans on the heights above. With great speed, Artillery Lieutenants Johann Engelhardt and Friedrich Fischer collected eighteen men, hitched eight horses to the two guns, and led them up the hill to "the first houses in the street." In a few minutes they opened fire on the Americans above them and got off twelve quick rounds against the American artillery. One Hessian shot hit the fore-horse on an American three-pounder. Sergeant John Greenwood saw the animal "struck in its belly and knocked over on its back. While it lay there kicking the cannon was stopped."

Under fire, the American artillery came into action on the high ground above the Hessian gunners. General Stirling watched as they "soon got two field pieces at play and several others in a short time." Captain Thomas Forrest's large Pennsylvania battery opened fire with its two big six-pounders and two five-and-a-half-inch howitzers. The New York batteries joined in. Captain Alexander Hamilton brought two guns into action, and Captain Sebastian Baumann's New York battery added three guns more. The gunners bent over their pieces in a heavy fall of wet snow, sheltering their powder and touchholes as best they could. The storm was beating down more violently than ever. Visibility was poor, and the guns were very wet. Merely to fire any weapon in that weather was an achievement.

The American artillery overpowered the Hessian guns and laid down a concentration of fire at the vital center of the battle. Solid iron shot bounded down King Street, toward the German artillery. Five horses were hit and fell terribly wounded in the street. Eight Hessian gunners went down. The rest were driven away from the guns by grapeshot and by heavy musketry from American infantry, who were firing from houses on their flank. The German artillerymen remembered that the American musketry was even more destructive than the batteries on the hill. Finally these brave Hessian gunners could stand no more. German Lieutenants Fischer and Engelhardt ordered their men to fall back. They abandoned the guns, retreated to the bottom of the town, and led their men across the bridge over Assunpink Creek to the hill beyond.

Behind the German guns, the grenadiers of the Rall regiment in King Street were now exposed to the American artillery. Ensign Carl Wilhelm Kleinschmidt remembered that "the enemy were firing on them with their cannon, and many men of the regiment had already been wounded." They recoiled in disorder. Colonel Rall appeared, always in the thick of the fight. He led them out of the line of fire, took them east through the house lots and a churchyard, and rallied the infantry behind the English Church in the center of the town. The Lossberg regiment gathered there as well.

Rall led both regiments of Hessian infantry east to a large apple orchard just beyond the houses and turned them north. His object was to move against the Americans on the heights above the town and to attack them on their flank. Over the noise of battle, the Hessian troops heard him shout, "Forward! Advance! Advance!" Both the Rall and Lossberg regiments followed him up the hill.

On the high ground above, George Washington saw the Hessian regiments rally in the apple orchard and watched them start up the hill toward his flank. With great speed and presence of mind, he instantly sent an order to Edward Hand's Pennsylvania Rifle Regiment and Haussegger's Pennsylvania and Maryland German regiment. They were told to shift to the east beyond the Hessians, who were advancing up the hill toward the Americans. Hand and Haussegger acted "with Spirit and Rapidity." They moved quickly beyond the Princeton Road and formed a line on the higher ground with a clear field of fire. That counterstroke defeated the Hessian design. If Colonel Rall had led his men forward to strike at what had been Washington's flank, the American regiments beyond the Princeton Road would now be on Rall's flank, and the German troops would be caught between two fires. Washington's quick reaction checked Rall's advance just as it was getting under way.

More bad news was brought to the Hessian commander. Colonel Rall learned that two Hessian guns had been abandoned before the enemy in King Street. Worse, they were the guns of his own regiment. Their loss would be a heavy blow to the honor of his unit. The Hessian colonel turned his men toward the center of the town, and shouted, "*Alle was meine Grenatir seyn, vor werds! All* who are my grenadiers, forward!" The men shared their colonel's concern for the honor of their regiment. Grenadier Reuber wrote proudly that the "grenadiers stormed to recapture the cannons." Many of these men loved and respected their brave colonel. They would have followed him to Hell, and that was where he led them.

With drums beating and colors flying, two regiments of Hessian infantry marched back toward King Street in the center of town, determined to rescue the guns and rout the rebels. They moved straight into a cone of American fire that came at them from three directions. Directly ahead were the infantry of Mercer's brigade, in houses and outbuildings where they were able to dry their muskets and fire from cover. Rall's regiments were in the open. In the rain and snow, many Hessians were unable to return fire with their wet weapons. To the Hessian right, Lord Stirling's American infantry moved down the hill against them, and the American artillery on the heights fired from the flank. On the Hessian left, St. Clair's brigade entered the town by the River Road, moved up King Street, and engaged the German troops from the other side. The American attackers used their artillery brilliantly as shock weapons, just as Henry Knox had intended. At the lower end of town, the New England battery came forward with St. Clair's troops and caught the advancing Hessians in a deadly crossfire.

With great courage, the Hessian infantry drove doggedly forward into King Street and recovered the German guns. "We got them back," Grenadier Reuber wrote triumphantly, but it was another thing to keep them. The Americans were fighting with a determination that the Hessians had not seen before. Sergeant Joseph White's crew worked their gun so hard that they shattered its carriage. White wrote, "The third shot we fired

broke the axle tree of the piece,—we stood there some time idle, they firing upon us."

Colonel Henry Knox rode up to Sergeant White's ruined gun,
looked toward the Hessian artillery, and said, "My brave lads, go up and
take those two held pieces sword in hand. There is a party going and you
must join them." The battery commander repeated the order, which was
sometimes necessary with these insubordinate Yankees. Captain John Allen
said, "You heard what the colonel said, Sergeant White. Now take your
men and join the others in the attack."

White's New Englanders joined the party and found that it consisted mainly of Virginians, "commanded by Captain Washington and Lieutenant Monroe." The Virginia infantry and New England gunners charged
side by side straight toward the Hessian guns. James Monroe wrote, "Captain Washington rushed forward, attacked and put the troops around the
cannon to flight and took possession of them." In the melee, William Washington went down, badly wounded in both hands. James Monroe took over
"at the head of the corps" and led it forward. He too was hit by a musket
ball, which severed an artery. He was carried from the field, bleeding dangerously. His life was saved by Doctor Riker, who had joined Monroe's
company as a volunteer the night before. The New Jersey physician
clamped Monroe's artery just in time to keep him from bleeding to death.

At the guns, Sergeant White took command. He remembered, "I
hallowed as loud as I could scream to the men to run for their lives right
up to the pieces. I was the first that reach them [the Hessian guns]. They
had all left it except one man tending the vent." White shouted, "Run, you
dog!" He raised his sword above the Hessian's head, who "looked up, and
saw it, then run." The American gunners seized the guns and turned one of
them toward the German infantry. White wrote, "We put in a canister of
shot (they had put in a cartridge before they left it,) and fired."

On the other side, Hessian grenadier Johann Reuber wrote, "the
rebels attacked us ferociously. Near Colonel Rall's quarters there was a barricade of boards and in front of that stood our two company cannon. As the
Americans were attempting to reach the cannon we of Rall's Grenadier
regiment encountered them, directly in front of Rall's headquarters. The
fight was furious. The rebels dismantled the barricade and now we lost the
greater part of our artillery and the rebels were about to use them."

The German troops suffered many killed and wounded. The Lossberg regiment lost seventy men in this struggle. The American infantry

were aiming at the Hessian officers and brought down four Lossberger captains. Colonel Rall was in the thick of it. As another junior officer went down, Rall turned to console him. Then the colonel himself was hit and "reeled in the saddle," shot twice in the side; both wounds were mortal. The dying German commander was helped off his horse, carried into the church, and laid upon a bench.

In the center of Trenton the battle became a bedlam of sound. The streets echoed with the thunder of artillery, the crash of iron on brick and stone, the noise of splintering wood and shattering glass, the roar of musketry, the clash of steel against steel, the mingled shouts and curses, and the cries of wounded men. On the vast scale of human slaughter this eighteenth-century battle was nothing to compare with other wars, but its very close combat of cold steel, massed musketry, and cannon at point-blank range created a scene of horror beyond imagining.

The Americans were appalled by the carnage that they had caused. Henry Knox wrote, "here succeeded a scene of war of which I had often conceived but never saw before. The hurry, fright, and confusion of the enemy was [not] unlike that which will be when the last trump shall sound." Sergeant Joseph White felt the same way: "My blood chill'd to see such horror and distress, blood mingling together, the dying groans, and 'Garments rolled in blood.' The sight was too much to bear."

The civilian inhabitants of Trenton were caught up in the violence. Among them was little Martha Reed, then a small child, who always remembered the horror of "that awful day," as she called it. "In the grey dawn, came the beating of drums, and the sound of firing," she wrote, "the soldiers quartered in our house, hastily decamped, all was uproar and confusion. My mother and we children hid in the cellar to escape the shots that fell about the house." Her family survived, but others were not so lucky. Martha Reed remembered that "our next door neighbor was killed on his doorstep," and "a bullet struck the blacksmith as he was in the act of closing himself in his cellar, and many other townspeople were injured by chance shots." One young woman was running from one house to another when a musket ball hit the high comb in her hair. She lived to tell the story and said that she was happy not to be half an inch taller. At least one American woman joined the fight. A German recalled that "the inhabitants shot at the Hessians from their houses. In fact even a woman fired out of her window and mortally wounded a captain."

Under heavy fire, the charge of the Hessians failed. They had fought valiantly but were overwhelmed by the weight of American fire.

Slowly, grudgingly, the German troops began to give way, and the broken German regiments retreated. Reuber, the Hessian grenadier, believed that the turning point was the loss of Colonel Rall. "If he had not been severely wounded they would not have taken us alive!" he wrote. A Lossberger thought differently. "Our muskets could not fire any more on account of the rain and snow and the rebels fired on us from, within the houses," one of them wrote, "the Regiment von Lossberg lost in this affair 70 men killed and wounded. . . . Our whole disaster was entirely due to Colonel Rall."

Some of the Hessians fled into buildings and basements. Most retreated to the east, away from the town, followed closely by the oncoming Americans, only fifty paces behind. Greenwood remembered that his men ran "after them pell mell. Some of the Hessians took refuge in a church at the door of which we stationed a guard to keep them in, and taking no further care of them for the present, advanced to find more, for many had run down into the cellars of the houses."

Greenwood's regiment advanced through the place where the fighting had been most severe. He wrote, "I passed two of their cannon, brass six-pounders, by the side of which lay seven dead Hessians, and a brass drum. This latter article was, I remember, of great curiosity to me and I stopped to look at it, but it was quickly taken possession of by one of our drummers, who threw away his own instrument." American troops left ranks and scoured the ground for souvenirs. Greenwood wrote that he "obtained a sword from one of the bodies," and "we then ran to join our regiment. He remembered that "General Washington, on horseback and alone, came up to our major and said, 'March on, my brave fellows, after me!' and rode off." Most American soldiers in this battle shared that memory of serving by the side of General Washington. They knew him not only as a leader but a comrade in arms.

The remnants of the Rall and Lossberg regiments retreated to the orchard east of town. They were now without their colonel, and many companies had lost their captains and lieutenants. These highly disciplined men kept some of their cohesion, but they were confused and surrounded. The fight drained out of them, and they did not know what to do.

American infantry and artillery moved forward around them, and the men in Haussegger's Pennsylvania and Maryland German regiment began to call "in German and English to stack their weapons and surrender." An American officer, perhaps Washington's aide George Baylor, rode toward the Hessians and spoke with the senior German officers, Lieutenant Colonel

Francis Scheffer of the Lossberg regiment and Major Yost Matthaus of the Rall regiment. He offered them surrender terms and agreed to carry away the brave Captain von Altenbockum, who had been wounded in the head.

The Hessians talked among themselves, then they lowered their proud colors to the snow and grounded weapons. Looking on was George Washington, who was standing with Lord Stirling near Captain Thomas Forrest's battery. Washington had ordered the artillery to shift from round shot to canister. Forrest was about to obey, then turned to the general:

"Sir," he said, "they have struck."

"Struck!" Washington repeated.

"Yes, their colours are down."

"So they are." Washington rode forward toward the Hessians. Forrest's men left their guns and followed him. It was said that the Americans mixed with the Hessians, and "after satisfying their curiosity a little, they began to converse familiarly in broken English and German."

Not part of this surrender was the Knyphausen regiment, the third Hessian unit at Trenton. At the start of the battle the Knyphausen men had marched to join Rall, but perhaps because of a misunderstood order, they countermarched to the southeast of town. They were behind the Quaker meetinghouse when Rall attacked into the center of Trenton. After he fell mortally wounded, and the Rall and Lossberg regiments were repulsed, the Knyphausen regiment tried to escape from the town across Assunpink Creek. Their acting commander, Major Friedrich von Dechow, led them toward the Stone Bridge, with three hundred troops and two guns.

They were too late. The bridge had been held by Hessian troops through the first hour of the battle, and many noncombatants escaped across it. Major von Dechow himself went to the bridge half an hour after the fighting began, found Sergeant Johannes Müller, who commanded the bridge guard, and ordered him to "hold out as long as possible." About half an hour later Müller and his eighteen bridge guards were attacked by "three battalions of the enemy."

These were Sargent's and Glover's brigades, mostly New England Yankees. They came forward quickly, "with their right on the Delaware, and with their left to the town, straight away to the bridge," Sergeant Müller recalled that the Americans carried "two flying colors," probably the Liberty flags that they had used in the New York campaign, or perhaps the Massachusetts and Connecticut flags. They overwhelmed Müller's guard, seized the bridge, and took a blocking position on the far side of Assunpink Creek. Sargent's Continental brigade moved up the Creek on the far bank, and Trenton was completely surrounded.

The Knyphausen regiment turned away from the bridge and marched up the creek in search of a ford. Their two guns sank deep in a patch of soft ground. While they struggled to free their artillery, American troops came up behind them, and others fired from across the creek. The Knyphausen men kept moving up the creek toward another ford, but that crossing was blocked as well. Some of the American infantry were so aggressive that they waded into the freezing creek "about mid-thigh" to attack the Hessians.

More American troops came out of the village and attacked the Knyphausen regiment from the rear and both flanks. The Hessians were trapped. Their acting commander, Major von Dechow, had come on the field still suffering from two wounds received at Fort Washington. Now he was hit again, mortally wounded in the hip. Dechow saw that the situation was hopeless, summoned his officers, and proposed to surrender. One said to him, "Major we cannot give ourselves up like this." Dechow replied, "My dear sirs, do as you like. I am wounded." He was carried off the field, escorted by "a file of sergeants" with "a white handkerchief tied to a musket."

As the Americans gathered around them, the officers and men of the Knyphausen regiment saw that resistance was hopeless. Looking on was Private Jacob Francis, an African American slave who had joined Sargent's brigade. Francis remembered that "the Hessians grounded their arms and left them there and marched down to the old ferry below the Assunpink, between Trenton and Lambertown."

Washington had heard the firing near the creek and rode to the sound of the guns. One of his officers remembered that "about half-way to the bridge he came upon some German troops who were assisting a badly wounded officer into a church." This was Major von Dechow. Then Sullivan's aide Major Wilkinson came riding up from the bridge with the news that the Knyphausen men had laid down their arms and the last remaining Hessian regiment had surrendered. Washington extended his hand and said, "Major Wilkinson, this is a glorious day for our country."

★   ★   ★   ★   ★

The defeat of the Hessian force at Trenton and a British force at Princeton a few days later gave Washington and the American cause the victory it so desperately needed. It gave Continental Congress a new confidence, and proved American soldiers could defeat European regulars. Enlistments for the Continental Army increased when 8,000 new recruits signed on as regulars. General Washington's successes in December of 1776 snatched victory from the jaws of defeat.

Narrative of a Revolutionary Soldier

PRIVATE JOSEPH PLUMB MARTIN

If buttercups buzz'd after the bee,
If boats were on land, churches on sea,
If ponies rode men and if grass ate the cows,
And cats should be chased into holes by the mouse,
If the mamas sold their babies
To the gypsies for half a crown;
If summer were spring and the other way round,
Then all the world would be upside down.
                    —"The World Turned Upside Down"

In 1776, fifteen-year-old Joseph Plumb Martin enlisted for a six-month term with the Connecticut State Troops, and saw action around the New York City area. When his enlistment ended he joined with the newly formed Continental Army for the remainder of the war. Joseph's seven years of service led him though many of the important engagements of the Revolutionary War. His memoirs, published anonymously in 1830, remain the best-kept record of the war by a private soldier. They speak not so much of battle as of everyday privations of the revolutionary soldier: the life-threatening cold, hunger, and disease; the bone-tiring road marches and uncertainties of war. His words have been an enduring testament to the true nature of the Revolution and the men and women who fought it.

He also gives the Continentals credit as a key element in winning the conflict, a subject hotly debated in the following years by a people and government suspicious of standing armies. The militia, while valuable and brave, "would not have answered so well as standing troops . . . they would not have endured the sufferings the army did; they would have considered themselves (as in reality they were and are) free citizens, not bound by any cords that were not of their own manufacturing, and when the hardships of fatigue, starvation, cold and nakedness . . . begun to seize upon them, in such awful array as they did on us, they would have instantly quitted the service in disgust; and who could blame them?" The Continentals "were there, and obliged to be; we could not go away when we pleased without exposing ourselves to military punishment." Simply put, Joseph Plumb Martin outlined the need for a professional standing army for the future of the United States.

In the following passage, Martin described his involvement in the Battle of Yorktown. In the late summer of 1781 General Washington moved his forces from New York to lay siege to the British army under Lord Cornwallis. The British prepared for a siege in a series of heavily-defended redoubts, and waited for reinforcements from either General Henry Clinton's forces in New York or from the British Navy. But the arrival of a French fleet under Admiral Comte de Grasse effectively cut them off from reinforcement and made their situation untenable.

Martin's unit attacked redoubt number ten on October 14, 1781, while French units assaulted redoubt number nine a short distance away. In a rare night action, the Americans advanced quietly with unloaded muskets and fixed bayonets to take the position by close assault. The loss of these redoubts made Lord Cornwallis' position critically vulnerable, and he surrendered on October 19.

With the sense that the American forces had bested their superiors, the British troops played the then-popular tune "The World Turned Upside Down," during the official surrender ceremony. British prime minister Lord Frederick North resigned on news of Cornwallis' surrender. The new British government signed the Treaty of Paris on September 3, 1783, which officially ended the revolution.

★   ★   ★   ★   ★

Soon after landing we marched to Williamsburg, where we joined General Lafayette, and very soon after, our whole army arriving, we prepared to move down and pay our old acquaintance, the British, at Yorktown, a visit. I doubt not but their wish was not to have so many of us come at once as their accommodations were rather scanty. They thought, "The fewer the better cheer." We thought, "The more the merrier." We had come a long way to see them and were unwilling to be put off with excuses. We thought the present time quite as convenient, at least for us, as any future time could be, and we accordingly persisted, hoping that, as they pretended to be a very courtly people, they would have the politeness to come out and meet us, which would greatly shorten the time to be spent in the visit, and save themselves and us much labor and trouble, but they were too impolite at this time to do so.

We marched from Williamsburg the last of September. It was a warm day [the twenty-eighth]. When we had proceeded about halfway to Yorktown we halted and rested two or three hours. Being about to cook some victuals, I saw a fire which some of the Pennsylvania troops had kindled a short distance off. I went to get some fire while some of my messmates made other preparations, we having turned our rum and pepper cook adrift. I had taken off my coat and unbuttoned my waistcoat, it being (as I said before) very warm. My pocketbook, containing about five dollars in money and some other articles, in all about seven dollars, was in my waistcoat pocket. When I came among the strangers they appeared to be uncommonly complaisant, asking many questions, helping me to fire, and chatting very familiarly. I took my fire and returned, but it was not long before I perceived that those kindhearted helpers had helped themselves to my pocketbook and its whole contents. I felt mortally chagrined, but there was no plaster for my sore but patience, and my plaster of that, at this time, I am sure, was very small and very thinly spread, for it never covered the wound.

Here, or about this time, we had orders from the Commander in Chief that, in case the enemy should come out to meet us, we should exchange but one round with them and then decide the conflict with the bayonet, as they valued themselves at that instrument. The French forces could play their part at it, and the Americans were never backward at trying its virtue. The British, however, did not think fit at that time to give us an opportunity to soil our bayonets in their carcasses, but why they did not we could never conjecture; we as much expected it as we expected to find them there.

We went on and soon arrived and encamped in their neighborhood, without let or molestation. Our Miners lay about a mile and a half from their works, in open view of them. Here again we encountered our old associate, Hunger. Affairs, as they respected provisions, &c., were not yet regulated. No eatable stores had arrived, nor could we expect they should until we knew what reception the enemy would give us. We were, therefore, compelled to try our hands at foraging again. We, that is, our corps of Miners, were encamped near a large wood. There was a plenty of shoats all about this wood, fat and plump, weighing, generally, from fifty to a hundred pounds apiece. We soon found some of them and as no owner appeared to be at hand and the hogs not understanding our inquiries (if we made any) sufficiently to inform us to whom they belonged, we made free with some of them to satisfy the calls of nature till we could be better supplied, if better we could be. Our officers countenanced us and that was all the permission we wanted, and many of us did not want even that.

We now began to make preparations for laying close siege to the enemy. We had holed him and nothing remained but to dig him out. Accordingly, after taking every precaution to prevent his escape, [we] settled our guards, provided fascines and gabions, made platforms for the batteries, to be laid down when needed, brought on our battering pieces, ammunition, &c. On the fifth of October we began to put our plans into execution.

One-third part of all the troops were put in requisition to be employed in opening the trenches. A third part of our Sappers and Miners were ordered out this night to assist the engineers in laying out the works. It was a very dark and rainy night. However, we repaired to the place and began by following the engineers and laying laths of pine wood end-to-end upon the line marked out by the officers for the trenches. We had not proceeded far in the business before the engineers ordered us to desist and remain where we were and be sure not to straggle a foot from the spot while they were absent from us. In a few minutes after their departure, there came a man alone to us, having on a surtout, as we conjectured, it being exceeding dark, and inquired for the engineers. We now began to be a little jealous for our safety, being alone and without arms, and within forty rods of the British trenches. The stranger inquired what troops we were, talked familiarly with us a few minutes, when, being informed which way the officers had gone, he went off in the same direction, after strictly charging us, in case we should be taken prisoners, not to discover to the enemy what troops we were. We were obliged to him for his kind advice, but we considered ourselves as standing in no great need of it, for we knew as well as he did that Sappers and Miners were allowed no quarters, at least, are entitled to none, by the laws of warfare, and of course should take care, if taken, and the enemy did not find us out, not to betray our own secret.

In a short time the engineers returned and the afore-mentioned stranger with them. They discoursed together some time when, by the officers often calling him "Your Excellency," we discovered that it was General Washington. Had we dared, we might have cautioned him for exposing himself too carelessly to danger at such a time, and doubtless he would have taken it in good part if we had. But nothing ill happened to either him or ourselves.

It coming on to rain hard, we were ordered back to our tents, and nothing more was done that night. The next night, which was the sixth of

October, the same men were ordered to the lines that had been there the night before. We this night completed laying out the works. The troops of the line were there ready with entrenching tools and began to entrench, after General Washington had struck a few blows with a pickax, a mere ceremony, that it might be said "General Washington with his own hands first broke ground at the siege of Yorktown." The ground was sandy and soft, and the men employed that night eat no "idle bread" (and I question if they eat any other), so that by daylight they had covered themselves from danger from the enemy's shot, who, it appeared, never mistrusted that we were so near them the whole night, their attention being directed to another quarter. There was upon the right of their works a marsh. Our people had sent to the western side of this marsh a detachment to make a number of fires, by which, and our men often passing before the fires, the British were led to imagine that we were about some secret mischief there, and consequently directed their whole fire to that quarter, while we were entrenching literally under their noses.

As soon as it was day they perceived their mistake and began to fire where they ought to have done sooner. They brought out a fieldpiece or two without their trenches, and discharged several shots at the men who were at work erecting a bomb battery, but their shot had no effect and they soon gave it over. They had a large bulldog and every time they fired he would follow their shots across our trenches. Our officers wished to catch him and oblige him to carry a message from them into the town to his masters, but he looked too formidable for any of us to encounter.

I do not remember, exactly, the number of days we were employed before we got our batteries in readiness to open upon the enemy, but think it was not more than two or three. The French, who were upon our left had completed their batteries a few hours before us, but were not allowed to discharge their pieces till the American batteries were ready. Our commanding battery was on the near bank of the [York] river and contained ten heavy guns; the next was a bomb battery of three large mortars; and so on through the whole line. The whole number, American and French, was ninety-two cannon, mortars and howitzers. Our flagstaff was in the ten-gun battery, upon the right of the whole. I was in the trenches the day that the batteries were to be opened. All were upon the tiptoe of expectation and impatience to see the signal given to open the whole line of batteries, which was to be the hoisting of the American flag in the ten-gun battery. About noon the much-wished-for signal went up. I confess I felt a secret pride swell in my heart when I saw the "star-spangled banner" waving majestically in the very faces of our implacable adversaries. It appeared like an omen of success to our enterprise, and so it proved in reality. A simultaneous discharge of all the guns in the line followed, the French troops accompanying it with "Huzza for the Americans!" It was said that the first shell sent from our batteries entered an elegant house formerly owned or occupied by the Secretary of State under the British government, and burned directly over a table surrounded by a large party of British officers at dinner, killing and wounding a number of them. This was a warm day to the British.

The siege was carried on warmly for several days, when most of the guns in the enemy's works were silenced. We now began our second parallel, about halfway between our works and theirs. There were two strong redoubts held by the British, on their left. It was necessary for us to possess those redoubts before we could complete our trenches. One afternoon, I, with the rest of our corps that had been on duty in the trenches the night but one before, were ordered to the lines. I mistrusted something extraordinary, serious or comical, was going forward, but what I could not easily conjecture.

We arrived at the trenches a little before sunset. I saw several officers fixing bayonets on long staves. I then concluded we were about to make a general assault upon the enemy's works, but before dark I was informed of the whole plan, which was to storm the redoubts, the one by the Americans and the other by the French. The Sappers and Miners were furnished with axes and were to proceed in front and cut a passage for the troops through the abatis, which are composed of the tops of trees, the small branches cut off with a slanting stroke which renders them as sharp as spikes. These trees are then laid at a small distance from the trench or ditch, pointing outwards, and the butts fastened to the ground in such a manner that they cannot be removed by those on the outside of them. It is almost impossible to get through them. Through these we were to cut a passage before we or the other assailants could enter.

At dark the detachment was formed and advanced beyond the trenches and lay down on the ground to await the signal for advancing to the attack, which was to be three shells from a certain battery near where we were lying. All the batteries in our line were silent, and we lay anxiously waiting for the signal. The two brilliant planets, Jupiter and Venus, were in close contact in the western hemisphere, the same direction that the signal was to be made in. When I happened to cast my eyes to that quarter, which was often, and I caught a glance of them, I was ready to spring on my feet, thinking they were the signal for starting. Our watch-word was "Rochambeau," the commander of the French forces' name, a good watchword, for being pronounced *Ro-sham-bow*, it sounded, when pronounced quick, like *rush-on-boys*.

We had not lain here long before the expected signal was given, for us and the French, who were to storm the other redoubt, by the three shells with their fiery trains mounting the air in quick succession. The word *up, up*, was then reiterated through the detachment. We immediately moved silently on toward the redoubt we were to attack, with unloaded muskets. Just as we arrived at the abatis, the enemy discovered us and directly opened a sharp fire upon us. We were now at a place where many of our large shells had burst in the ground, making holes sufficient to bury an ox in. The men, having their eyes fixed upon what was transacting before them, were every now and then falling into these holes. I thought the British were killing us off at a great rate. At length, one of the holes happening to pick me up, I found out the mystery of the huge slaughter.

As soon as the firing began, our people began to cry, "The fort's our own!" and it was "Rush on boys." The Sappers and Miners soon cleared a passage for the infantry, who entered it rapidly. Our Miners were ordered not to enter the fort, but there was no stopping them. "We will go," said they. "Then go to the d———l," said the commanding officer of our corps, "if you will." I could not pass at the entrance we had made, it was so crowded. I therefore forced a passage at a place where I saw our shot had cut away some of the abatis; several others entered at the same place. While passing, a man at my side received a ball in his head and fell under my feet, crying out bitterly. While crossing the trench, the enemy threw hand grenades (small shells) into it. They were so thick that I at first thought them cartridge papers on fire, but was soon undeceived by their cracking. As I mounted the breastwork, I met an old associate hitching himself down into the trench. I knew him by the light of the enemy's musketry, it was so vivid. The fort was taken and all quiet in a very short time. Immediately after the firing ceased, I went out to see what had become of my wounded friend and the other that fell in the passage. They were both dead. In the heat of the action I saw a British soldier jump over the walls of the fort next the river and go down the bank, which was almost perpendicular and twenty or thirty feet high. When he came to the beach he made off for the town, and if he did not make good use of his legs I never saw a man that did.

All that were in the action of storming the redoubt were exempted from further duty that night. We laid down upon the ground and rested the remainder of the night as well as a constant discharge of grape and canister shot would permit us to do, while those who were on duty for the day completed the second parallel by including the captured redoubts within it. We returned to camp early in the morning, all safe and sound, except one of our lieutenants, who had received a slight wound on the top of the shoulder by a musket shot. Seven or eight men belonging to the infantry were killed, and a number wounded. . . .

We were on duty in the trenches twenty-four hours, and forty-eight hours in camp. The invalids did the camp duty, and we had nothing else to do but to attend morning and evening roll calls and recreate ourselves as we pleased the rest of the time, till we were called upon to take our turns on duty in the trenches again. The greatest inconvenience we felt was the want of good water, there being none near our camp but nasty frog ponds where all the horses in the neighborhood were watered, and we were forced to wade through the water in the skirts of the ponds, thick with mud and filth, to get at water in any wise fit for use, and that full of frogs. All the springs about the country, although they looked well, tasted like copperas water or like water that had been standing in iron or copper vessels. . . .

In the morning, while the relieves were coming into the trenches, I was sitting on the side of the trench, when some of the New York troops coming in, one of the sergeants stepped up to the breastwork to look about him. The enemy threw a small shell which fell upon the outside of the works; the man turned his face to look at it. At that instant a shot from the enemy, which doubtless was aimed for him in particular as none others were in sight of them, passed just by his face without touching him at all. He fell dead into the trench. I put my hand on his forehead and found his skull was shattered all in pieces and the blood flowing from his nose and mouth, but not a particle of skin was broken. I never saw an instance like this among all the men I saw killed during the whole war.

After we had finished our second line of trenches there was but little firing on either side. After Lord Cornwallis had failed to get off, upon the seventeenth day of October (a rather unlucky day for the British) he requested a cessation of hostilities for, I think, twenty-four hours, when commissioners from both armies met at a house between the lines to agree upon articles of capitulation. We waited with anxiety the termination of the armistice and as the time drew nearer our anxiety increased. The time at length arrived—it passed, and all remained quiet. And now we concluded that we had obtained what we had taken so much pains for, for which we had encountered so many dangers, and had so anxiously wished. Before night we were informed that the British had surrendered and that the siege was ended.

The next day we were ordered to put ourselves in as good order as our circumstances would admit, to see (what was the completion of our present wishes) the British army march out and stack their arms. The trenches, where they crossed the road leading to the town, were leveled and all things put in order for this grand exhibition. After breakfast, on the nineteenth, we were marched onto the ground and paraded on the right-hand side of the road, and the French forces on the left. We waited two or three hours before the British made their appearance. They were not always so dilatory, but they were compelled at last, by necessity, to appear, all armed, with bayonets fixed, drums beating, and faces lengthening. They were led by General [Charles] O'Hara, with the American General Lincoln on his right, the Americans and French beating a march as they passed out between them. It was a noble sight to us, and the more so, as it seemed to promise a speedy conclusion to the contest. The British did not make so good an appearance as the German forces, but there was certainly some allowance to be made in their favor. The English felt their honor wounded, the Germans did not greatly care whose hands they were in. The British paid the Americans, seemingly, but little attention as they passed them, but they eyed the French with considerable malice depicted in their countenances. They marched to the place appointed and stacked their arms; they then returned to the town in the same manner they had marched out, except being divested of their arms. After the prisoners were marched off into the country, our army separated, the French remaining where they then were and the Americans marching for the Hudson.

During the siege, we saw in the woods herds of Negroes which Lord Cornwallis (after he had inveigled them from their proprietors), in love and pity to them, had turned adrift, with no other recompense for their confidence in his humanity than the smallpox for their bounty and starvation and death for their wages. They might be seen scattered about in every direction, dead and dying, with pieces of ears of burnt Indian corn in the hands and mouths, even of those, that were dead. After the siege was ended, many of the owners of these deluded creatures came to our camp and engaged some of our men to take them up, generally offering a guinea a head for them. Some of our Sappers and Miners took up several of them that belonged to a Colonel Banister; when he applied for them they refused to deliver them to him unless he would promise not to punish them. He said he had no intention of punishing them, that he did not blame them at all, the blame lay on Lord Cornwallis. I saw several of those miserable wretches delivered to their master; they came before him under a very powerful fit of the ague. He told them that he gave them the free choice either to go with him or remain where they were, that he would not injure a hair of their heads if they returned with him to their duty. Had the poor souls received a reprieve at the gallows they could not have been more overjoyed than they appeared to be at what he promised them; their ague fit soon left them. I had a share in one of them by assisting in taking him up; the fortune I acquired was small, only one dollar. I received what was then called its equivalent in paper money, if money it might be called; it amounted to twelve hundred (nominal) dollars, all of which I afterwards paid for one single quart of rum. To such a miserable state had all paper stuff called money depreciated.

Our corps of Sappers and Miners were now put on board vessels to be transported up the bay. I was on board a small schooner; the captain of our company and twenty others of our men were in the same vessel. There was more than twenty tons of beef on board, salted in bulk in the hold. We were obliged to remain behind to deal out this beef in small quantities to the troops that remained here. I remained part of the time on board and part on shore for eighteen days after all the American troops were gone to the northward, and none remaining but the French. It now began to grow cold, and there were two or three cold rainstorms. We suffered exceedingly while we were compelled to stay on shore, having no tents nor any kind of fuel, the houses in the town being all occupied by the French troops.

Our captain at length became tired of this business and determined to go on after the other troops at all events. We accordingly left Yorktown and set our faces towards the Highlands of New York.

★   ★   ★   ★   ★

Following the war, Martin took up land in Maine near the mouth of the Penobscot River in what became the town of Prospect. By age fifty-nine he and his wife and five children were destitute, living only on his soldier's pension of $96 a year and whatever money they could earn. At age seventy he published his wartime memoir, which only sold a few copies and was soon forgotten. He died in May, 1850. His book was rediscovered in the 1960s and recognized as one of the best and most complete diaries of that era.

Old Hickory's Finest Hour

THOMAS FLEMING

The brave man inattentive to his duty, is worth little more to his
country than the coward who deserts in the hour of danger.
—Andrew Jackson

The War of 1812 is best remembered by Americans today for the creation
of the "Star-Spangled Banner." Originally written as a poem by Francis
Scott Key, it describes the siege of Fort McHenry at the entrance to Baltimore harbor in September of 1814. Naval artillery pounded the fort
through the night. Only when dawn arrived on the following day did people see the American flag still flying—the Americans had refused to surrender, and the British withdrew. It was a glorious moment for the United
States in a costly and unsuccessful war.

Two years earlier a confederation of allies in Congress under
Henry Clay convinced President James Madison and most of Congress to
declare war on Britain for seizing American ships at sea, impressments of
American citizens into the Royal Navy, and the refusal to surrender forts in
the northwest territories promised at the Treaty of Paris in 1783. The war,
however, was a disaster from the start. In 1812, the regular army consisted of
fewer than 12,000 men. Congress authorized the expansion of the army to
35,000 men, but the service was voluntary and unpopular, and there was an
almost total lack of trained and experienced officers. The American attempts to invade Canada ended in failure as war raged across the frontier.

The fledgling American Navy was unable to challenge the enemy
fleets at sea, giving the British complete freedom to sail the American coast
and raid at will. In August of 1814, the British landed an army to attack
Washington, where they soundly defeated the hastily-assembled milita defending the capital. The White House and capital buildings were torched

in retaliation for the Americans' burning of York (Toronto) a year earlier. The victory at Baltimore the following month only resulted in a British withdrawal from Maryland. British Vice Admiral Alexander Cochrane withdrew his forces to the Caribbean where they would prepare to attack their next target: New Orleans.

New Orleans was the jewel of the American south and the crucial hub of trade for cotton and other goods that flowed down the Mississippi. Capture of this vital port would give the British control of the Mississippi and place the United States between British forces in Cananda and in the south along the river delta. An attack from British Canada into the New England states, already on the point of secession, would end the war. The war in Europe had come to an end. Napoleon was exiled on the island of Elba. Thousands of veteran British solders were now free to deploy to the Americas, and New Orleans seemed ripe for the taking.

Defense of the the city fell to Major General Andrew Jackson who commanded a force of 700 U.S. Army regulars. He faced a city on the verge of hysteria as news of the impending British attack spread. His command would prove that the right man in the right place and time can change everything. Jackson was a tough and highly intelligent officer. His nickname "Old Hickory" was in reference to his bravery at the Battle of Horseshoe Bend earlier that spring against the Creek Indians. He had served in the Continental Army as a runner at the age of fourteen. Imprisoned after the fall of Charleston he nearly starved to death, and received a lifetime scar from a British officer who slashed him for refusing to polish his boots. During the war, Jackson's entire immediate family died of sickness and starvation, and the experience inspired in him a deep hatred for the British.

Jackson's presence in New Orleans that November was electrifying to the terrified people. His ranks grew as hundreds of men from all walks of life volunteered to serve under him as militia. His expert knowledge of military science gave the Americans a fighting chance to repel an attack. Thomas Fleming, writing for the *Military History Quarterly*, describes the scene.

★　　★　　★　　★　　★

In mid-September 1814, a letter was surreptitiously delivered to William C. C. Claiborne, governor of Louisiana. It came from a man he detested: Jean Lafitte, ruler of the island of Grand Terre and the Bay of Barataria near the mouth of the Mississippi River. Lafitte had grown rich and powerful as a pirate who preyed on American, English, and Spanish commerce during the second decade of the Napoleonic wars. In 1813, Claiborne had posted a notice declaring his readiness to give anyone who seized the suave brigand a reward of five hundred dollars. Lafitte retaliated by posting around New Orleans an offer of five thousand dollars to anyone who delivered Claiborne to him at Grand Terre.

The letter from the outlaw made Claiborne's scalp tingle, not with rage but with panic. Lafitte informed the governor that he had just received an offer from one Nicholas Lockyer, captain of His Majesty's sloop *Sophia*, to join a British force in an assault on New Orleans. The expedition was intended to create a British colony along the Gulf of Mexico to match the one Great Britain already had in Canada. The conquest would neatly encircle the treacherous Americans, who had declared war on Great Britain in 1812 while it was embroiled in its death grapple with Napoleon Bonaparte.

Now Napoleon was beaten and in exile on the island of Elba. The veteran troops who had helped batter the French dictator into submission were rendezvousing in Jamaica before coming to America to settle affairs. Captain Lockyer urged Lafitte to join him in rescuing the French citizens of Louisiana from American "oppression." Control of New Orleans, near the Mississippi's mouth, would make the British the virtual rulers of the burgeoning American heartland, whose economy depended on the tons of cotton and grain shipped down the river each year for export. Lafitte had asked the British captain to give him two weeks to think it over. The pirate chieftain then promptly sent the letter to Claiborne with an offer to side with the Americans if he and his men were granted amnesty for their previous sanguinary careers.

To counter the British, Governor Claiborne had only half a dozen gunboats and a fourteen-gun schooner—a fleet that a single Royal Navy frigate could annihilate in five minutes. His army consisted of little more than seven hundred Regulars, commanded by an imperious stranger from distant Tennessee, forty-seven-year-old Maj. Gen. Andrew Jackson, with whom the governor was barely on speaking terms.

In the eleven years since Claiborne had assumed governorship of the territory that Thomas Jefferson had purchased from Napoleon, the pompous bureaucrat had done little to conciliate the local French and Spanish Creoles to American rule. Instead, the governor specialized in writing self-pitying letters to Washington blaming everyone but himself for his unpopularity. "I am not at the head of a United and Willing people," he moaned. "Our country is filled with spies and traitors."

His attempts to organize a militia in New Orleans had been met with defiance and ridicule. When the French consul urged his fellow Gauls to respond to Claiborne's pleas, his windows were smashed. Militia from the northern part of the state, disgusted by the inertia of the locals, had deserted in droves. Dampening everyone's spirits was an acute shortage of guns and ammunition.

While Governor Claiborne chewed his fingernails, New Englanders far to the north were gathering in Hartford, Connecticut, to discuss the possibility of seceding from the United States rather than continuing "Mr. Madison's War." Pint-sized President James Madison, Jefferson's successor, had been a disaster as a national leader. He had allowed Congress to vote Alexander Hamilton's Bank of the United States out of business in 1811, on the eve of declaring war on the British. As a result, the federal government was now broke. So worthless was the guaranty of the United States that Secretary of War James Monroe was reduced to riding from bank to bank in Washington, begging for loans to which he pledged his own credit.

New Englanders had opposed the declaration of war. They had been disenchanted with the federal government since President Jefferson's harebrained 1807 embargo, which banned American ships from trading with anyone, lest the English or the French attack them. Madison had maintained a modified version of this policy, which one critic compared to cutting a man's throat to cure a nosebleed. Since the start of the war, a series of disastrous attempts to conquer Canada had turned Yankee disenchantment with federal incompetence to disgust and calls for secession.

That sentiment reached a climax of sorts in late August 1814 when the British landed a small army in Maryland, routed a ragtag American force at Bladensburg, and spent several days in Washington burning the chief executive's mansion, the Capitol, and other government buildings. A few days later, the king's men captured huge amounts of undefended war materiel in nearby Alexandria. Only an American naval victory on Lake Champlain turned back another British army descending from Canada to support New England's secessionists.

Even farther from New Orleans, in Ghent, Belgium, another group of Americans, led by John Quincy Adams, son of the second president, was locked in bitter argument with British commissioners, trying to negotiate a peace treaty. The British kept insisting on the principle of *uti possidetis* (winner keeps what he holds), an absolute right to navigate the Mississippi, and the privilege of creating a satellite Indian nation in the heart of the Northwest Territory. Faced with what amounted to an end to their sovereignty, the Americans could only keep rejecting the terms and hope for good news from the battlefronts.

Clearly, a great deal depended on Maj. Gen. Andrew Jackson's response to the crisis unfolding in Louisiana. The lean, hawk-eyed Tennessean, known to his admirers as "Old Hickory," had won a national reputation when he crushed the powerful Creek Indian Nation earlier in 1814 and forced them to cede twenty-three million acres to land-hungry Americans. But how would he fare against soldiers and commanders who had defeated Napoleon Bonaparte? New Orleans sophisticates were not favorably impressed. One Creole lady, who had seen Bonaparte's generals strutting in their gorgeous uniforms in Europe, called Jackson "an ugly old Kaintuck flat-boatman."

Jackson, however, had one asset many better-dressed generals lacked: audacity. In September, when Claiborne received Lafitte's letter of warning, Old Hickory was in the port city of Mobile, which American forces had only recently taken from the Spanish. Rumors of the projected British invasion had already reached him. He was convinced that the British would try to seize Mobile, march overland to Baton Rouge, and descend on New Orleans from the north. Jackson had already sent urgent messages to the Tennessee veterans of the Creek War, ordering them to join him without delay.

Seizing Mobile and marching overland was, in fact, the British plan, but its execution was botched by egregious overconfidence. Relying on intelligence that Louisiana was virtually undefended, the commander of the expedition, Vice Adm. Sir Alexander Cochrane, sent a four-ship squadron and a company of Royal Marines commanded by Lt. Col. Edward Nicholls to nearby Pensacola in theoretically neutral Spanish West Florida. There the British began arming and training Creek warriors. Nicholls dispatched Captain Lockyer to woo Lafitte and his Baratarians and issued a windy proclamation telling the Creoles that he had come to liberate them from "a faithless imbecile government." With the help of a dark night and some money, he had the gasconade posted all over New Orleans.

On September 12, Nicholls assaulted Fort Bowyer, guarding the mouth of Mobile Bay. Jackson had garrisoned the weak twelve-gun fortification, which the British had predicted they would capture in twenty minutes, with 130 American Regulars. They amazed the British, and possibly themselves, by beating off the attack and sinking a frigate in the process. Nicholls retreated to Pensacola. Without waiting for orders from the all-but-defunct federal government, Old Hickory launched a pre-emptive strike on this enemy beachhead. With two thousand mounted Tennesseans commanded by one of his ablest lieutenants—huge, combative General John Coffee—plus seven hundred Regulars and a detachment of Mississippi Territory dragoons, Jackson smashed into Pensacola on November 7 after an hour of hard fighting. Dismayed by the ferocity of the American attack, the British fled to their ships.

The Spanish and the Creeks were totally cowed by this defeat. The Spanish governor, who had previously written sneering letters to Jackson, was soon signing himself "Your most faithful and grateful servant, who kisses your hand." At least as important, word of the redcoats' flight quickly spread through the southwest, giving new confidence to militiamen from Baton Rouge to Nashville.

Garrisoning Pensacola with two regiments, Jackson double-timed his little army back to Mobile, where he found panicky letters from Claiborne and others, begging him to come immediately to New Orleans to invigorate the city's defenders. Meanwhile, the governor, in an act of incredible stupidity, had allowed the local naval commander, Commodore Daniel Todd Patterson, to attack Jean Lafitte at Grand Terre. With more than two thousand men under his command, Lafitte could have wiped up the Gulf of Mexico with Patterson's little flotilla and its seventy-man force of Regulars. Instead, still hoping for American amnesty, he and his elder brother Pierre retreated to nearby islands, allowing Patterson to capture eighty of their men and their eldest brother, Alexandre Frederic, who sailed under the name Dominique You. Patterson plundered the pirate headquarters of merchandise worth half a million dollars and claimed it as spoils of war.

At first, Jackson approved of the commodore's foray. In a proclamation he issued to stiffen Creole spines, the general asked how anyone could have confidence in the British, who were ready to court an alliance with the "hellish banditti" of Barataria. But when he reached New Orleans, he learned that most of the Creoles sympathized with the Lafittes and considered the expedition another of "Claibo's" blunders. Jackson was still inclined to denounce the pirates—until he talked to an old friend, Edward Livingston.

An adroit lawyer, Livingston had served in Congress with Jackson and earned his trust in the tumultuous political wars of the late 1790s. Livingston urged the general to make a deal with the Lafittes and do his utmost to conciliate the Creoles. As Jackson grasped the degree of disaffection in the city and its environs, he agreed to appear at a welcoming ceremony in the central square, the Place d'Armes, to encourage local loyalty. The impact of the ramrod-straight, grim-visaged general and his promise to "drive their enemies into the sea, or perish in the effort" was, one awed Creole wrote, "electric." Males of all ages now rushed to join the militia.

While American control of Mobile and Pensacola denied the British a port from which to disembark an army, Jackson knew that he was dealing with an enemy that was expert in amphibious operations. There was nothing to prevent them from landing elsewhere along the six hundred miles of Gulf coast. In fact, they could choose from no less than six possible routes to the city. Jackson did not have the manpower to defend them all—and he was astonished to discover "the total ignorance among all descriptions of persons . . . of the topography of the country."

As the American general considered his options, Admiral Cochrane's fifty-ship armada carrying fifteen hundred marines and 5,498 veteran troops debouched from Negril Bay, Jamaica. The fifty-six-year-old Cochrane had never forgiven the Americans for killing his brother, Major Charles Cochrane, at the Battle of Yorktown in 1781. The admiral was a veteran campaigner in the Caribbean, with the capture of several French islands, most notably Martinique, on his escutcheon. His British army counterpart was thirty-three-year-old, black-whiskered Maj. Gen. John Keane, who had served as a brigadier under Arthur Wellesley, duke of Wellington, in Spain, where he had acquired a reputation for recklessness.

The unofficial motto of the expedition was "Beauty and Booty." The first word referred to the exotic ladies of New Orleans, already world famous; the second to the fifteen million dollars worth of cotton and other goods in the city's bulging warehouses. In spite of the repulses at Pensacola and Mobile, optimism was high. Many officers brought their wives along on the transports, giving the expedition a holiday air. Admiral Cochrane had promised everyone that they would celebrate a glorious Christmas in New Orleans.

Ignoring a debilitating attack of dysentery and the miseries of lead poisoning from a bullet lodged in his shoulder since 1813 (a byproduct of a street brawl with political enemies in Nashville), Old Hickory spent the first weeks of December touring and strengthening New Orleans' defenses. He paid particular attention to Fort Saint Philip, fifty miles below the city. This bastion, with its twenty-eight 24-pounders, was the key to blocking an enemy attempt to sail up the Mississippi to attack the city. Additional batteries were erected for insurance at English Turn, a huge bend in the river fourteen miles below New Orleans. Axmen were put to work blocking the numerous bayous feeding off the great river that an amphibious enemy might use.

Aboard his flagship HMS *Tonnant*, Admiral Cochrane was studying maps and intelligence reports received from numerous spies within the city, most of them Spanish Creoles who hoped an English victory would return Louisiana to Spain. Brushing aside General Keane's doubts, the admiral decided the route of choice was via Lake Bourgne. This broad, shallow arm of the Gulf came within six miles of the Mississippi River just above English Turn. From there, the invaders would have several options, including a right turn into nearby Lake Pontchartrain, which would enable them to attack New Orleans from the north. Or they might find a bayou that would allow them to reach solid ground and a road along the river leading directly to the city from the south.

Aware of Lake Bourgne's potential, Jackson and Commodore Patterson had stationed five of their six gunboats on its muddy waters. Admiral Cochrane saw these impudent six-gun creatures as so many gnats to swat away. He lowered forty-five attack barges, each armed with a cannon and equipped with planked-up sides to protect the crews from musketry. With Captain Lockyer in command, they attacked the American flotilla on December 14.

The American commander, Lieutenant Thomas Catesby Jones, had dispatched a tender to warn Jackson of the British onslaught. In spite of an ill wind that had grounded his flagship and another gunboat, Jones decided to fight it out with the oncoming oar-powered squadron. By the time the battle ended two hours later, ten Americans were dead, thirty-five wounded, including Jones, and the rest captured. The British victors had seventeen dead. Captain Lockyer was among their seventy-seven wounded.

Although he had been defeated, Jones had bought Old Hickory precious time to prepare for the British thrust, now that Lake Bourgne was clearly the route of choice. The American commander rushed a very Jacksonian message to General Coffee, whom he had stationed at Baton Rouge: "You must not sleep until you reach me." Other messengers headed up the Mississippi to urge militia from Tennessee and Kentucky, supposedly en route, to hurry forward without a moment's delay. Even more vital was the anticipated arrival of a shipment of guns and ammunition the federal government had dispatched from Pittsburgh months earlier. Next, Jackson tried to deal with the panic that swept New Orleans at the news of the gunboats' annihilation on Lake Bourgne. He issued a proclamation declaring martial law and appeared before the Louisiana State Legislature, which was rife with defeatism. The Tennessean urged it to adjourn for two or three weeks, leaving him in charge. The legislators refused and threw in a condemnation of martial law as a violation of their rights. Totally alienated from Governor Claiborne, they had begun to dislike the pugnacious Jackson too. The legislature wanted to retain the option of surrendering the city rather than have it destroyed in a climactic battle.

Livingston, still urging Jackson to meet with Lafitte, persuaded the legislature to pass a resolution offering the Baratarians amnesty. That enabled Jackson to change his mind without eating his words about dealing with pirates. There is no record of his meeting with Lafitte, but Jean and his brother Pierre were soon part of the general's staff, and their brother, Dominique You, was commanding a battery of cannons hoisted from the buccaneers' ships. Even more valuable was their contribution of seventy-five hundred badly needed flints and five hundred muskets.

On December 20, the advance guard of General Coffee's two-thousand-man brigade reached New Orleans. The rest arrived there two days later. A few hours behind them came three thousand Tennessee militiamen commanded by Jackson's good friend Maj. Gen. William Carroll. During their five-week trip down the river, Carroll had drilled his men constantly. The militiamen had also scooped up eleven hundred muskets, part of the slow-moving federal shipment from Pittsburgh. That same day, December 22, Major Thomas Hinds arrived with a regiment of blue-coated Mississippi Territory dragoons. All Jackson needed now was the twenty-three-hundred-man Kentucky militia force, which was somewhere on the river. On December 23, he scribbled a letter to his wife, Rachel, ending with a reassuring, "All's well."

The general had barely sealed the letter when three mud-stained men burst into his headquarters on Royal Street to tell him that the British army had materialized only eight miles below the city without a shot being fired at them. There was nothing between them and New Orleans—not a fort, not a gun, not a soldier.

From the flabbergasted Jackson's point of view, the British had done the impossible. Two officers, disguised as locals, had found the one bayou leading from Lake Bourgne to the Mississippi River that the Creoles, ignoring Jackson's repeated orders, had failed to block. Suitably named Bienvenue, it had welcomed (with an assist from the smaller Bayou Mazant and a connecting canal) the midnight passage of General Keane, 2,080 men, and two guns to firm ground on the Villeré plantation along the Mississippi.

At dawn on December 23, they had surrounded and taken prisoner the militia detachment supposedly guarding the bayou. The commander of the detachment, Major Gabriel Villeré, had made a daring escape and was among the messengers who brought the grim news to headquarters.

The general's reaction was vintage Jackson. "I will smash them, so help me God!" he roared. Instead of frantically throwing up entrenchments, which would have shaken the spirit of his raw soldiers, as soon as darkness fell on December 23, Jackson attacked. He ordered Carroll and his Tennessee militia into New Orleans to act as his reserve, while he threw 2,131 troops at the British. The American attack was led by the Seventh and Forty-fourth U.S. Infantry, John Coffee's division of Tennesseans, and a battalion of free black refugees from Haiti that Jackson had recruited over the objections of the Creoles. For artillery, he ordered Patterson to send the fourteen-gun schooner USS *Carolina* down the river until it was opposite the British camp.

Surprise was total. The overconfident British were cooking their dinners over blazing fires when *Carolina*'s guns blasted sheets of grapeshot into their camp. The American Regulars, free blacks, and some Creole militia rushed down the road along the levee, supported by two 6-pounder guns, while Coffee's veterans swung left through a cypress swamp to outflank the enemy. But darkness, river fog, difficult terrain, and fierce British resistance soon turned the battle into a melee fought by platoons and detachments, which was described by one participant as being "hand to hand, bayonet to bayonet, sabre to sabre." In his headquarters at the Villeré mansion, a distraught General Keane could make no sense of what was happening. "What kind of fighting is this?" he cried to an aide.

By midnight, Coffee and his men had shot their way through the British camp almost to the river. But they now found themselves under flank attack by companies from the second British brigade coming down the Bayou Bienvenue. Ahead of them Colonel William Thornton of the Eighty-fifth Regiment had recovered from the initial shock of the American attack and organized a formidable defense in a ditch between the old and new levees. Coffee readily obeyed Jackson's order to fall back. Two deserters had told the commander that the British had six thousand men and all of them were coming down the Bayou Bienvenue. Jackson was convinced that this was the main British attack, and he could not risk losing even part of the force he had thrown at the enemy.

In the light of dawn, both sides counted their losses. American casualties were twenty-four killed, one hundred fifteen wounded, and seventy-four captured. British losses were forty-six killed, one hundred sixty-seven wounded, and sixty-four captured. Among the captured British was Major Samuel Mitchell of the Ninety-fifth Regiment, the man who had put the torch to the American Capitol in August.

On December 24, a shaken General Keane abandoned his plan to attack New Orleans that day, even though he now had forty-seven hundred men under his immediate command. He reasoned that Jackson must have gathered a formidable army; Keane could not imagine risking such a reckless night attack without a large reserve. In the British ranks Jackson's audacity had taken a toll. Lieutenant George Robert Gleig of the Eighty-fifth said that the losses included "our finest soldiers and best officers." Among them was Gleig's close friend, Captain Charles Grey, shot through the head by a rifle ball. Compounding the Britons' misery was the weather. It had turned bitterly cold. The worst sufferers were two regiments of Jamaican blacks who were wearing summer uniforms. Further demoralizing the British was *Carolina*, still offshore, hurling grapeshot and cannonballs into their camp. To counter her heavy guns, Keane had nothing but fieldpieces.

General Jackson, using the Mississippi dragoons as his eyes, soon learned that the British were entrenching rather than continuing to advance. After deciding to imitate them, Jackson led his men back two miles to the Rodriguez Canal, a muddy ditch about twenty feet wide and four feet deep bordering the Chalmette plantation. He ordered them to start throwing up a rampart behind the canal. By the end of the day a wall of mud and logs extended six hundred yards from the river to a cypress swamp. Jackson, seldom off his horse, ordered the digging to continue through the night.

On Christmas Day a salvo of artillery fire from the British sailed toward the American earthworks. Was it the expected attack? No. Jackson's dragoons informed him the British were welcoming the arrival of a new general. According to rumor, it was no less than the duke of Wellington. In fact, it was the duke's brother-in-law, thirty-seven-year-old Maj. Gen. Sir Edward Pakenham. The conqueror of Guadeloupe, and a brilliant subordinate of Wellington in Spain, Pakenham had been appointed to supersede the unsuccessful Keane. As an index of British intentions, Pakenham reportedly carried in his dispatch case a commission as governor of Louisiana and the promise of an earldom for his anticipated victory. Popular with the troops, he was seemingly imbued with Wellington's aura.

General Pakenham found nothing merry about this Christmas Day. He had grave doubts about Admiral Cochrane's route of attack via Lake Bourgne and the Bayou Bienvenue. The British army was trapped on an isthmus three-quarters of a mile wide, between the Mississippi and a virtually impassable swamp, with the narrow, twelve-mile-long bayou the only link to the lake and the fleet. Now that they had lost the element of surprise, they were faced with sustaining their army along a watery supply line eighty miles long, with open boats as the only means of transport.

When Pakenham hinted at his dissatisfaction, Admiral Cochrane informed him that if the general was not willing to attack this American rabble in arms, he would do it with his sailors and marines and assign the army the job of carrying the baggage into New Orleans. Pakenham decided the army's honor was now at stake and sat down with his staff to plan offensive operations.

The general's first decision was to get rid of *Carolina*. His artillery commander, Colonel Alexander Dickson, assured him he could manage it with relatively light field guns as soon as he built a furnace for hot shot. At dawn on December 27 his guns opened fire with incandescent rounds on the schooner. Jackson had told the captain to retire up the river—orders that should have been sent twenty-four hours earlier. But the wind was feeble and the current strong. After being hit by the first few rounds, the vessel almost instantly became an inferno. As flames curled around her magazine, the crew abandoned ship. Soon afterward *Carolina* exploded with a blast that drew cheers from the watching British regiments.

British gunners now turned their attention to the merchant ship *Louisiana*, a mile up the river. She had been equipped with twenty-four-pounders manned by a crew impressed from the hundreds of idle seamen on the New Orleans waterfront. Ignoring the whizzing hot shot, *Louisiana*'s crew used their longboat and cables on shore to haul their ship up the river and out of range.

Satisfied, Pakenham ordered the army to launch an assault across the plain of Chalmette the following day. He knew another twenty-seven hundred men under Maj. Gen. John Lambert would soon arrive to reinforce him. But he was also driven by the knowledge that the fleet could not feed his men for long, and they could not survive on the meager pickings from the nearby plantations. He was confident that his artillery could shatter Jackson's mud earthwork, exposing the "dirty-shirts" (his troops' name for Jackson's Tennesseans) to British bayonets.

On the crisp, cold morning of December 28, the British advanced in two columns. General Keane led three infantry regiments and some riflemen along the river while veteran Maj. Gen. Samuel Gibbs led another column toward Jackson's opposite flank, which was anchored in the cypress swamp. Cannons belched at the American defenses, supplemented by shrieking Congreve rockets, weapons designed to panic green troops. Jackson steadied his men by shouting that the Congreves were nothing but "toys to amuse children."

Out in the river, *Louisiana* lay silent. The British hot shot battery opened on her, but the range was too great for accuracy. As Keane's column came within six hundred yards of the American parapet, Commodore Patterson growled, "Fire!" A terrific cascade of metal tore into the British ranks. Simultaneously, the batteries along the American parapet cut loose with what one British soldier called "As destructive a fire of artillery as I have ever witnessed." Several Britons ruefully noted the battery commanded by Dominique You was among the most deadly. Adding to the chaos was hot shot that set fire to several nearby Chalmette plantation buildings, which an enterprising American had booby-trapped the night before. The buildings exploded, showering the stunned British troops with debris.

The American gunners now concentrated on the British artillery. They swiftly knocked out two 6-pounders and sent the crew of two 9-pounders scrambling for cover. But on the American left, out of range of *Louisiana*'s guns, Gibbs' column made progress. He sent a regiment into the swamp, where they outfought two hundred Tennesseans, killing their commander. A detachment of sixty Choctaw Indians recruited by Jackson slowed their progress, but it looked to Gibbs as if a determined assault could turn the American flank.

As messengers reached Jackson with reports of his endangered left flank, an emissary from Claiborne brought even more alarming news from New Orleans. The legislature was debating whether to surrender the city to the British. The Creoles had heard that Jackson planned to burn New Orleans if he was forced to retreat, and they feared that the city's destruction would be the signal for a slave rebellion. Old Hickory's response was vintage Jackson: "Tell him [the governor] to investigate. If he finds it's true . . . blow up the legislature!"

Meanwhile, in the center of the battlefield, General Pakenham saw his left column in disarray and many of his cannons dismounted. Out of touch with General Gibbs on the right, the British commander had a fateful loss of nerve, and he ordered a withdrawal. Gibbs and his regimental colonels were infuriated.

Pakenham now turned to Admiral Cochrane to rescue the campaign. The army's light artillery could not match the twenty-four- and thirty-two-pounders aboard *Louisiana* and on the American ramparts.

Could the sailors bring heavier guns from the fleet? Cochrane instantly rapped out an order, and his men began the herculean task of rowing ten 18- and four 24-pounders in open boats eighty miles across shallow Lake Bourgne and up Bayou Bienvenue. Equally daunting was the task of mounting the guns in the oozy soil, which turned to water when a shovel reached eight inches below the surface.

Nevertheless, after three days and nights of constant labor the big guns were ready by the morning of January 1, 1815. Artillery chief Alexander Dickson and Pakenham's chief engineer, Colonel John Fox Burgoyne, illegitimate son of the British general who had surrendered at Saratoga, improvised above-ground emplacements by filling sugar hogsheads from nearby plantations with mud. Burgoyne also dug entrenchments to protect the troops during the coming artillery duel.

As morning fog lifted on January 1, the British guns thundered. The overconfident Americans were celebrating New Year's Day with a dress parade. They scrambled frantically for their weapons as cannonballs and Congreve rockets hissed and shrieked around them. At first the British guns had the better part of the duel. They disabled three American guns. Within half an hour, however, American shots began knocking the hogsheads to pieces, and the recoil of the big British naval guns hurled several of them off their platforms.

Although not a single British gun was disabled, Pakenham lost twenty-seven men to American fire. After three hours the British guns fell silent. They had run out of ammunition.

Once more a glum Pakenham gave the order to withdraw. American artillerymen made the movement impossible until dark. A cold rain began to fall, and the shivering men had to endure it—and the humiliation of another setback—for the rest of the day. At nightfall the British veterans were so dispirited they refused to drag a ten-gun center battery to safety. An aide had to awaken Pakenham, who rushed to the scene to issue orders personally. In his journal, a morose Lieutenant Gleig reported the army was "disheartened and discontented."

The British high command was not in a much better frame of mind—until good news came from the fleet: General Lambert and his twenty-seven hundred fresh men were at the mouth of Lake Bourgne. Pakenham ordered them brought up Bayou Bienvenue immediately. He also pounced on an offer from Admiral Cochrane to bring enough boats up the bayou to ferry part of the army across the river. On the opposite bank, only untried Creole militia protected Patterson's guns.

General Jackson also welcomed reinforcements. On January 4, the missing Kentucky militiamen, 2,368 strong, began to arrive. But the general was dismayed to learn that they had only seven hundred guns. Worse, the militiamen were in terrible shape, ragged and half-starved. Jackson procured warm clothes from New Orleans and persuaded the mayor to part with enough rusty Spanish muskets from the city's armory to equip another four hundred, but they were placed well in the rear of his line, along with their unarmed comrades, as a reserve.

Pakenham, meanwhile, was planning an assault that would take a leaf from Jackson's book. He was sending one of his most aggressive colonels, William Thornton of the Eighty-fifth, with fourteen hundred men to attack the militia on the west bank. They had orders to seize Patterson's guns and enfilade the American breastwork. Meanwhile, Keane was to lead a demonstration along the river, drawing the fire of the American artillery concentrated on their right, while Gibbs with twenty-one hundred men was to make the main attack on their left. One of Pakenham's black regiments was ordered to divert Coffee's men by luring them into the cypress swamp. The newly arrived Lambert and his troops were to remain in the center of the battlefield, ready to strike toward whatever flank seemed most promising. All these hammerblows and feints were to be executed in the predawn darkness, when the accuracy of American cannons and rifles would be negligible.

It was a good, even masterful, plan. But on January 8, the day of the attack, things started going wrong almost immediately. Thornton's boats became mired in mud when a dam constructed by Cochrane's naval engineers collapsed, and the water in the canal that was supposed to float them into the Mississippi ran the other way, toward Lake Bourgne. Thornton got only 450 of his fourteen hundred men across the river. In Gibbs' column, the Forty-fourth Regiment was supposed to carry fascines to fill in the Rodriguez Canal and scaling ladders to mount the enemy's breastwork. As the column moved forward, Gibbs discovered they had neither of these essentials. He sent the Forty-fourth back to get them, spurred by sulfurous curses at their colonel, Thomas Mullins.

In the center, an anxious Pakenham waited for the sound of gunfire across the river. Thornton's attack was supposed to be the signal for the advance on the right. The darkness was ebbing into a foggy dawn. In another hour, his columns would be murderously visible to the waiting Americans. His aide urged him to postpone the attack. With desperate fatalism, the general shook his head and ordered two rockets fired to signal the advance. General Gibbs, still without fascines or scaling ladders, went forward anyway. On the opposite shore, Thornton and his men were just getting out of their boats. Misjudging the strength of the Mississippi's current, they had been driven a thousand yards downstream, away from the American guns.

At first, Pakenham's men seemed to be finally favored by good luck. They advanced amid swirling fog. Behind his breastwork, Jackson knew they were coming. He had his forty-four hundred men ready, their rifles and cannons loaded, as the beat of British drums thudded through the mist. By now, his mud rampart was between fourteen and twenty feet thick. He had no worries about British artillery. Tensely, he sent orders right and left along the line to keep heads down until he gave the order to fire.

Abruptly, almost as if an invisible hand had drawn a curtain back, the fog lifted and the winter sun glittered on the redcoats' ranks. Jackson's cannons boomed, and the hissing shots tore terrible gaps in the British columns. As Gibbs' formation came within three hundred yards, Brig. Gen. John Adair, the commander of the Kentuckians, summoned one of his best marksmen. He pointed to an officer on a gray horse in front of Gibbs' men. "Snuff his candle," he said. A second later, a bullet tore through Major John Whittaker's left ear and exited his temple. He toppled into the mud. That feat of marksmanship was followed by a blast of fire from the rest of the American line. A British quartermaster, watching from the balcony of a nearby house, saw the Forty-fourth Regiment, laboring forward with the fascines and ladders, "literally swept from the face of the earth." The survivors abandoned their burdens and ran for their lives.

Near the river, in spite of harassing fire from Patterson's guns on the west bank, the British scored a surprising victory. Lieutenant Colonel Robert Rennie led a flank battalion toward an exposed American redoubt from which his troops could enfilade the Rodriguez Canal line. He captured it and waited for General Keane's far-larger column to rush to his support. The chance to break through the supposedly impregnable American right flank now seemed more than possible.

To his dismay, Rennie saw Keane's column, largely the kilted Ninety-third Highlanders, angling right, toward Gibbs. Keane was reacting to the near-annihilation of the Forty-fourth Regiment. More volleys poured from the American rampart. As soon as a soldier fired, he stepped down to reload and another man took his place. In minutes the Twenty-first Regiment in Gibbs' column disintegrated as totally as had the Forty-fourth. Its colonel was dead, and the survivors were running for the rear.

A choleric General Gibbs galloped to the front to rally the panicky regiments behind the Twenty-first. At about the same time, General Keane went down with a bullet in his groin. His Highlanders took fearful losses as they struggled across the muddy plain toward Gibbs' faltering column. Gibbs, at the head of the column, saw a few brave men from the Twenty-first Regiment and members of the rifle brigade trying to cut steps in the American rampart with their bayonets. "If I live until tomorrow, I will hang Colonel Mullins from one of these trees!" Gibbs roared. A moment later, four bullets smashed into his head and body.

Pakenham, seeing Gibbs' men in disarray and the Highlanders wavering under the deadly American fire, rode forward to take command of the situation. As he called to the Highlanders to follow him, grapeshot shattered his knee and a bullet killed his horse. Struggling to his feet, he mounted an aide's horse and shouted, "Come on, brave Ninety-third!" A bullet struck him in the spine. He toppled into his aide's arms and was carried to the rear, croaking a final order, "Have Lambert bring up the reserve." In the forward redoubt, meanwhile, a desperate Rennie led a doomed assault with his handful of men. He was instantly shot dead, and most of his men met the same fate.

Across the river, a very different drama was unfolding. Leading his 450 men in a bayonet charge, Colonel William Thornton routed eight hundred Creole militiamen and about two hundred Kentuckians that Jackson had sent to reinforce them. Their commander, a fat Massachusetts loudmouth named Brig. Gen. David B. Morgan, ran as fast as his men. A cursing Commodore Patterson had to spike his nine-gun battery on the riverbank and follow the scampering amateurs. The British discovered that several of the guns were not badly damaged and could quickly be repaired and turned loose on Jackson's line. If Thornton had been able to bring his entire fourteen-hundred-man division across the river on schedule, he would have drastically altered the outcome of the battle.

But this startling development could not alter the situation on the plain of Chalmette. By the time Thornton's men reached Patterson's guns, Pakenham and Gibbs were dying, Keane was incapacitated, and more than half of the attacking army were dead or wounded. The rest were a panicked rabble, bereft of officers and courage.

In the center of the field, General John Lambert and his two reserve regiments had watched the carnage with appalled disbelief. In his campaigns in Spain and France, the forty-two-year-old Lambert had never seen anything like the murderous accuracy of Jackson's riflemen. Told that he was now in command, Lambert conferred briefly with Admiral Cochrane at a nearby plantation house. The admiral urged a renewed attack. Lambert walked out of the room without responding to him and ordered Thornton's men to return to the east bank. For Lambert, the battle was over.

Jackson was enormously relieved when he received a message from Lambert asking for a cease-fire to bury the dead and succor the wounded. Jackson agreed to the proposal but only on the east bank. On the west bank he wanted the freedom to take the offensive. But a closer look at the corpse-carpeted plain of Chalmette made him realize that was a needless worry. The British army was out of business.

Pakenham's assault had consumed 3,326 men. Of those, 828 were killed and 2,468 were wounded—with more than half of the latter listed as "permanently disabled," a medical term that usually meant an amputated leg or arm. The remainder were taken prisoner. The losses in individual regiments make the slaughter even more apparent. The Highlanders lost 868 men out of a thousand. In Gibbs' column the light infantry lost 650 out of 862. Only 134 survived from the 816 men in the luckless, badly led Forty-fourth Regiment. Jackson's men, behind their mud rampart, had lost only eight men killed and fourteen wounded. Old Hickory could only express a sense of wonder at these numbers. "The unerring hand of Providence shielded my men," he said.

On January 9, American work parties joined the British in burying the dead. They also busily collected more than fifteen hundred enemy rifles and muskets, which Jackson distributed to his weaponless Kentuckians. The British retreated halfway down the isthmus on which they had fought the battle but showed no sign of departing. Meanwhile, fifty miles down the Mississippi, Jackson soon had a more realistic worry. A Royal Navy flotilla was attacking Fort Saint Philip.

Admiral Cochrane had ordered this foray after the failure of the British artillery on January 1. Two bomb ships, escorted by three sloops and a schooner, began bombarding the fort on the ninth. In command of the strongpoint was Major Walter J. Overton, with a garrison of 346 men. Staying out of range of the Americans' cannons, the British hurled more than a thousand shells into the fort during the next week. A lack of fuses for his mortars left Overton helpless to fire back. But on January 15, fuses, powder, and other supplies from Jackson's army arrived. The American mortars soon silenced one of the bomb ships and drove the other one down the river. On the morning of January 18 the British retreated, leaving the fort a shambles. But only two defenders had been killed, and the garrison was still full of fight.

That night, on the Villeré and adjoining de la Ronde plantations, the British army began a silent withdrawal. The engineers had labored for seven days to build a road along the Bayou Bienvenue. By morning the entire army had struggled through the mud to the shore of Lake Bourgne. They spent another miserable week in the muck and cold waiting to be ferried by Admiral Cochrane's weary oarsmen to the ships at the mouth of the lake.

In Washington, D.C., another act in the drama was reaching a climax. President James Madison waited anxiously for news from New Orleans—and from Hartford, Connecticut, where the New England convention to discuss secession was still in session. A letter that had left New Orleans on December 24 reported that the British had made a surprise landing with six thousand men and were marching on the city. On February 3, three delegates set out from Hartford to hand the president an ultimatum demanding that the federal government abandon all direction of the war, leaving its conduct up to individual states or combinations of states. It was not quite secession, but it was a big step toward it.

At Gadsby's Hotel in Baltimore, only a day's travel from Washington, the delegates heard a bustle in the streets. People were shouting and shooting off guns. News of Jackson's January 8 victory had arrived. By the time the delegates reached Washington, a huge celebration was in progress. The New Englanders found rooms in a boardinghouse in Georgetown and waited for the excitement to subside so they could proceed with their embassy. The war was not over.

It certainly did not appear to be over for the British army and navy as they sailed along the Gulf Coast toward Fort Bowyer, at the head of Mobile Bay. Even General Keane, recovering from his wound, agreed that with another fifty-six hundred men they could easily capture Mobile and attack New Orleans overland from the north. After all, victory went to the winner of the last battle, and the British were optimistic after they easily captured Fort Bowyer. Nearby Mobile was practically in their hands.

The next day, however, a British frigate hauled into the anchorage and dispatched a gig to Admiral Cochrane's flagship. It brought astonishing news from England. On December 24, the British and Americans had signed a treaty of peace at Ghent! It called for a *status quo ante* settlement—all boundaries would be restored to both sides as they existed at the outbreak of the war. Moderates in the British cabinet had seized on the September 11, 1814, American victory on Lake Champlain to convince the hard-liners it was time to make a peace of reconciliation.

The news reached Washington on February 14 and triggered another wild celebration. The delegates from the Hartford Convention waited in vain to hear from President Madison. After ten days they slunk out of the capital, and the Hartford Convention became a footnote in history textbooks.

Almost the last man to accept the news of peace as worthy of celebration was Andrew Jackson. He stubbornly refused to disband his army until he heard that both countries had ratified the treaty. This led to some spectacular brawls with the restless natives of New Orleans and with Governor Claiborne. But the general never deviated from his opinion that when dealing with "perfidious Albion," an American should keep up his guard.

Jackson emerged from his victory at New Orleans a national hero. He was able to parlay his popularity into a political base of power that propelled him to the presidency in 1828. As Jackson was leaving the White House at the end of his second term in 1837, a congressman asked him if there had been any point to the Battle of New Orleans. After all, it had been fought after the peace treaty was signed. The old warrior gave him one of his patented steely glares and said: "If General Pakenham and his ten thousand matchless veterans could have annihilated my little army . . . he would have captured New Orleans and sentried all the contiguous territory, though technically the war was over . . . .Great Britain would have immediately abrogated the Treaty of Ghent and would have ignored Jefferson's transaction with Napoleon."

Was he right? We will never know for certain. Old Hickory settled the argument in advance by winning the battle.

★   ★   ★   ★   ★

Unknown to anyone in the United States at the time of the battle, the Treaty of Ghent had been signed two weeks earlier in Paris on January 8. By the terms of the treaty, however, the war was not officially over until ratifications were exchanged on February 17, 1815 and proclaimed the following day. If the British had succeeded in taking New Orleans, they would have used it to gain concessions from the Americans. The victory at New Orleans helped bring the United States together as a nation, and propelled Andrew Jackson to the presidency in 1828.

Dispatches from the Mexican War

GEORGE WILKINS KENDALL

In war nothing is impossible, provided you use audacity.
—Major General George Patton

The Mexican war came in 1845 over the issue of Texas, recently annexed by the United States. Texas claimed the Rio Grande River as its southern border, yet the Mexican government under Santa Anna understandably refused to accept the loss of their territory. President James K. Polk ordered General Zachary Taylor to place troops between the Nueces and Rio Grande rivers. Taylor marched his men past the Nueces and deployed along the Rio Grande against the warnings of Mexican leaders. On April 24, 1846 Mexican cavalry attacked and captured a small American detachment near the Rio Grande. Two other border clashes at Palo Alto and Resaca de la Palma moved the president to request a declaration of war that was approved by Congress on May 23.

General Taylor led the advance across the Rio Grande, winning the Battle of Monterrey in September 1846. President Antonio López de Santa Anna personally marched north to fight Taylor but was defeated at the battle of Buena Vista on February 22, 1847. President Polk sent a second army under U.S. General Winfield Scott in March, transported to the port of Veracruz by sea, to begin an invasion of the Mexican heartland. Scott won the siege of Veracruz and marched toward Mexico City, winning the battles of Cerro Gordo and Chapultepec, occupying Mexico City in September.

Covering the advance under General Winfield Scott was the talented journalist George Wilkins Kendall. He was an exponent of war with Mexico. When hostilities began, he worked by first traveling with General Zachary Taylor, and then as aide to General William Worth in Winfield Scott's campaigns. He sent his paper, the *Daily Picayune,* the latest news by means of pony expresses and steamers, sometimes giving information to the government in advance of the official dispatches. His narrative accounts became famous and were widely copied, thus earning him a reputation as the first war correspondent.

The following is Kendall's reportage on the attacks to seize the defenses around Mexico City during the battle of Molino del Rey on September 8, 1847. The infantry captured the approaches to the castle Chapultepec, which protected the western approaches to Mexico City. On September 13, he would witness the climactic engagement of the war as American soldiers stormed Chapultepec ensuring the fall of Mexico City.

★　　★　　★　　★　　★

Tacubaya, September 7, 1847

This morning the enemy is making preparations for our reception in real earnest. At any early hour long lines of infantry were seen emerging from the city, filing past Chapultepec, and taking up positions at the Molino del Rey, at a strong work known as the Powder Magazine, and as is supposed at the foundry where the Mexicans cast all their cannon. I might here mention that Chapultepec is about three miles directly west of the city, that the Molino is about one thousand yards father west, and that the other positions occupied by the Mexicans stretch along at intervals in the same direction. Chapultepec itself is on a steep hill or mound, noted as the residence of Montezuma, is fortified, and is also said to be mined. From the archbishop's palace to this work is but little over or under one mile; from the former to the Molino about twelve hundred yards. The palace is nearly south of Chapultepec, which brings the new positions of the enemy directly to the left as our army faces them. Close reconnaissances of their works have been made this morning by Capt. Mason, and as the destruction of the foundry is considered of paramount importance, it has been determined upon to attack the enemy tonight. A hard resistance is anticipated, as large bodies, both of cavalry and infantry, are in plain view. Four pieces of cannon have been discovered in position, and it is thought the enemy has several others so masked that they cannot be seen.

In the meantime the greatest enthusiasm exists in the army—all appear anxious again to attack an enemy whose cowardice has no parallel, and whose treachery and duplicity would shame the veriest barbarians. Unpopular as was the armistice from the first with all, and uncalled for as they deemed it, its shameful violation by the Mexicans has served but to inflame, while the infamous intentions of the Mexican leaders in signing it, now rendered so palpable, has incensed both our officers and men to a degree that the enemy will feel in any encounter that may now take place.

Night, 9 o'clock.—The plan of attack has just been settled upon at a council of officers held at Gen. Worth's. Col. Garland's brigade is to move on the right in the direction of the Molino, watching Chapultepec and to be governed by circumstances. A storming party of 500 picked men under Maj. Wright, and conducted by Capt. Mason, is to attack the work supposed to be the foundry. Capt. Huger, with two 24-pounders, is to open upon the building as soon as it is light enough to see. Col. McIntosh, now that Col. Clarke is disabled, commands the 2d brigade of Worth's division, and will attack the enemy's right, Duncan's light battery and a large dragoon force under Maj. Sumner will act according to circumstances. To strengthen the movement, Gen. Cadwalader's brigade is also to take a part, and will probably attack in the centre. There are many who do not approve of the attack. They think that Chapultepec should be included in the programme of the performances, but of this Gen. Scott should be the best judge.

Yours, Etc.,

G. W. K.

Daily Picayune, October 17, 1847

Tacubaya, September 8, 1847

Forenoon, 10 o'clock.—I have just returned from another battlefield—one on which the victory of the American arms was complete, and on which our troops contended against an enemy immensely superior in number and strongly posted. Gen. Worth commenced the attack at early daylight, and in less than two hours every point was carried, all the cannon of the enemy were in our possession, an immense quantity of ammunition captured, and nearly 1000 men, among them fifty-three officers, taken prisoners.

For more than an hour the battle raged with a violence not surpassed since the Mexican war commenced, and so great the odds opposed that for some time the result was doubtful. The force of the enemy has been estimated at from 12,000 to 15,000, strongly posted behind breastworks, and to attack them our small force of scarcely 3000 was obliged to approach on an open plain and without the least cover; but their dauntless courage carried them over every obstacle, and notwithstanding the Mexicans fought with a valor rare for them, they were finally routed from one point or another until all were driven and dispersed. The defeat was total.

But to gain this victory our own loss has been uncommonly severe—it has been purchased with the blood of some of the most gallant spirits of the army. The 5th Infantry has suffered the most. This regiment along with the 6th and 8th, was engaged in the attack upon a strong work on the enemy's right, and was opposed to such superior numbers that it was compelled to retire along with the others. The celebrated Col. Martin Scott was killed in this attack, along with Lieuts. Burwell and Strong, while Col. McIntosh and many other officers were badly wounded. The worse than savage miscreants in the fort, after our men retired, set up a yell and came out and massacred such of our wounded as were unable to get off. In this way poor Burwell lost his life. Fully were they avenged, however; for within half an hour Duncan's battery, aided by the fall of another of their works, drove the dastardly wretches in full flight across the fields. No one knew or even surmised the strength of the place: it was an old fort, constructed long since, and was one of the main defences of the line of works.

On the enemy's left, and nearer Chapultepec, our loss was also great, although not as severe. It was here that Col. Wm. M. Graham, as brave a spirit as ever lived, was killed: Capts. Merrill and Ayers also fell in this part of the field. The wonder now is how anyone could come out safe under such a terrible fire as the enemy poured from his entire line of works. Nothing but the daring and impetuosity of our men, who rushed onward while their comrades were falling thick around them, gained the victory— had they once faltered all would have been lost.

The broken ground on the right of the enemy, cut up by deep ravines, saved many of Santa Anna's troops in their flight: yet as it was our dragoons killed and captured many of the fugitives. Large bodies of the Mexican cavalry approached the scene of strife several times, but they were driven like sheep by Duncan's battery.

The Mexican loss has been even more severe than our own. Gen. Balderas, Gen. León, and many other officers are numbered among the dead, while the interior of their works, the tops of the houses from which they fought, and the ground over which they fled are strewn with lifeless bodies. Such was the panic that many of our officers say that a few fresh troops might have taken Chapultepec itself almost without a struggle; but other than a few shots fired at that point from some of the captured cannon, no demonstration was made.

After the battle was over Gen. Scott came out, accompanied by his staff, and also by Mr. Trist. The Mexicans at the time were throwing shells at some of the wagons Gen. Worth had sent out to pick up the dead and wounded. They had placed a howitzer in position on Chapultepec at the close of the action, and now, seeing no enemy within reach, the cowardly wretches opened upon the ambulances and those who were gathering the bodies of their wounded and lifeless comrades. On seeing this worse than savage outrage, one of our officers, with a sarcastic expression of countenance, asked whether Mr. Trist had any new peace propositions in his pockets. Mackintosh did not come out after the battle to gain more time for his friend Santa Anna, nor worm out fresh intelligence of the strength and movements of our army, in order that he might be of service to the Mexicans by communicating it.

The Mexican prisoners say that Santa Anna himself was on the ground in the rear of their works, but left at the commencement of the rout. They admit that their entire force was 15,000; it is certain that including killed, wounded, prisoners and dispersed their loss has been near 5,000. Many of them were regulars, the 11th and 12th Infantry Regiments suffering most. The commander of the latter, Col. Tenorio, is a prisoner in our hands; some fourteen officers belonging to the former are also prisoners, but the commander, Gen. Perez, escaped.

The foundry, in which several moulds for casting cannon and other apparatus were found, was entirely demolished, and after ascertaining this, Gen. Scott, not wishing to hold the position, ordered all the forces to retire. The whole affair, as a military movement, is severely criticized by many of our officers. They contend that no result has been gained commensurate with the immense loss we have sustained in the battle. This is a matter I do not feel myself qualified to discuss, but it must be certain that the *morale* upon the Mexicans, of a defeat so disgraceful and so disastrous, must be important. They have now, (it is 5 o'clock in the afternoon,) returned to their positions; and if Santa Anna was on the ground as is stated, and can find no one to lay the blame upon, he may twist the whole affair into a victory—*on paper*. It will not be the first time he has done this thing.

Since I commenced this letter I have been out endeavoring to obtain a full list of the killed and wounded officers, but so far have been unable. Knowing the deep anxiety felt in the United States by the families of all, this shall be my first care. The entire loss in Gen. Worth's division, out of some 1,800 or 2,000 that went into action, will not fall much short of 600. The Dragoons and Gen. Cadwalader's brigade did not suffer so severely in comparison. What the next movement is to be no one knows, but it is thought the city will be attacked immediately.

Yours, Etc.,

G. W. K.

Daily Picayune, October 14, 1847

Tacubaya, September 10, 1847

We have accounts from Mexico, brought in by Frenchmen and other foreigners, to the effect that Santa Anna's loss at El Molino was much more severe than anyone here had anticipated. They say that during the afternoon of the 8th no less than 1500 wounded men came into the city, while the number of killed was over 600. The slaughter from the batteries of Col. Duncan and Capt. Drum must have been terrific. Santa Anna, it is said, would have laid all the blame of the defeat upon Gen. León, but that officer, unfortunately for him, died. He has since torn epaulets from the shoulders of Col. Miguel Andrade, commander of the celebrated regiment of Hussars, accuses him of everything, has thrown him into prison, and denied him all communication. He must have some one to break out upon.

Everything looks quiet today, but the Mexicans are busily employed in fortifying at every point. At Chapultepec they can be seen at work, while they are also repairing the damage done at El Molino and other points on that line. On the Piedad road they have strong works, while at the Niño Perdido and San Antonio Abad entrances to the city they are also fortifying with the greatest vigor. Gen. Pillow's division, as also Col. Riley's brigade, attached to that of Gen. Twiggs, occupy the village of La Piedad and neighborhood, in plain sight and in fact under the guns of the enemy. Gen. Worth remains here in Tacubaya, but he is sending all his sick and wounded to Mixcoac, out of the range of the guns of Chapultepec. No one knows what point will be first attacked, but this question will soon be determined. The next blow struck will be hard, and all hope decisive. It must read strange, the story that some 7 or 8000 men have set themselves down before a strongly fortified city of over 200,000 inhabitants, with an army of at least 25,000 men to defend it; but the tale is a true one and the proud capital of Mexico must fall.

Yours, Etc.,

G. W. K.

Daily Picayune, October 14, 1847

Tacubaya, September 12, 1847

At early daylight this morning a heavy cannonade was opened upon the stronghold of Chapultepec, which was increased during the day as additional siege guns were placed in position. The Mexicans returned the fire with great spirit at intervals during the day, but with little effect other than dismounting one of our guns—I cannot learn that a man has been killed at any of the batteries. Several of the Voltigeurs, while skirmishing with the enemy's sharpshooters at the foot of Chapultepec, were wounded, but none of them severely. A 10½-inch mortar was opened upon the place during the afternoon, and as several shells have been seen to fall and explode directly within the enemy's works it is certain that great damage has been caused. A firing of heavy guns has also been heard in the direction of La Piedad, showing that the Mexicans have been diverted in that quarter.

At dusk this evening several loads of scaling ladders were sent down towards the foot of Chapultepec, and the movements of our infantry and other light corps would indicate that the strong works upon the crest are to be stormed early tomorrow. A large portion of the entire army will be brought to the struggle, and it is thought the contest will be terrible. I have little time to write.

> Yours, Etc.,
> G.W.K.
> *Daily Picayune,* October 14, 1847

City of Mexico, September 14, 1847

Another victory, glorious in its results and which has thrown additional lustre upon the American arms, has been achieved today by the army under Gen. Scott—the proud capital of Mexico has fallen into the power of a mere handful of men compared with the immense odds arrayed against them, and Santa Anna, instead of shedding his blood as he had promised, is wandering with the remnant of his army no one knows whither.

The apparently impregnable works on Chapultepec, after a desperate struggle, were triumphantly carried—Gens. Bravo and Monterde, besides a host of officers of different grades, taken prisoners; over 1000 non-commissioned officers and privates, all their cannon and ammunition, are in our hands; the fugitives soon were in full flight towards the different works which command the entrance to the city, and our men at once were in hot pursuit.

Gen. Quitman, supported by Gen. Smith's brigade, took the road by the Chapultepec aqueduct towards the Belén gate and the Ciudadela; Gen. Worth, supported by Gen. Cadwalader's brigade, advanced by the San Cosmé aqueduct towards the garita of that name. Both routes were cut up by ditches and defended by breastworks, barricades, and strong works of every description known to military science; yet the daring and impetuosity of our men overcame one defence after another, and by nightfall every work to the city's edge was carried. Gen. Quitman's command, after the rout at Chapultepec, was the first to encounter the enemy in force. Midway between the former and the Belén gate, Santa Anna had constructed a strong work; but this was at once vigorously assaulted by Gen. Quitman, and aided by a flank fire from two of Duncan's guns, which Gen. Worth had ordered to approach as near as possible from the San Cosmé road, the enemy was again routed and in full flight. They again made a stand from their strong fortifications at and near the Belén garita, opening a tremendous fire not only of round shot, grape and shell, but of musketry; yet boldly Gen. Quitman advanced, stormed and carried the works, although at great loss, and then every point on this side the city was in our possession. In this onslaught two of our bravest officers were killed—Capt. Drum and Lieut. Benjamin.

Meanwhile Gen. Worth was rapidly advancing upon San Cosmé. At the English burying ground the enemy had constructed a strong work. It was defended by infantry for a short time, but could not resist the assault of our men—the affrighted Mexicans soon fled to another line of works nearer the city, and thus Gen. Worth was in possession of the entrance to San Cosmé. As his men advanced towards the garita, the enemy opened a heavy fire of musketry from the house tops, as well as of grape, canister and shell from their batteries, thus sweeping the street completely. At this juncture the old Monterey game, of burrowing and digging through the houses, was adopted. On the right, as our men faced the enemy, the aqueduct afforded a partial shelter; on the left, the houses gave some protection; but many were still killed or wounded by the grape which swept every part, as well as by the shells which were continually bursting in every direction. About 3 o'clock the work of the pick-axe and the crow-bar, under the direction of Lieut. G. W. Smith, of the Sappers and Miners, had fairly commenced, and every minute brought our men nearer the enemy's last stronghold. In the meantime two mountain howitzers were fairly lifted to the top of one of the houses and into the cupalo of the church, from which they opened a plunging and most effective fire, while one of Duncan's guns, in charge of Lieut. Hunt, was run up under a galling fire to a deserted breastwork, and at once opened upon the garita. In this latter daring feat, four men out of eight were either killed or wounded, but still the piece was most effectively served. The work of the Miners was still going on. In one house which they had entered, by the pick-axe, a favorite aide of Santa Anna's was found. The great man had just fled, but had left his friend and his supper! Both were well cared for—the latter was devoured by our hungry officers; the former, after doing the honors of the table, was made a close prisoner. Just as dark was setting in, our men had dug and mined their way almost up to the very guns of the enemy, and now, after a short struggle, they were completely routed and driven with the loss of everything. The command of the city by the San Cosmé route was attained.

During the night, Gen. Quitman commenced the work of throwing up breastworks and erecting batteries, with the intention of opening a heavy cannonade upon the Ciudadela with the first light this morning. At 10 o'clock at night Gen. Worth ordered Capt. Huger to bring up a 24-pounder and a 10-inch mortar to the garita or gate of San Cosmé, and having ascertained the bearings and distance of the grand plaza and palace, at once opened upon those points. The heavy shells were heard to explode in the very heart of the city. At a little after midnight Major Palacios, accompanied by two or three members of the municipal council of the city, arrived at Gen. Worth's headquarters, and in great trepidation informed him that Santa Anna and his grand army had fled, and that they wished at once to surrender the capital! They were referred to the commander-in-chief, and immediately started for Tacubaya; but in the meantime the firing upon the town ceased.

At 7 o'clock this morning Gen. Scott, with his staff, rode in and took quarters in the national palace, on the top of which the regimental flag of the gallant Rifles and the stars and stripes were already flying. An immense crowd of blanketed leperos, the scum of the capital, were congregated in the plaza as the commander-in-chief entered it. They pressed upon our soldiers, and eyed them as though they were beings of another world. So much were they in the way, and with such eagerness did they press around, that Gen. Scott was compelled to order our Dragoons to clear the plaza. They were told, however, not to injure or harm a man in the mob—they were all our friends!

About five minutes after this, and while Gen. Worth was returning to his division near the Alameda, he was fired upon from a house near the Convent of San Francisco. Some of the cowardly Polkas, who had fled the day previous without discharging their guns, now commenced the assassin game of shooting at every one of our men they saw, from windows, as well as from behind the parapets on the azoteas or tops of the houses. In half an hour's time our good friends, the leperos, in the neighborhood of the hospital of San Andres and the church of Santa Clara, also commenced discharging muskets and throwing bottles and rocks from the azoteas. I have neglected to mention that just previous to this Col. Garland had been severely wounded by a musket, fired by some miscreant from a window.

For several hours this cowardly war upon our men continued, and during this time many were killed or wounded. It was in this species of fighting that Lieut. Sidney Smith received his death wound. The division of Gen. Twiggs in one part of the city, and Gen. Worth in another, were soon actively engaged in putting down the insurrection. Orders were given to shoot every man in all the houses from which the firing came, while the guns of the different light batteries swept the streets in all directions. As the assassins were driven from one house they would take refuge on another; but by the middle of the afternoon they were all forced back to the barriers and suburbs. Many innocent persons have doubtless been killed during the day, but this could not be avoided. Had orders been given at the outset to blow up and demolish every house or church from which one man was fired upon, the disturbances would have been at once quelled. At it is, I trust that the lesson the rabble and their mischievous leaders have received today may deter them from future outrages.

On entering the palace Gen. Scott at once named Gen. Quitman governor of Mexico—a most excellent appointment. Some wag immediately proclaimed aloud in the plaza as follows: "Gen. John A Quitman of Mississippi, has been appointed governor of Mexico, vice Gen. Jose Maria Tornel resigned—*very suddenly!*" It seems that the valiant Tornel ran off at an early hour, and his magnificent house has been converted into a hospital for our wounded officers.

Yours, Etc.,

G. W. K.

Daily Picayune, October 14, 1847

Mexico, September 17, 1847

The Mexican loss it is impossible to ascertain, but it has been immense. Among the killed at Chapultepec were Gen. Juan Nepomecuno Perez, Col. Juan Cano, a distinguished officer of engineers, and Lieut. Lucian Calvo, one of Gen. Bravo's aides. Gen. Saldaña was badly wounded, as were many other distinguished officers. Five generals, three colonels, seven lieutenant colonels, and near one hundred majors, captains and lieutenants, were taken prisoners, together with 800 or more rank and file. At the garitas of Belén and San Cosmé many officers were killed or wounded, but their names are not known.

The total number of deserters hung at San Angel and Mixcoac was *fifty*, and well did they deserve their fate. Thirty of them were hung at Mixcoac on the morning of the 13th. They were compelled to stand upon the gallows until the flag they had deserted was flying from Chapultepec, and were then all swung off at the same time. Not one of them complained that his fate was undeserved.

It is no time now to mention the hundreds of cases of individual gallantry noticed at the different battles, but I cannot help paying a passing compliments to the noted chaplain, Parson McCarty, as he is called by all. The worthy man was seen in all parts, and where the danger was the greatest, comforting the wounded and exhorting the wavering to press forward, and all the time regardless of his own safety. No man exerted himself more to ensure a victory, no man is more entitled to special commendation.

We are still without any positive or definite information as regards Santa Anna's great army, but all agree that it is disorganized and broken up. There is a report that Gen. Herrera has reached Querétaro with 4000 men in a body, but it requires confirmation.

Yours, Etc.,

G. W. K.

Daily Picayune, October 15, 1847

★ ★ ★ ★ ★

The Treaty of Guadalupe Hidalgo was signed on February 2, 1848, ending the war and giving the United States undisputed control of Texas, California, Nevada, Utah, and parts of Colorado, Arizona, New Mexico and Wyoming. Zachary Taylor would later become President in 1849.

A Day: Hospital Sketches, Fredericksburg

LOUISA MAY ALCOTT

Let us cross over the river and rest under the shade of the trees.
—Lt. Gen. Thomas J. Jackson

The American Civil War came at a time when great technological changes had revolutionized military weaponry. Rifled muskets and advancements in artillery maximized the range and firepower brought to bear upon an enemy. These advances, however, were not matched by changes in tactics that still relied on Napoleonic-era concepts of massed infantry and bayonet charges, which led to the horrific casualties of Civil War engagements as thousands of men fell before murderous gunfire at close ranges.

Medical science had not kept pace with the advancement of military technology either. Surgeons were still unaware of the dangers of infection, and used instruments that went unsterilized from patient to patient. Operations were mostly a crude affair. Doctors were forced to amputate any limb smashed by musket balls or shell fragments. If a man was wounded in the abdomen, there was nothing surgeons could do. The sheer number of wounded men often overwhelmed the field hospitals. Disease and infection were rampant, and only about half of those admitted with serious wounds would survive.

Women would play a vital role in hospitals in both the Confederacy and the Union. The attitude toward women was another aspect of the times that had not changed, and as such, only a handful served with the army as regular nurses. The Army Nurse Corps was not established until 1901. It was tradition for women to volunteer as nurses, and they did so by the thousands. Others would volunteer as cooks, suppliers, and laundry workers. Some became spies for their cause. A special few would disguise themselves as men to serve in combat. Dr. Mary Walker, who volunteered as a surgeon, was awarded the Medal of Honor by President Johnson. The majority, however, were unsung heroes of the Civil War who left home and family to do what they could to ease the suffering.

Louisa May Alcott was already an active feminist, abolitionist, and writer when she volunteered to serve as a nurse at the Union Hospital in Georgetown, D.C. Already writing for the *Atlantic Monthly*, she also wrote letters home that were later edited into a published work called *Hospital Sketches*. The following chapter, "A Day," describes her first encounter with the arrival of mass casualties from the battlefield at Fredericksburg. Her writing is the powerful story of her shocking loss of innocence in war, and a reminder of the dedication of the nurses who devoted themselves to the care of the wounded. Thousands more like her would serve in her footsteps, and now continue to serve in the highest stations of the U.S. Army.

★   ★   ★   ★   ★

T HEY'VE come! they've come! hurry up, ladies—you're wanted."

"Who have come? the rebels?"

This sudden summons in the gray dawn was somewhat startling to a three days' nurse like myself, and, as the thundering knock came at our door, I sprang up in my bed, prepared

> "To gird my woman's form,
> And on the ramparts die,"

if necessary; but my room-mate took it more coolly, and, as she began a rapid toilet, answered my bewildered question,—

"Bless you, no child; it's the wounded from Fredericksburg; forty ambulances are at the door, and we shall have our hands full in fifteen minutes."

"What shall we have to do?"

"Wash, dress, feed, warm and nurse them for the next three months, I dare say. Eighty beds are ready, and we were getting impatient for the men to come. Now you will begin to see hospital life in earnest, for you won't probably find time to sit down all day, and may think yourself fortunate if you get to bed by midnight. Come to me in the ball-room when you are ready; the worst cases are always carried there, and I shall need your help."

So saying, the energetic little woman twirled her hair into a button at the back of her head, in a "cleared for action" sort of style, and vanished, wrestling her way into a feminine kind of pea-jacket as she went.

I am free to confess that I had a realizing sense of the fact that my hospital bed was not a bed of roses just then, or the prospect before me one of unmingled rapture. My three days' experiences had begun with a death, and, owing to the defalcation of another nurse, a somewhat abrupt plunge into the superintendence of a ward containing forty beds, where I spent my shining hours washing faces, serving rations, giving medicine, and sitting in a very hard chair, with pneumonia on one side, diptheria on the other, five typhoids on the opposite, and a dozen dilapidated patriots, hopping, lying, and lounging about, all staring more or less at the new "nuss," who suffered untold agonies, but concealed them under as matronly an aspect as a spinster could assume, and blundered through her trying labors with a Spartan firmness, which I hope they appreciated, but am afraid they didn't. Having a taste for "ghastliness," I had rather longed for the wounded to arrive, for rheumatism wasn't heroic, neither was liver complaint, or measles; even fever had lost its charms since "bathing burning brows" had been used up in romances, real and ideal; but when I peeped into the dusky street lined with what I at first had innocently called market carts, now unloading their sad freight at our door, I recalled sundry reminiscences I had heard from nurses of longer standing, my ardor experienced a sudden chill, and I indulged in a most unpatriotic wish that I was safe at home again, with a quiet day before me, and no necessity for being hustled up, as if I were a hen and had only to hop off my roost, give my plumage a peck, and be ready for action. A second bang at the door sent this recreant desire to the right about, as a little woolly head popped in, and Joey, (a six years' old contraband,) announced—

"Miss Blank is jes' wild fer ye, and says fly round right away. They's comin' in, I tell yer, heaps on 'em—one was took out dead, and I see him,—hi! warn't he a goner!"

With which cheerful intelligence the imp scuttled away, singing like a blackbird, and I followed, feeling that Richard was *not* himself again, and wouldn't be for a long time to come.

The first thing I met was a regiment of the vilest odors that ever assaulted the human nose, and took it by storm. Cologne, with its seven and seventy evil savors, was a posy-bed to it; and the worst of this affliction was, every one had assured me that it was a chronic weakness of all hospitals, and I must bear it. I did, armed with lavender water, with which I so besprinkled myself and premises, that, like my friend Sairy, I was soon known among my patients as "the nurse with the bottle." Having been run over by three excited surgeons, bumped against by migratory coal-hods, water-pails, and small boys, nearly scalded by an avalanche of newly-filled tea-pots, and hopelessly entangled in a knot of colored sisters coming to wash, I progressed by slow stages up stairs and down, till the main hall was reached, and I paused to take breath and a survey. There they were! "our brave boys," as the papers justly call them, for cowards could hardly have been so riddled with shot and shell, so torn and shattered, nor have borne suffering for which we have no name, with an uncomplaining fortitude, which made one glad to cherish each as a brother. In they came, some on stretchers, some in men's arms, some feebly staggering along propped on rude crutches, and one lay stark and still with covered face, as a comrade gave his name to be recorded before they carried him away to the dead house. All was hurry and confusion; the hall was full of these wrecks of humanity, for the most exhausted could not reach a bed till duly ticketed and registered; the walls were lined with rows of such as could sit, the floor covered with the more disabled, the steps and doorways filled with helpers and lookers on; the sound of many feet and voices made that usually quiet hour as noisy as noon; and, in the midst of it all, the matron's motherly face brought more comfort to many a poor soul, than the cordial draughts she administered, or the cheery words that welcomed all, making of the hospital a home.

The sight of several stretchers, each with its legless, armless, or desperately wounded occupant, entering my ward, admonished me that I was there to work, not to wonder or weep; so I corked up my feelings, and returned to the path of duty, which was rather "a hard road to travel" just then. The house had been a hotel before hospitals were needed, and many of the doors still bore their old names; some not so inappropriate as might be imagined, for my ward was in truth a *ball-room*, if gun-shot wounds could christen it. Forty beds were prepared, many already tenanted by tired men who fell down anywhere, and drowsed till the smell of food roused them. Round the great stove was gathered the dreariest group I ever saw— ragged, gaunt and pale, mud to the knees, with bloody bandages untouched since put on days before; many bundled up in blankets, coats being lost or useless; and all wearing that disheartened look which proclaimed defeat, more plainly than any telegram of the Burnside blunder. I pitied them so much, I dared not speak to them, though, remembering all they had been through since the route at Fredericksburg, I yearned to serve the dreariest of them all. Presently, Miss Blank tore me from my refuge behind piles of one-sleeved shirts, odd socks, bandages and lint; put basin, sponge, towels, and a block of brown soap into my hands, with these appalling directions:

"Come, my dear, begin to wash as fast as you can. Tell them to take off socks, coats and shirts, scrub them well, put on clean shirts, and the attendants will finish them off, and lay them in bed."

If she had requested me to shave them all, or dance a hornpipe on the stove funnel, I should have been less staggered; but to scrub some dozen lords of creation at a moment's notice, was really—really—. However, there was no time for nonsense, and, having resolved when I came to do everything I was bid, I drowned my scruples in my wash-bowl, clutched my soap manfully, and, assuming a business-like air, made a dab at the first dirty specimen I saw, bent on performing my task *vi et armis* if necessary. I chanced to light on a withered old Irishman, wounded in the head, which caused that portion of his frame to be tastefully laid out like a garden, the bandages being the walks, his hair the shrubbery. He was so overpowered by the honor of having a lady wash him, as he expressed it, that he did nothing but roll up his eyes, and bless me, in an irresistible style which was too much for my sense of the ludicrous; so we laughed together, and when I knelt down to take off his shoes, he "flopped" also, and wouldn't hear of my touching "them dirty craters. May your bed above be aisy darlin', for the day's work ye ar doon! —Whoosh! there ye are, and bedad, it's hard tellin' which is the dirtiest, the fut or the shoe." It was; and if he hadn't been to the fore, I should have gone on pulling, under the impression that the "fut" was a boot, for trousers, socks, shoes and legs were a mass of mud. This comical tableau produced a general grin, at which propitious beginning I took heart and scrubbed away like any tidy parent on a Saturday night. Some of them took the performance like sleepy children, leaning their tired heads against me as I worked, others looked grimly scandalized, and several of the roughest colored like bashful girls. One wore a soiled little bag about his neck, and, as I moved it, to bathe his wounded breast, I said,

"Your talisman didn't save you, did it?"

"Well, I reckon it did, marm, for that shot would a gone a couple a inches deeper but for my old mammy's camphor bag," answered the cheerful philosopher.

Another, with a gun-shot wound through the cheek, asked for a looking-glass, and when I brought one, regarded his swollen face with a dolorous expression, as he muttered—

"I vow to gosh, that's too bad! I warn't a bad looking chap before, and now I'm done for; won't there be a thunderin' scar? and what on earth will Josephine Skinner say?"

He looked up at me with his one eye so appealingly, that I controlled my risibles, and assured him that if Josephine was a girl of sense, she would admire the honorable scar, as a lasting proof that he had faced the enemy, for all women thought a wound the best decoration a brave soldier could wear. I hope Miss Skinner verified the good opinion I so rashly expressed of her, but I shall never know.

The next scrubbee was a nice looking lad, with a curly brown mane, and a budding trace of gingerbread over the lip, which he called his beard, and defended stoutly, when the barber jocosely suggested its immolation. He lay on a bed, with one leg gone, and the right arm so shattered that it must evidently follow: yet the little Sergeant was as merry as if his afflictions were not worth lamenting over; and when a drop or two of salt water mingled with my suds at the sight of this strong young body, so marred and maimed, the boy looked up, with a brave smile, though there was a little quiver of the lips, as he said,

"Now don't you fret yourself about me, miss; I'm first rate here, for it's nuts to lie still on this bed, after knocking about in those confounded ambulances, that shake what there is left of a fellow to jelly. I never was in one of these places before, and think this cleaning up a jolly thing for us, though I'm afraid it isn't for you ladies."

"Is this your first battle, Sergeant?"

"No, miss; I've been in six scrimmages, and never got a scratch till this last one; but it's done the business pretty thoroughly for me, I should say. Lord! what a scramble there'll be for arms and legs, when we old boys come out of our graves, on the Judgment Day: wonder if we shall get our own again? If we do, my leg will have to tramp from Fredericksburg, my arm from here, I suppose, and meet my body, wherever it may be."

The fancy seemed to tickle him mightily, for he laughed blithely, and so did I; which, no doubt, caused the new nurse to be regarded as a light-minded sinner by the Chaplain, who roamed vaguely about, informing the men that they were all worms, corrupt of heart, with perishable bodies, and souls only to be saved by a diligent perusal of certain tracts, and other equally cheering bits of spiritual consolation, when spirituous ditto would have been preferred.

"I say, Mrs.!" called a voice behind me; and, turning, I saw a rough Michigander, with an arm blown off at the shoulder, and two or three bullets still in him—as he afterwards mentioned, as carelessly as if gentlemen were in the habit of carrying such trifles about with them. I went to him, and, while administering a dose of soap and water, he whispered, irefully:

"That red-headed devil, over yonder, is a reb, damn him! You'll agree to that, I'll bet? He's got shet of a foot, or he'd a cut like the rest of the lot. Don't you wash him, nor feed him, but jest let him holler till he's tired. It's a blasted shame to fetch them fellers in here, along side of us; and so I'll tell the chap that bosses this concern; cuss me if I don't."

I regret to say that I did not deliver a moral sermon upon the duty of forgiving our enemies, and the sin of profanity, then and there; but, being a red-hot Abolitionist, stared fixedly at the tall rebel, who was a copperhead, in every sense of the word, and privately resolved to put soap in his eyes, rub his nose the wrong way, and excoriate his cuticle generally, if I had the washing of him.

My amiable intentions, however, were frustrated; for, when I approached, with as Christian an expression as my principles would allow, and asked the question—"Shall I try to make you more comfortable, sir?" all I got for my pains was a gruff—

"No; I'll do it myself."

"Here's your Southern chivalry, with a witness," thought I, dumping the basin down before him, thereby quenching a strong desire to give him a summary baptism, in return for his ungraciousness; for my angry passions rose, at this rebuff, in a way that would have scandalized good Dr. Watts. He was a disappointment in all respects, (the rebel, not the blessed Doctor,) for he was neither fiendish, romantic, pathetic, or anything interesting; but a long, fat man, with a head like a burning bush, and a perfectly expressionless face: so I could dislike him without the slightest drawback, and ignored his existence from that day forth. One redeeming trait he certainly did possess, as the floor speedily testified; for his ablutions were so vigorously performed, that his bed soon stood like an isolated island, in a sea of soap-suds, and he resembled a dripping merman, suffering from the loss of a fin. If cleanliness is a near neighbor to godliness, then was the big rebel the godliest man in my ward that day.

Having done up our human wash, and laid it out to dry, the second syllable of our version of the word war-fare was enacted with much success. Great trays of bread, meat, soup and coffee appeared; and both nurses and attendants turned waiters, serving bountiful rations to all who could eat. I can call my pinafore to testify to my good will in the work, for in ten minutes it was reduced to a perambulating bill of fare, presenting samples of all the refreshments going or gone. It was a lively scene; the long room lined with rows of beds, each filled by an occupant, whom water, shears, and clean raiment, had transformed from a dismal ragamuffin into a recumbent hero, with a cropped head. To and fro rushed matrons, maids, and convalescent "boys," skirmishing with knives and forks; retreating with empty plates; marching and counter-marching, with unvaried success, while the clash of busy spoons made most inspiring music for the charge of our Light Brigade:

> *"Beds to the front of them,*
> *Beds to the right of them,*
> *Beds to the left of them,*
> *Nobody blundered.*
> *Beamed at by hungry souls,*
> *Screamed at with brimming bowls,*
> *Steamed at by army rolls,*
> *Buttered and sundered.*
> *With coffee not cannon plied,*
> *Each must be satisfied,*
> *Whether they lived or died;*
> *All the men wondered."*

Very welcome seemed the generous meal, after a week of suffering, exposure, and short commons; soon the brown faces began to smile, as food, warmth, and rest, did their pleasant work; and the grateful "Thankee's" were followed by more graphic accounts of the battle and retreat, than any paid reporter could have given us. Curious contrasts of the tragic and comic met one everywhere; and some touching as well as ludicrous episodes, might have been recorded that day. A six foot New Hampshire man, with a leg broken and perforated by a piece of shell, so large that, had I not seen the wound, I should have regarded the story as a Munchausenism, beckoned me to come and help him, as he could not sit up, and both his bed and beard were getting plentifully anointed with soup. As I fed my big nestling with corresponding mouthfuls, I asked him how he felt during the battle.

"Well, 'twas my fust, you see, so I ain't ashamed to say I was a trifle flustered in the beginnin', there was such an allfired racket; for ef there's anything I do spleen agin, it's noise. But when my mate, Eph Sylvester, caved, with a bullet through his head, I got mad, and pitched in, licketty cut. Our part of the fight didn't last long; so a lot of us larked round Fredericksburg, and give some of them houses a pretty consid'able of a rummage, till we was ordered out of the mess. Some of our fellows cut like time; but I warn't a-goin' to run for nobody; and, fust thing I knew, a shell bust, right in front of us, and I keeled over, feelin' as if I was blowed higher'n a kite. I sung out, and the boys come back for me, double quick; but the way they chucked me over them fences was a caution, I tell you. Next day I was most as black as that darkey yonder, lickin' plates on the sly. This is bully coffee, ain't it? Give us another pull at it, and I'll be obleeged to you."

I did; and, as the last gulp subsided, he said, with a rub of his old handkerchief over eyes as well as mouth:

"Look a here; I've got a pair a earbobs and a handkercher pin I'm a goin' to give you, if you'll have them; for you're the very moral o' Lizy Sylvester, poor Eph's wife: that's why I signalled you to come over here. They ain't much, I guess, but they'll do to memorize the rebs by."

Burrowing under his pillow, he produced a little bundle of what he called "truck," and gallantly presented me with a pair of earrings, each representing a cluster of corpulent grapes, and the pin a basket of astonishing fruit, the whole large and coppery enough for a small warming-pan. Feeling delicate about depriving him of such valuable relics, I accepted the earrings alone, and was obliged to depart, somewhat abruptly, when my friend stuck the warming-pan in the bosom of his night-gown, viewing it with much complacency, and, perhaps, some tender memory, in that rough heart of his, for the comrade he had lost.

Observing that the man next him had left his meal untouched, I offered the same service I had performed for his neighbor, but he shook his head.

"Thank you, ma'am; I don't think I'll ever eat again, for I'm shot in the stomach. But I'd like a drink of water, if you ain't too busy."

I rushed away, but the water-pails were gone to be refilled, and it was some time before they reappeared. I did not forget my patient patient, meanwhile, and, with the first mugful, hurried back to him. He seemed asleep; but something in the tired white face caused me to listen at his lips for a breath. None came. I touched his forehead; it was cold: and then I knew that, while he waited, a better nurse than I had given him a cooler draught, and healed him with a touch. I laid the sheet over the quiet sleeper, whom no noise could now disturb; and, half an hour later, the bed was empty. It seemed a poor requital for all he had sacrificed and suffered,—that hospital bed, lonely even in a crowd; for there was no familiar face for him to look his last upon; no friendly voice to say, Good bye; no hand to lead him gently down into the Valley of the Shadow; and he vanished, like a drop in that red sea upon whose shores so many women stand lamenting. For a moment I felt bitterly indignant at this seeming carelessness of the value of life, the sanctity of death; then consoled myself with the thought that, when the great muster roll was called, these nameless men might be promoted above many whose tall monuments record the barren honors they have won.

All having eaten, drank, and rested, the surgeons began their rounds; and I took my first lesson in the art of dressing wounds. It wasn't a festive scene, by any means; for Dr P., whose Aid I constituted myself, fell to work with a vigor which soon convinced me that I was a weaker vessel, though nothing would have induced me to confess it then. He had served in the Crimea, and seemed to regard a dilapidated body very much as I should have regarded a damaged garment; and, turning up his cuffs, whipped out a very unpleasant looking housewife, cutting, sawing, patching and piecing, with the enthusiasm of an accomplished surgical seamstress; explaining the process, in scientific terms, to the patient, meantime; which, of course, was immensely cheering and comfortable. There was an uncanny sort of fascination in watching him, as he peered and probed into the mechanism of those wonderful bodies, whose mysteries he understood so well. The more intricate the wound, the better he liked it. A poor private, with both legs off, and shot through the lungs, possessed more attractions for him than a dozen generals, slightly scratched in some "masterly retreat;" and had any one appeared in small pieces, requesting to be put together again, he would have considered it a special dispensation.

The amputations were reserved till the morrow, and the merciful magic of ether was not thought necessary that day, so the poor souls had to bear their pains as best they might. It is all very well to talk of the patience of woman; and far be it from me to pluck that feather from her cap, for, heaven knows, she isn't allowed to wear many; but the patient endurance of these men, under trials of the flesh, was truly wonderful. Their fortitude seemed contagious, and scarcely a cry escaped them, though I often longed to groan for them, when pride kept their white lips shut, while great drops stood upon their foreheads, and the bed shook with the irrepressible tremor of their tortured bodies. One or two Irishmen anathematized the doctors with the frankness of their nation, and ordered the Virgin to stand by them, as if she had been the wedded Biddy to whom they could administer the poker, if she didn't; but, as a general thing, the work went on in silence, broken only by some quiet request for roller, instruments, or plaster, a sigh from the patient, or a sympathizing murmur from the nurse.

It was long past noon before these repairs were even partially made; and, having got the bodies of my boys into something like order, the next task was to minister to their minds, by writing letters to the anxious souls at home; answering questions, reading papers, taking possession of money and valuables; for the eighth commandment was reduced to a very fragmentary condition, both by the blacks and whites, who ornamented our hospital with their presence. Pocket books, purses, miniatures, and watches, were sealed up, labelled, and handed over to the matron, till such times as the owners thereof were ready to depart homeward or campward again. The letters dictated to me, and revised by me, that afternoon, would have made an excellent chapter for some future history of the war; for, like that which Thackeray's "Ensign Spooney" wrote his mother just before Waterloo, they were "full of affection, pluck, and bad spelling;" nearly all giving lively accounts of the battle, and ending with a somewhat sudden plunge from patriotism to provender, desiring "Marm," "Mary Ann," or "Aunt Peters," to send along some pies, pickles, sweet stuff, and apples, "to yourn in haste," Joe, Sam, or Ned, as the case might be.

My little Sergeant insisted on trying to scribble something with his left hand, and patiently accomplished some half dozen lines of hieroglyphics, which he gave me to fold and direct, with a boyish blush, that rendered a glimpse of "My Dearest Jane," unnecessary, to assure me that the heroic lad had been more successful in the service of Commander-in-Chief Cupid than that of Gen. Mars; and a charming little romance blossomed instanter in Nurse Periwinkle's romantic fancy, though no further confidences were made that day, for Sergeant fell asleep, and, judging from his tranquil face, visited his absent sweetheart in the pleasant land of dreams.

At five o'clock a great bell rang, and the attendants flew, not to arms, but to their trays, to bring up supper, when a second uproar announced that it was ready. The new comers woke at the sound; and I presently discovered that it took a very bad wound to incapacitate the defenders of the faith for the consumption of their rations; the amount that some of them sequestered was amazing; but when I suggested the probability of a famine hereafter, to the matron, that motherly lady cried out: "Bless their hearts, why shouldn't they eat? It's their only amusement; so fill every one, and, if there's not enough ready to-night, I'll lend my share to the Lord by giving it to the boys." And, whipping up her coffee-pot and plate of toast, she gladdened the eyes and stomachs of two or three dissatisfied heroes, by serving them with a liberal hand; and I haven't the slightest doubt that, having cast her bread upon the waters, it came back buttered, as another large-hearted old lady was wont to say.

Then came the doctor's evening visit; the administration of medicines; washing feverish faces; smoothing tumbled beds; wetting wounds; singing lullabies; and preparations for the night. By twelve, the last labor of love was done; the last "good night" spoken; and, if any needed a reward for that day's work, they surely received it, in the silent eloquence of those long lines of faces, showing pale and peaceful in the shaded rooms, as we quitted them, followed by grateful glances that lighted us to bed, where rest, the sweetest, made our pillows soft, while Night and Nature took our places, filling that great house of pain with the healing miracles of Sleep, and his diviner brother, Death.

★ ★ ★ ★ ★

Louisa May Alcott served as a nurse for only six weeks before contracting typhoid fever. The doctors of the time treated the disease with calomel, a mercury-laden drug to cure typhoid. The effects of the mercury poisoned her for the rest of her life. She went on to publish her most famous story *Little Women* in 1868. The book was an instant success and ensured her future as a writer. She also became an active suffragist for the women's vote. She died in May of 1888 in Boston from the effects of mercury poisoning.

Bayonet: Forward!

JOSHUA LAWRENCE CHAMBERLAIN

At that crisis, I ordered the bayonet. The word was enough.
—Col. Joshua L. Chamberlain, 1863

The battle of Gettysburg, fought over July 1–3, 1863, was arguably the most strategically significant battle in American history. General Lee decided to advance into northern territory with his Army of Northern Virginia following his victory at Chancellorsville in May. An invasion of the north would interrupt the Union's plans to campaign that summer and relieve pressure on the besieged city of Vicksburg in Mississippi. Lee's army could forage and capture vitally-needed supplies while giving the Virginia farmers time to grow and harvest their crops. Most importantly, a victory on northern soil would threaten Philadelphia, Baltimore, Washington, or New York, and help gain southern recognition by foreign powers. A victory for Lee could bring an end to the war as the peace movement in the northern states was growing. The high-water mark of the Confederacy was at hand.

The first day of the battle saw the Confederates win the field, forcing the Union regiments off McPherson's Ridge near the town of Gettysburg. Union forces had withdrawn to the high ground south of town along Cemetery Ridge, defending Culp's Hill to the northeast, and Little Round Top to the south. At 3:00 PM on July 2, however, Maj. General Sickle in command of III Corps moved his men forward 800 meters to the west without orders to obtain higher ground for his artillery. This left the Little Round Top undefended. Late in the afternoon, Brigadier General Gouverneur K. Warren was sent by General Meade to deal with the gap in the line that had formed between General Sickle's and Hancock's Corps. Climbing Little Round Top, Warren found only a small Signal Corps station there. He saw the glint of bayonets in the sun to the southwest and realized that a Confederate assault into the Union flank was imminent.

The Confederates of General John Bell Hood's division were coming. General Lee assigned Longstreet's II Corps for an all-out attack on the Union left flank. If they could take the Little Round Top, Confederate artillery would command the entire battlefield. Warren sent his staff officers racing to find help. Maj. Gen. George Sykes, who commanded V Corps quickly dispatched a messenger to order his 1st Division, commanded by Maj. Gen. James Barnes, to Little Round Top. Before the messenger could reach Barnes, he encountered Colonel Strong Vincent, leading the lead brigade, who seized the initiative and directed his four regiments to Little Round Top without waiting for permission from Barnes.

He and a staff officer galloped ahead to reconnoiter and guided his four regiments into position. On the western slope he placed the 16th Michigan, and then proceeding counterclockwise were the 44th New York, the 83rd Pennsylvania, and finally, at the end of the line on the southern slope, the 20th Maine. Arriving only ten minutes before the Confederates, Vincent instructed his brigade to take cover and wait, and ordered Colonel Joshua Lawrence Chamberlain, commanding the 20th Maine, to hold his position, the extreme left of the Army of the Potomac, at all costs. Chamberlain and his 385 men waited for the advancing wave of Confederate soldiers now only a few hundred yards away.

Col. Joshua Chamberlain had commanded the 20th Maine Volunteer Regiment since it was formed at the outbreak of the Civil War. They had already seen action at Fredericksburg, Antietam, and Chancellorsville. Before the war, Chamberlain was a professor of rhetoric at Bowdoin College in Maine. Here then was a legend in the making, a citizen soldier and his volunteer regiment at the crucible of the largest battle ever fought in North America. The following chapter is taken from Chamberlain's account of the action for Little Round Top, "Through Blood and Fire at Gettysburg," published in *Hearst's Magazine* in 1913.

★   ★   ★   ★   ★

Through Blood and Fire at Gettysburg

Nightfall brought us to Hanover, Pennsylvania, and to a halt. And it was the evening of the first day of July, 1863. All day we had been marching north from Maryland, searching and pushing out on all roads for the hoped-for collision with Lee eagerly, hurriedly, yet cautiously, with skirmishers and flankers out to sound the first challenge, and our main body ready for the call. Fanwise our divisions had been spread out to cover Washington, but more was at stake than the capital city of the Union: there was that important political and international question, the recognition of the Southern Confederacy as independent by France and England. This recognition, denying the very contentions of the North from the beginning would have been almost fatal to it. And Lee need not win a decided victory in the field to bring about the recognition: his capture and occupation of an important and strategic point in the North would have been enough.

All day, ever and again, we had seen detachments of Lee's cavalry; even as we passed an outlying field to our encampment the red slanting sunlight fell softly across the grim relics of a cavalry fight of the afternoon; the survivors of which had swept on, and pursuing.

Worn and famished we stacked arms in camping order, hoping to bivouac beside them, and scampered like madcaps for those two prime factors of a desultory supper—water and fence-rails; for the finding of which the Yankee volunteer has an aptitude which should be ranked among the spiritual intuitions, though in their old-school theology most farmers of our acquaintance were inclined to reckon the aptitude among the carnal appetites of the totally depraved. Some of the forage wagons had now got up, and there was a brief rally at their tail ends for quick justice to be dispensed. But the unregenerate fires had hardly blackened the coffee-dippers, and the hardtack hardly been hammered into working order by the bayonet shanks, when everything was stopped short by whispers of disaster away on the left: the enemy had struck our columns at Gettysburg, and driven it back with terrible loss; Reynolds, the commander, had been killed, and the remnant scarcely able to hold on to the hillsides unless rescue came before morning. These were only rumors flitting owl-like, in the gathering shadows. We could not quite believe them, but they deepened our mood.

To the March! On to Gettysburg!

Suddenly the startling bugle-call from unseen headquarters! "The General!" it rang! "To the march! No moment of delay!"

Word was coming, too. Staff officers dashed from corps, to division, to brigade, to regiment, to battery, and the order flew like the hawk, and not the owl. "To Gettysburg!" it said, a forced march of sixteen miles. But what forced it? And what opposed? Not supper, nor sleep, nor sore feet and aching limbs.

In a moment, the whole corps was in marching order; rest, rations, earth itself forgotten; one thought,—to be first on that Gettysburg road. The iron-faced veterans were transformed to boys. They insisted on starting out with colors flying, so that even the night might know what manner of men were coming to redeem the day.

All things, even the most common, were magnified and made mysterious by the strange spell of night. At a turn of the road a staff-officer, with an air of authority, told each colonel as he came up, that McClellan was in command again, and riding ahead of us on the road. Then wild cheers rolled from the crowding column into the brooding sky, and the earth shook under the quickened tread. Now from a dark angle of the roadside came a whisper, whether from earthly or unearthly voice one cannot feel quite sure, that the august form of Washington had been seen that afternoon at sunset riding over the Gettysburg hills. Let no one smile at me! I half believed it myself,— so did the powers of the other world draw nigh!

But there were wayside greetings such as we had never met before. We were in a free state, and among friendly people. All along the road, citizens came out to contemplate this martial array with a certain awe, and greet us with hearty welcome. But, most of all, our dark way was illumined by groups of girls in sweet attire gathered on the embowered lawns of modest homes, with lights and banners and flowers, and stirring songs whose import and effect were quite other than impersonal. Those who were not sisters of the muse of song waved their welcome in the ripple of white handkerchiefs—which token the gallant young gentlemen of the staff were prompt to take as summons to parley, and boldly rode up to meet with soft, half-tone scenes under the summer night: those meetings looked much like proposals for exchange of prisoners, or unconditional surrender. And others still, not daring quite so much, but unable to repress the gracious impulse of giving, offered their silent benediction in a cup of water. And we remembered then with what sanction it was that water had been turned to wine in Cana of Galilee!

Our Battlefield, a Thirst for Blood

Snatching an hour's sleep by the roadside just before dawn, we reached at about seven o'clock in the morning the heights east of Gettysburg, confronting the ground over which the lost battle of the first day had ebbed. After a little, we were moved to the left, across Rock Creek and up the Baltimore Pike to an open field more nearly overlooking the town. On our front and left were the troops of the Eleventh and First Corps; on a commanding height to our right was strongly established the Twelfth Corps of our army. Told to rest awhile, we first resumed the homely repast so sharply interrupted the evening before. Next we stretched ourselves on the ground to make up lost sleep, and rest our feet after a twenty-four hours scarcely broken march, and get our heads level for the coming test.

We knew that a great battle was soon to be fought, a desperate and momentous one. But what much more impressed my mind was the great calm, the uncertainty of overture, and seeming lack of tactical plan for the tremendous issue. We were aware that other troops were coming up, on one side and the other; but we had no means of knowing or judging which side would take the offensive and which the defensive, or where the battle would begin. All the forenoon we had no other intimation as to this, than the order given in an impressive tone to hold ourselves ready to take part in an attack on our right; but whether to be begun by us or the enemy, we neither knew, nor could guess.

We were on Cemetery Hill, the apex of the angle made by an extended ridge, on the right bending sharply back for a mile to end in a lofty wooded crest known as Culp's Hill, and on the left running southerly from the Cemetery, declining somewhat in its course till at the distance of two miles or more it makes an abrupt and rugged rise in a rocky spur, 500 feet high, named Little Round Top.

This was as now the outpost of a steep and craggy peak southward, one hundred and fifty feet higher, terminating the range, named Great Round Top. These landmarks for the whole region near and far, to the west and north especially in a military point of view commanded the entire ground available for a great battle.

Within the wings of this sharp-beaked ridge there entered and met in the town two great thoroughfares, the Baltimore Pike and Taneytown Road, perfectly commanded by the Little Round Top. The latter road opened the direct way to Washington, and in the aspect of affairs was our only practicable line of retreat in case of disaster. Our Second Corps, Hancock's, had taken position on the ridge, from the Cemetery southerly; and on the extension on this line our Third Corps, Sickles', was forming—its left, we were told, resting on the northern slope of Little Round Top. This formation indicated a defensive attitude for us, and deepened our confidence in Meade.

Opposite Cemetery Ridge occupied by us, westerly, something like a mile away, is another ridge, extending from behind the upper limits of the town to nearly opposite the Great Round Top. This is known as

Seminary Ridge, so named from the Lutheran Seminary on its northern slope. Between these two ridges comes another great thoroughfare, the Emmitsburg Road, entering the town close past the base of Cemetery Hill—thus all three thoroughfares mentioned converged. Along this ridge Hill's Confederate Corps had established itself, and up this Emmitsburg Road from Chambersburg, Longstreet's Corps were advancing. Ewell's Confederate Corps held the town, and Early's Division extended northerly and easterly around to the front of Culp's Hill. Their attack, it is curious to observe, was from the north and east—from the direction of York and Hanover—so quickly and completely had Lee turned from his first, and so far successful, attempt to occupy the northern cities, to face the army of the Potomac now threatening their rear.

Our orders and expectations still kept us looking anxiously to the right, where yesterday's battle had left off, and the new one was to begin. But all was as yet uncertain. We were told that General Meade was now conferring with his Corps commanders as to the best point and part for the battle to open. But this symposium was cut short, and a plan of opening announced by a thunder burst of artillery from the rocks and woods away in front of the Round Tops, where we least of all expected it. A crash of musketry followed.

Double-Quick to the Havoc of Battle

So the awakening bugle sounded "To the left! At utmost speed!" Down to the left we pushed—the whole Fifth Corps—our brigade nearest and leading; at the double-quick, straight for the strife; not seeking roads, nor minding roughness of ground, thorn-hedges, stone fences, or miry swamps mid-way, earth quaking, sky ablaze, and a deepening uproar as we drew near. We soon saw that our Third Corps was not where we thought—between the Second Corps and the Round Tops—but had been moved forward a mile it seemed, almost to the Emmitsburg Road.

The fight was desperate already. We passed along its rear, first getting a glimpse of the Peach Orchard on the right, where our troops were caught between Heth's Corps on Seminary Ridge and Longstreet's Corps fast arriving on the Emmitsburg Road—and the havoc was terrible. We passed on to the Wheat-field where heroic men standing bright as golden grain were ravaged by Death's wild reapers from the woods. Here we halted to be shown our places. We had a momentary glimpse of the Third Corps left in front of Round Top, and the fearful struggle at the Devil's

Den, and Hood's out-flanking troops swarming beyond. Our halt was brief, but our senses alert. I saw our First and Second Brigades go on to the roaring woods, between the Peach Orchard and the Wheatfield.

The Race to Little Round Top

In another instant, a staff officer from General Warren rushed up to find Sykes, our Corps Commander, to beg him to send a brigade at least, to seize Little Round Top before the enemy's surging waves should overwhelm it. Other supplications were in the air; calling for aid everywhere. Our Vincent, soldierly and self-reliant, hearing this entreaty for Round Top, waited word from no superior, but taking the responsibility ordered us to turn and push for Round Top at all possible speed, and dashed ahead to study how best to place us. We broke to the right and rear, found a rude log bridge over Plum Run, and a rough farm-road leading to the base of the mountain. Here, as we could, we took the double-quick.

Now we learned that Warren, chief engineer of our army, sent by Meade to see how things were going on the left, drawn to Little Round Top by its evident importance, found to his astonishment that it was unoccupied except by a little group of signal-men, earnestly observing the movements over in the region of the Emmitsburg Road beyond the Devil's Den. Warren, to test a surmise, sent word to a battery of ours in position below, to throw a solid shot into a mass of woods in that vicinity. The whir of the shot overhead brought out the glitter of many musket-barrels and bayonets in the slanting sunlight—the revelation of fact, the end of dreams. In a moment more, the fierce attack fell on our Third Corps' left, lashed the Devil's Den into a seething cauldron, leaving free a large Confederate force to sweep past for the base of the Round Tops. They would make short work in taking the height, and Warren did likewise in his call for the race.

Earnestly we scanned that rugged peak which was to be the touch stone of that day's battle. It bore a rough forbidding face, wrinkled with jagged ledges, bearded with mighty boulders; even the smooth spots were strewn with fragments of rock like the play-ground or battleground of giants in the elemental storms of old. Straggling trees wrestled with the rocks for a foot-hold; some were in a rich vein of mould and shot up stark and grim. Altogether it was a strange and solemn place, looking forlorn, and barren now but to be made rich enough soon with precious blood, and far-wept tears.

As we mounted its lower gradient, Longstreet's batteries across Plum Run had us in full view, and turned their whole force upon our path, to sweep the heights free of us till their gray line, now straining towards them, could take them by foot or hand. Shells burst overhead and brought down tree-tops as the hissing fragments fell; or glanced along the shelving ledges and launched splinters of rock to multiply their terrors; solid shot swept close above our heads, their compressed, burning breath driving the men's breath like lead to the bottom of their breasts.

At that fiery moment three brothers of us were riding abreast, and a solid shot driving close past our faces disturbed me. "Boys," I said, "I don't like this. Another such shot might make it hard for Mother. Tom, go to the rear of the regiment, and see that it is well closed up! John, pass up ahead and look out a place for our wounded." Tom, the youngest lieutenant of Company G, was serving as adjutant of the regiment; John, a little older, was sent out by the Christian Commission for this battle, and I had applied for him. We had no surgeon; the old ones were gone, and the new ones not come. So I pressed him into field hospital service, with Chaplain French and the ambulance men, under charge of Hospital Steward Baker.

Hold the Line at All Costs

As we neared the summit of the mountain, the shot so raked the crest that we had to keep our men below it to save their heads, although this did not wholly avert the visits of tree-tops and splinters of rock and iron, while the boulders and clefts and pitfalls in our path made it seem like the replica of the evil "den" across the sweetly named Plum Run.

Reaching the southern face of Little Round Top, I found Vincent there, with intense poise and look. He said with a voice of awe, as if translating the tables of the eternal law, "I place you here! This is the left of the Union line. You understand. You are to hold this ground at all costs!" I did understand—full well; but had more to learn about costs.

The regiment coming up "right in front" was put in position by a quite uncommon order, "on the right by file into line"; both that we should thus be facing the enemy when we came to a front, and also be ready to commence firing as fast as each man arrived. This is a rather slow style of formation, but this time it was needful. Knowing that we had no supports on the left, I despatched a stalwart company under the level-headed Captain Morrill in that direction, with orders to move along up the valley to our front and left, between us and the eastern base of the Great Round Top, to keep within supporting distance of us, and to act as the exigencies of the battle should require.

Do Duty or Be Shot

The Twentieth Maine Regiment had 358 men equipped for duty in the ranks with twenty-eight officers. They were all well-seasoned soldiers, and what is more, well rounded men, body and brain. One somewhat important side-note must have place here, in order properly to appreciate the mental and moral attitude of the men before us. One hundred and twenty of these men from the Second Maine were recruits, whom some recruiting officer had led into the belief that they should be discharged with their regiment at the end of its term of service. In their enthusiasm they had not noticed that they were signing enlistment papers for "three years of the war"; and when they had been held in the field after the discharge of the regiment they had refused to do military duty, and had been sequestered in a prisoners' camp as mutineers, waiting court-martial. The exigency of our movement the last of May had not permitted this semi-civil treatment: and orders from the Secretary of War had directed me to take these men up on my rolls and put them to duty. This made it still harder for them to accept, as they had never enlisted in this regiment. However, they had been soon brought over to me under guard of the One Hundred and Eighteenth Pennsylvania, with fixed bayonets; with orders to me to take them into my regiment and "make them do duty, or shoot them down the moment they refused"; these had been the very words of the Corps Commander in person. The responsibility, I had thought, gave me some discretionary power. So I had placed their names on our rolls, distributed them by groups, to equalize companies, and particularly to break up the "esprit de corps" of banded mutineers. Then I had called them together and pointed out to them the situation, that they could not be entertained as civilian guests by me; that they were by authority of the United States on my rolls as soldiers, and I should treat them as soldiers should be treated; that they should lose no rights by obeying orders, and would see what could be done for their claim. It is pleasant to record that all but one or two had gone back manfully to duty, to become some of the best soldiers in the regiment, as I was to prove this very day.

Not a Man Wavers Now

The exigency was great. I released the pioneers and provost guard altogether, and sent them to their companies. All but the drummer boys and hospital attendants went into the ranks. Even the cooks and servants not liable to such service, asked to go in. Others whom I knew to be sick or footsore, and had given a pass to "fall out" on the forced marches of the day and night before, came up, now that the battle was on, dragging themselves along on lame and bleeding feet, finding their regiment with the sagacity of the brave, and their places where need is greatest and hearts truest. "Places?" Did any of these heroic men ever leave them?—although for all too many we passed their names at evening roll all thereafter, with only the heart's answer, "Here forever!"

Our line looked towards the Great Round Top, frowning above us, not a gunshot away, and raising grave thoughts of what might happen if the enemy should gain foothold there, even if impracticable for artillery.

We had enough of that, as it was. For the tremendous cannonade from across the Plum Run gorge was still pounding the Little Round Top crests; happily, not as yet striking my line, which it would have enfiladed if it got the range.

The other regiments of the brigade were forming on our right; the Eighty-third Pennsylvania, the Forty-fourth New York, and the Sixteenth Michigan. I was observing and meditating as to the impending and the possible, when something of the real was substituted by a visit from Colonel Rice. He thought it would be profitable for us to utilize these few minutes by going to the clearer space on the right of his regiment to take a look at the aspect of things in the Plum Run valley—the direction of the advance on our front. It was a forewarning indeed. The enemy had already turned the Third Corps left, the Devil's Den was a smoking crater, the Plum Run gorge was a whirling maelstrom; one force was charging our advanced batteries near the Wheat-field; the flanking force was pressing past the base of the Round Tops; all rolling towards us in tumultuous waves.

It was a stirring, not to say, appalling sight; here a whole battery of shot and shell cutting a ragged chasm through a serried mass, flinging men and horses like drift aside; there, a rifle volley at close range, with reeling shock, hands tossed in air, muskets dropped with death's quick relax, or clutched with last, convulsive energy, men falling like grass before the scythe—others with manhood's proud calm and rally; there, a little group kneeling above some favorite officer slain,—his intense spirit still animating the fiery steed pressing headlong with empty saddle to the van; here, a defiant regiment of ours, broken, slaughtered, captured; or survivors of both sides crouching among the rocks for shelter from the terrible crossfire where there is no rear! But all advancing—all the frenzied force, victors and vanquished, each scarcely knowing which—surging and foaming towards us; death around, behind, before, and madness everywhere!

Yes, brave Rice! it was well for us to see this; the better to see it through. A look into each other's eyes; without a word, we resumed our respective places.

A Lull, Then the Crash of Hell

Ten minutes had not passed. Suddenly the thunder of artillery and crash of iron that had all the while been roaring over the Round Top crests stopped short.

We understood this, too. The storming lines, that had swept past the Third Corps' flank, had got up the base of Little Round Top, and under the range and reach of their guns. They were close upon us among the rocks, we knew, unseen, because so near.

In a minute more came the roll of musketry. It struck the exposed right center of our brigade.

Promptly answered, repulsed, and renewed again and again, it soon reached us, still extending. Two brigades of Hood's Division had attacked—Texas and Alabama. The Fourth Alabama reached our right, the Forty-seventh Alabama joined and crowded in, but gradually, owing to their echelon advance. Soon seven companies of this regiment were in our front. We had all we could stand. My attention was sharply called, now here, now there. In the thick of the fight and smoke, Lieutenant Nichols, a bright officer near our center, ran up to tell me something queer was going on in his front, behind those engaging us.

The Gray Is Flanking Us!

I sprang forward, mounted a great rock in the midst of his company line, and was soon able to resolve the "queer" impression into positive knowledge. Thick groups in gray were pushing up along the smooth dale between the Round Tops in a direction to gain our left flank. There was no mistaking this. If they could hold our attention by a hot fight in front while they got in force on that flank, it would be bad for us and our whole defence. How many were coming we could not know. We were rather too busy to send out a reconnaissance. If a strong force should gain our rear, our brigade would be caught as by a mighty shears-blade, and be cut and crushed. What would follow it was easy to foresee. This must not be. Our orders to hold that ground had to be liberally interpreted. That front had to be held, and that rear covered. Something must be done,—quickly and cooly. I called the captains and told them my tactics: To keep the front at the hottest without special regard to its need or immediate effect, and at the same time, as they found opportunity, to take side steps to the left, coming gradually into one rank, file-closers and all. Then I took the colors with their guard and placed them at our extreme left, where a great boulder gave token and support; thence bending back at a right angle the whole body gained ground leftward and made twice our original front And were not so long doing it. This was a difficult movement to execute under such a fire, requiring coolness as well as heat. Of rare quality were my officers and men. I shall never cease to admire and honor them for what they did in this desperate crisis.

To the Rescue or All Is Lost!

Now as an important element of the situation, let our thoughts turn to what was going on meanwhile to the right of us. When Warren saw us started for Little Round Top, looking still intently down, he saw Hood's two brigades breaking past the Third Corps' left and sweeping straight for Little Round Top. Then he flew down to bring reinforcement for this vital place and moment. He came upon the One Hundred and Fortieth New York, of Weed's Brigade of our Second Division, just going in to Sickles' relief, and dispatched it headlong for Round Top. Weed was to follow, and Ayres' whole division—but not yet. Warren also laid hold of Hazlett, with his battery, D of the Fifth Regulars, and sent him to scale those heights—if in the power of man so to master nature. Meantime the tremendous blow of the Fourth and Fifth Texas struck the right of our brigade, and our Sixteenth Michigan reeled and staggered back under the shock. Confusion followed. Vincent felt that all was lost unless the very gods should intervene. Sword aloft and face aflame, he rushed in among the broken companies in desperate effort to rally them, man by man. By sheer force of his superb personality he restored a portion of his line, and was urging up the rest "Don't yield an inch now, men, or all is lost!" he cried, when an answering volley scorched the very faces of the men, and Vincent's soul went up in a chariot of fire. In that agonizing moment, came tearing up the One Hundred and Fortieth New York, gallant Patrick H. O'Rorke at the head. Not waiting to load a musket or form a line, they sprang forward into that turmoil. Met by a withering volley that killed its fine young colonel and laid low many of his intrepid officers and a hundred of his men, this splendid regiment, as by a providence we may well call divine; saved us all in that moment of threatened doom.

To add a tragic splendor to this dark scene, in the midst of it all, the indomitable Hazlett was trying to get his guns—ten-pounder rifled Parrotts—up to a working place on the summit close beyond. Finally he was obliged to take his horses entirely off, and lift his guns by hand and handspike up the craggy steep, whence he launched death and defiance wide and far around.

The roar of all this tumult reached us on the left, and heightened the intensity of our resolve. Meanwhile the flanking column worked around to our left and joined with those before us in a fierce assault, which lasted with increasing fury for an intense hour. The two lines met and broke and mingled in the shock. The crush of musketry gave way to cuts and thrusts, grapplings and wrestlings. The edge of conflict swayed to and from, with wild whirlpools and eddies. At times I saw around me more of the enemy than of my own men: gaps opening, swallowing, closing again with sharp convulsive energy; squads of stalwart men who had cut their way through us, disappearing as if translated. All around, strange, mingled roar-shouts of defiance, rally, and desperation; and underneath, murmured entreaty and stifled moans; gasping prayers, snatches of Sabbath song, whispers of loved names; everywhere men torn and broken, staggering, creeping quivering on the earth, and dead faces with strangely fixed eyes staring stark into the sky. Things which cannot be told—nor dreamed.

How men held on, each one knows, not I. But manhood commands admiration. There was one fine young fellow, who had been cut down early in the fight with a ghastly wound across his forehead, and who I had thought might possibly be saved with prompt attention. So I had sent him back to our little field hospital, at least to die in peace. Within a half-hour, in a desperate rally I saw that noble youth amidst the rolling smoke as an apparition from the dead, with bloody bandage for the only covering of his head, in the thick of the fight, high-borne and pressing on as they that shall see death no more. I shall know him when I see him again, on whatever shore!

The Colors Stand Alone

So, too, another. In the very deepest of the struggle our shattered line had pressed the enemy well below their first point of contact, and the struggle to regain it was fierce, I saw through a sudden rift in the thick smoke our colors standing alone. I first thought some optical illusion imposed upon me. But as forms emerged through the drifting smoke, the truth came to view. The cross-fire had cut keenly; the center had been almost shot away, only two of the color-guard had been left, and they fighting to fill the whole space; and in the center, wreathed in battle smoke, stood the Color-Sergeant, Andrew Tozier. His color-staff planted in the ground at his side, the upper part clasped in his elbow, so holding the flag upright, with musket and cartridges seized from the fallen comrade at his side he was defending his sacred trust in the manner of the songs of chivalry. It was a stirring picture—its import still more stirring. That color must be saved, and that center too. I sent first to the regiment on our right for a dozen men to help us here, but they could not spare a man. I then called my young brother, Tom, the adjutant, and sent him forward to close that gap somehow; if no men could be drawn from neighboring companies, to draw back the salient angle and contract our center. The fire down there at this moment was so hot I thought it impossible for him to get there alive; and I dispatched immediately after him Sergeant Thomas whom I had made a special orderly, with the same instructions. It needed them both; and both came back with personal proofs of the perilous undertaking. It was strange that the enemy did not seize that moment and point of weakness. Perhaps they saw no weakness. Perhaps it was awe or admiration that held them back from breaking in upon that sublime scene.

When that mad carnival lulled,—from some strange instinct in human nature and without any reason in the situation that can be seen— when the battling edges drew asunder, there stood our little line, groups and gaps, notched like saw-teeth, but sharp as steel, tempered in infernal heats like a magic sword of the Goths. We were on the appointed and entrusted line. We had held ground—flat "at all costs!"

But sad surprise! It had seemed to us we were all the while holding our own, and had never left it. But now that the smoke dissolved, we saw our dead and wounded all out in front of us, mingled with more of the enemy. They were scattered all the way down to the very feet of the baffled hostile line now rallying in the low shrubbery for a new onset. We could not wait for this. They knew our weakness now. And they were gathering force. No place for tactics now! The appeal must be to primal instincts of human nature!

Down the Death-Strewn Slope!

"Shall they die there, under the enemy's feet, and under your eyes?" Words like those brokenly uttered, from heart to heart, struck the stalwart groups holding together for a stand, and roused them to the front quicker than any voice or bugle of command. These true-hearted men but a little before buffeted back and forth by superior force, and now bracing for a into the face of the rallied and recovering foe, and hurled them, tore them from above our fallen as the tiger avenges its young. Nor did they stop till they had cleared the farthest verge of the field, redeemed by the loving for the lost—the brave for the brave. Now came a longer lull. But this meant, not rest, but thought and action. First, it was to gather our wounded, and bear them to the sheltered lawn for saving life, or peace in dying; the dead, too that not even our feet should do them dishonor in the coming encounter. Then—such is heavenly human pity—the wounded of our Country's foes; brothers in blood for us now, so far from other caring; borne to like refuge and succor by the drummer-boys who had become angels of the field. In this lull I took a turn over the dismal field to see what could be done for the living, in ranks or recumbent; and came upon a manly form and face I well remembered. He was a sergeant earlier in the field of Antietam and of Fredericksburg; and for refusing to perform some menial personal service for a bullying quarter-master in winter camp, was reduced to the ranks by a commander who had not carefully investigated the case. It was a degradation, and the injustice of it rankled in his high-born spirit. But his well-bred pride would not allow him to ask for justice as a favor. I had kept this in mind, for early action. Now he was lying there, stretched on an open front where a brave stand had been made, face to the sky, a great bullet-hole in the middle of his breast, from which he had loosened the clothing to ease his breathing, and the rich blood was pouring in a stream. I bent down over him. His face lightened; his lips moved. But I spoke first, "My dear boy, it has gone hard with you. You shall be cared for!" He whispered. "Tell my mother I did not die a coward!" It was the prayer of home-bred manhood poured out with his life-blood. I knew and answered him, "You die a sergeant; I promote you for faithful service and noble courage on the field of Gettysburg!" This was all he wanted. No word more. I had him borne from the field, but his high spirit had passed to its place. It is needless to add that as soon as a piece of parchment could be found after that battle, a warrant was made out promoting George Washington Buck to sergeant in the terms told him; and this evidence placed the sad, proud mother's name on the rolls of the Country's benefactors.

The Last Cartridge and Bare Steel

The silence and the doubt of the momentary lull were quickly dispelled. The formidable Fifteenth Alabama, repulsed and as we hoped dispersed, now in solid and orderly array—still more than twice our numbers—came rolling through the fringe of chaparral on our left. No dash; no yells; no demonstrations for effect; but settled purpose and determination! We opened on them as best we could. The fire was returned, cutting us to the quick. The Forty-Seventh Alabama had rallied on our right. We were enveloped in fire, and sure to be overwhelmed in fact when the great surge struck us. Whatever might be other where, what was here before us was evident; these far out-numbering, confident eyes, yet watching for a sign of weakness. Already I could see the bold flankers on their right darting out and creeping and crawling like under the smoke to gain our left, thrown back as it was. It was for us, then, once for all. Our thin line was broken, and the enemy were in rear of the whole Round Top defense—infantry, artillery, humanity itself—with the Round Top and the day theirs. Now, too, our fire was slackening; our last rounds of shot had been fired; what I had sent for could not get to us. I saw the faces of my men one after another, when they had fired their last cartridge, turn anxiously towards mine for a moment; then square to the front again. To the front for them lay death; to the rear what they would die to save. My thought was running deep. I was combining the elements of a "forlorn hope," and had just communicated this to Captain Ellis J. Spear of the wheeling flank, on which the initiative was to fall. Just then—so will a little incident fleck a brooding cloud of doom with a tint of human tenderness—brave, warm-hearted Lieutenant Melcher, of the Color Company, whose Captain and nearly half his men were down, came up and asked if he might take his company and go forward and pick up one or two of his men left wounded on the field, and bring them in before the enemy got too near. This would be a most hazardous move in itself and in this desperate moment, we could not break our line. But I admired him. With a glance, he understood, I answered, "Yes, sir, in a moment! I am about to order a charge!"

Not a moment was to be lost! Five minutes more of such a defensive, and the last roll-call would sound for us! Desperate as the chances were, there was nothing for it, but to take the offensive. I stepped to the colors. The men turned towards me. One word was enough,—"BAYONET!" It caught like fire and swept along the ranks. The men took it up with a shout,—one could not say, whether from the pit, or the song of the morning star! It were vain to order "Forward." No mortal could have heard it in the mighty hosanna that was winging the sky. Nor would he want to hear. There are things still as of the first creation, "whose seed is in itself." The grating clash of steel in fixing bayonets told its own story; the color rose in front; the whole line quivered for the start; the edge of the left-wing rippled, swung, tossed among the rocks, straightened, changed curve from cimetar to sickle-shape; and the bristling archers swooped down upon the serried host—down into the face of half a thousand! Two hundred men!

It was a great right wheel. Our left swung first. The advancing foe stopped, tried to make a stand amidst the trees and boulders, but the frenzied bayonets pressing through every space, forced a constant settling to the rear. Morrill with his detached company and the remnants of our valorous sharpshooters, who had held the enemy so long in check on the slopes of the Great Round Top, now fell upon the flank of the retiring crowd, and it turned to full retreat, some up amidst the crags of Great Round Top, but most down the smooth vale towards their own main line on Plum Run. This tended to mass them before our center. Here their stand was more stubborn. At the first dash the commanding officer I happened to confront, coming on fiercely, sword in one hand and big navy revolver in the other, fires one barrel almost in my face; but seeing the quick saber-point at his throat, reverses arms, gives sword and pistol into my hands and yields himself prisoner. I took him at his word, but could not give him further attention. I passed him over into the custody of a brave sergeant at my side, to whom I gave the sword as emblem of his authority, but kept the pistol with its loaded barrels, which I thought might come handy soon, as indeed it did.

Ranks were broken; many retired before us somewhat hastily; some threw their muskets to the ground even loaded: sunk on their knees, threw up their hands, calling out, "We surrender. Don't kill us!" As if we wanted to do that! We kill only to resist killing. And these were manly men, whom we would befriend, and by no means kill, if they came our way in peace and good will. Charging right through and over these, we struck the second line of the Forty-seventh Alabama doing their best to stand, but offering little resistance. Their Lieutenant-Colonel as I passed—and a fine gentleman was Colonel Bulger—introduced himself as my prisoner, and as he was wounded, I had him cared for as best we could. Still swinging to the right as a great gate on its hinges, we swept the front clean of assailants. We were taking in prisoners by scores—more than we could hold, or send to the rear, so that many made final escape up Great Round Top. Half way down to the throat of the vale I came upon Colonel Powell of the . . . Fifth Texas, a man of courtly bearing, who was badly wounded. I sent him to the Eighty-third Pennsylvania, nearest to us and better able to take care of him than we were.

Two for Every Man of Us

When we reached the front of the Forty-fourth New York, I thought it far enough. Beyond on the right the Texas Brigade had rallied or rendezvoused, I took thought of that. Most of the fugitives before us, rather than run the gauntlet of our whole brigade, had taken the shelter of the rocks of Great Round Top, on our left, as we now faced. It was hazardous to be so far out, in the very presence of so many baffled but far from beaten veterans of Hood's renowned division. A sudden rush on either flank might not only cut us off, but cut in behind us and seize that vital point which it was our orders and our trust to hold. But it was no light task to get our men to stop. They were under the momentum of their deed. They thought they were "on the road to Richmond." They had to be reasoned with, persuaded, but at last faced about and marched back to that dedicated crest with swelling hearts.

Not without sad interest and service was the return. For many of the wounded had to be gathered up. There was a burden, too, of the living. Nearly four hundred prisoners remained in our hands—two for every man of ours.

$$\star \quad \star \quad \star \quad \star \quad \star$$

The Union defense of Little Round Top stopped General Longstreet's I Corps advance on the left flank dead in its tracks. The 20th Maine would be pulled back on July 3 to rest in the center of the battlefield atop Cemetery Ridge in time to face the onslaught of Pickett's charge. Chamberlain would receive the Medal of Honor for his actions at Little Round Top in 1893. He would serve four terms as Governor of Maine and return to teaching at Bowdoin College. He died due to complications of lingering war wounds at the age of 85, in 1914.

Appomattox

ULYSSES S. GRANT

He was consummately modest and quietly confident . . . It was
a primary law with Grant that he should never in the smallest
way appear to be pressing for honors.
                                        —William S. McFeely

By the spring of 1865 the Confederacy lay in ruins. On April 3, Richmond fell to Union troops as General Robert E. Lee led his Army of
Northern Virginia in retreat from Petersburg and Richmond to the
west, pursued by General Ulysses S. Grant and the Army of the Potomac. A running battle ensued as each army moved farther west in an
effort to outflank the enemy, and to avoid a flanking movement in turn.
On April 7, Grant initiated a series of dispatches seeking to discuss
terms for the surrender of Lee's army. Lee still hoped to elude his pur-
suers and would not surrender. His forces would make one last stand in
an effort to break free.

Early on April 9, the remnants of John B. Gordon's corps and
Fitzhugh Lee's cavalry formed a line of battle at Appomattox Court
House. Lee determined to make one last attempt to escape the closing
Union pincers and reach his supplies at Lynchburg. At dawn the Confederates advanced, initially gaining ground against Sheridan's cavalry. The
arrival of Union infantry, however, stopped the advance in its tracks. Lee's
army was now surrounded on three sides. Lee had few choices left but to
seek terms from General Grant. They agreed to meet at the home of
Wilmer McLean, who coincidentally was the same man who had been
forced to lend his home to General P. G. T. Beauregard at the First Battle
of Bull Run.

The meeting was of vast importance for the future of the country. The agreements they would reach would set in motion a complete end to the war. Lee had other options greatly feared by Union generals; 175,000 Confederate soldiers were still in arms across the south, including General Joseph E. Johnston's army in North Carolina. Lee could order them to disperse and fight a geurilla war against the Union that would continue the fighting for years and cost thousands more lives. By April of 1865, however, Robert E. Lee was the true leader of the Confederacy. Whatever example he made would be followed and it was his intention to lay down their arms in accordance with honor.

Dressed in an immaculate uniform, Lee arrived at McLean's home shortly after noon on April 9, 1865. Grant, in haste, arrived in a dusty private's uniform with only his shoulder boards to indicate his rank. Grant was a tanner's son from Ohio who graduated from West Point in the middle ranking of his 1843 class. Lee hailed from the aristocratic background of a First Family of Virginia and graduated second in the West Point class of 1829. Yet they had served in the same campaign together in the Mexican war, and Lee remembered him. Grant's terms were generous—all officers and men were to be paroled and allowed to return home. The horses would return with the men to help them on their farms. Grant ordered his supply trains to be opened to feed the starving Confederates. It was an honorable peace.

The following chapter is Grant's recollection of the event, from a memoir he wrote in the last months of his life. Grant's memoirs are considered a masterpiece, both for their writing style and their historical content.

★   ★   ★   ★   ★

On the 8th I had followed the Army of the Potomac in rear of Lee. I was suffering very severely with a sick headache, and stopped at a farmhouse on the road some distance in rear of the main body of the army. I spent the night in bathing my feet in hot water and mustard, and putting mustard plasters on my wrists and the back part of my neck, hoping to be cured by morning. During the night I received Lee's answer to my letter of the 8th, inviting an interview between the lines on the following morning. But it was for a different purpose from that of surrendering his army, and I answered him as follows:

Headquarters Armies of the U. S.,
April 9, 1865 GENERAL R. E. LEE
Commanding C. S. A.

Your note of yesterday is received. As I have no authority to treat on the subject of peace, the meeting proposed for ten A.M. to-day could lead to no good. I will state, however, General, that I am equally anxious for peace with yourself, and the whole North entertains the same feeling. The terms upon which peace can be had are well understood. By the South laying down their arms they will hasten that most desirable event, save thousands of human lives, and hundreds of millions of property not yet destroyed. Sincerely hoping that all our difficulties may be settled without the loss of another life, I subscribe myself, etc.

U. S. GRANT,

Lieutenant-General

I proceeded at an early hour in the morning, still suffering with the headache, to get to the head of the column. I was not more than two or three miles from Appomattox Court House at the time, but to go direct I would have to pass through Lee's army, or a portion of it. I had therefore to move south in order to get upon a road coming up from another direction.

When the white flag was put out by Lee, as already described, I was in this way moving towards Appomattox Court House, and consequently could not be communicated with immediately, and be informed of what Lee had done. Lee, therefore, sent a flag to the rear to advise Meade and one to the front to Sheridan, saying that he had sent a message to me for the purpose of having a meeting to consult about the surrender of his army, and asked for a suspension of hostilities until I could be communicated with. As they had heard nothing of this until the fighting had got to be severe and all going against Lee, both of these commanders hesitated very considerably about suspending hostilities at all. They were afraid it was not in good faith, and we had the Army of Northern Virginia where it could not escape except by some deception. They, however, finally consented to a suspension of hostilities for two hours to give an opportunity of communicating with me in that time, if possible. It was found that, from the route I had taken, they would probably not be able to communicate with me and get an answer back within the time fixed unless the messenger should pass through the rebel lines. Lee, therefore, sent an escort with the officer bearing this message through his lines to me.

April 9, 1865

GENERAL:—I received your note of this morning on the picket-line whither I had come to meet you and ascertain definitely what terms were embraced in your proposal of yesterday with reference to the surrender of this army. I now request an interview in accordance with the offer contained in your letter of yesterday for that purpose.

R. E. LEE
General

When the officer reached me I was still suffering with the sick headache; but the instant I saw the contents of the note I was cured. I wrote the following note in reply and hastened on:

April 9, 1865

GENERAL R. E. LEE,
Commanding C. S. Armies.

Your note of this date is but this moment (11.50 A.M.) received, in consequence of my having passed from the Richmond and Lynchburg road to the Farmville and Lynchburg road. I am at this writing about four miles west of Walker's Church and will push forward to the front for the purpose of meeting you. Notice sent to me on this road where you wish the interview to take place will meet me.

U. S. GRANT,
Lieutenant-General

I was conducted at once to where Sheridan was located with his troops drawn up in line of battle facing the Confederate Army near by. They were very much excited, and expressed their view that this was all a ruse employed to enable the Confederates to get away. They said they believed that Johnston was marching up from North Carolina now, and Lee was moving to join him; and they would whip the rebels where they now were in five minutes if I would only let them go in. But I had no doubt about the good faith of Lee, and pretty soon was conducted to where he was. I found him at the house of a Mr. [Wilmer] McLean, at Appomattox Court House, with Colonel [Charles] Marshall, one of his staff officers, awaiting my arrival. The head of his column was occupying a hill, on a portion of which was an apple orchard, beyond a little valley which separated it from that on the crest of which Sheridan's forces were drawn up in line of battle to the south.

Before stating what took place between General Lee and myself, I will give all there is of the story of the famous apple tree.

Wars produce many stories of fiction, some of which are told until they are believed to be true. The war of the rebellion was no exception to this rule, and the story of the apple tree is one of those fictions based on a slight foundation of fact. As I have said, there was an apple orchard on the side of the hill occupied by the Confederate forces. Running diagonally up the hill was a wagon road, which, at one point, ran very near one of the trees, so that the wheels of vehicles had, on that side, cut off the roots of this tree, leaving a little embankment. General Babcock, of my staff, reported to me that when he first met General Lee he was sitting upon this embankment with his feet in the road below and his back resting against the tree. The story had no other foundation than that. Like many other stories, it would be very good if it was only true.

I had known General Lee in the old army, and had served with him in the Mexican War; but did not suppose, owing to the difference in our age and rank, that he would remember me, while I would more naturally remember him distinctly, because he was the chief of staff of General Scott in the Mexican War.

When I had left camp that morning I had not expected so soon the result that was then taking place, and consequently was in rough garb. I was without a sword, as I usually was when on horseback on the field, and wore a soldier's blouse for a coat, with the shoulder straps of my rank to indicate to the army who I was. When I went into the house I found General Lee. We greeted each other, and after shaking hands took our seats. I had my staff with me, a good portion of whom were in the room during the whole of the interview.

What General Lee's feelings were I do not know. As he was a man of much dignity, with an impassable face, it was impossible to say whether he felt inwardly glad that the end had finally come, or felt sad over the result, and was too manly to show it. Whatever his feelings, they were entirely concealed from my observation; but my own feelings, which had been quite jubilant on the receipt of his letter, were sad and depressed. I felt like anything rather than rejoicing at the downfall of a foe who had fought so long and valiantly, and had suffered so much for a cause, though that cause was, I believe, one of the worst for which a people ever fought, and one for which there was the least excuse. I do not question, however, the sincerity of the great mass of those who were opposed to us.

General Lee was dressed in a full uniform which was entirely new, and was wearing a sword of considerable value, very likely the sword which had been presented by the State of Virginia; at all events, it was an entirely different sword from the one that would ordinarily be worn in the field. In my rough traveling suit, the uniform of a private with the straps of a lieutenant-general, I must have contrasted very strangely with a man so handsomely dressed, six feet high and of faultless form. But this was not a matter that I thought of until afterwards.

We soon fell into a conversation about old army times. He remarked that he remembered me very well in the old army, and I told him that as a matter of course I remembered him perfectly, but from the difference in our rank and years (there being about sixteen years' difference in our ages), I had thought it very likely that I had not attracted his attention sufficiently to be remembered by him after such a long interval. Our conversation grew so pleasant that I almost forgot the object of our meeting. After the conversation had run on in this style for some time, General Lee called my attention to the object of our meeting, and said that he had asked for this interview for the purpose of getting from me the terms I proposed to give his army. I said that I meant merely that his army should lay down their arms, not to take them up again during the continuance of the war unless duly and properly exchanged. He said that he had so understood my letter.

Then we gradually fell off again into conversation about matters foreign to the subject which had brought us together. This continued for some little time, when General Lee again interrupted the course of the conversation by suggesting that the terms I proposed to give his army ought to be written out. I called to General [Ely S.] Parker, secretary on my staff, for writing materials, and commenced writing out the following terms:

Appomattox C. H., Va.,
Ap'l 9th, 1865
EN. R. E. LEE
Comd'g C. S. A.

GEN.: In accordance with the substance of my letter to you of the 8th inst., I propose to receive the surrender of the Army of N. Va. on the following terms, to wit: Rolls of all the officers and men to be made in duplicate. One copy to be given to an officer designated by me, the other to be retained by such officer or officers as you may designate. The officers to give their individual paroles not to take up arms against the Government of the United States until properly exchanged, and each company or regimental commander sign a like parole for the men of their commands. The arms, artillery and public property to be parked and stacked, and turned over to the officer appointed by me to receive them. This will not embrace the side-arms of the officers, nor their private horses or baggage. This done, each officer and man will be allowed to return to their homes, not to be disturbed by United States authority so long as they observe their paroles and the laws in force where they may reside.

Very respectfully,

U. S. GRANT

Lt.-Gen.

When I put my pen to the paper I did not know the first word that I should make use of in writing the terms. I only knew what was in my mind, and I wished to express it clearly, so that there could be no mistaking it. As I wrote on, the thought occurred to me that the officers had their own private horses and effects, which were important to them, but of no value to us; also that it would be an unnecessary humiliation to call upon them to deliver their side arms.

No conversation, not one word, passed between General Lee and myself, either about private property, side arms, or kindred subjects. He appeared to have no objections to the terms first proposed; or if he had a point to make against them he wished to wait until they were in writing to make it. When he read over that part of the terms about side arms, horses and private property of the officers, he remarked, with some feeling, I thought, that this would have a happy effect upon his army.

Then, after a little further conversation, General Lee remarked to me again that their army was organized a little differently from the army of the United States (still maintaining by implication that we were two countries); that in their army the cavalrymen and artillerists owned their own horses; and he asked if he was to understand that the men who so owned their horses were to be permitted to retain them. I told him that as the terms were written they would not; that only the officers were permitted to take their private property. He then, after reading over the terms a second time, remarked that that was clear.

I then said to him that I thought this would be about the last battle of the war—I sincerely hoped so; and I said further I took it that most of the men in the ranks were small farmers. The whole country had been so raided by the two armies that it was doubtful whether they would be able to put in a crop to carry themselves and their families through the next winter without the aid of the horses they were then riding. The United States did not want them and I would, therefore, instruct the officers I left behind to receive the paroles of his troops to let every man of the Confederate army who claimed to own a horse or mule take the animal to his home. Lee remarked again that this would have a happy effect. He then sat down and wrote out the following letter:

Headquarters Army of Northern Virginia,
April 9, 1865

GENERAL:—I received your letter of this date containing the terms of the surrender of the Army of Northern Virginia as proposed by you. As they are unsubstantially the same as those expressed in your letter of the 8th inst., they are accepted. I will proceed to designate the proper officers to carry the stipulations into effect.

R. E. LEE,
General
LIEUTENANT-GENERAL U. S. GRANT.

While duplicates of the two letters were being made, the Union generals present were severally presented to General Lee.

The much talked of surrendering of Lee's sword and my handing it back, this and much more that has been said about it is the purest romance. The word sword or side arms was not mentioned by either of us until I wrote it in the terms. There was no premeditation, and it did not occur to me until the moment I wrote it down. If I had happened to omit it, and General Lee had called my attention to it, I should have put it in the terms precisely as I acceded to the provision about the soldiers retaining their horses.

General Lee, after all was completed and before taking his leave, remarked that his army was in a very bad condition for want of food, and that they were without forage; that his men had been living for some days on parched corn exclusively, and that he would have to ask me for rations and forage. I told him "certainly," and asked for how many men he wanted rations. His answer was "about twenty-five thousand": and I authorized him to send his own commissary and quartermaster to Appomattox Station, two or three miles away, where he could have, out of the trains we had stopped, all the provisions wanted. As for forage, we had ourselves depended almost entirely upon the country for that.

Generals Gibbon, Griffin and Merritt were designated by me to carry into effect the paroling of Lee's troops before they should start for their homes—General Lee leaving Generals Longstreet, Gordon and Pendleton for them to confer with in order to facilitate this work. Lee and I then separated as cordially as we had met, he returning to his own lines, and all went into bivouac for the night at Appomattox.

Soon after Lee's departure I telegraphed to Washington as follows:

Headquarters Appomattox C. H., Va.,
April 9th, 1865 4.30 P.M. HON. E. M. Stanton
Secretary of War, Washington.

General Lee surrendered the Army of Northern Virginia this afternoon on terms proposed by myself. The accompanying additional correspondence will show the conditions fully.

U. S. GRANT
Lieut.-General

When news of the surrender first reached our lines our men commenced firing a salute of a hundred guns in honor of the victory. I at once sent word, however, to have it stopped. The Confederates were now our prisoners, and we did not want to exult over their downfall.

I determined to return to Washington at once, with a view to putting a stop to the purchase of supplies, and what I now deemed other useless outlay of money. Before leaving, however, I thought I would like to see General Lee again; so next morning I rode out beyond our lines towards his headquarters, preceded by a bugler and a staff-officer carrying a white flag.

Lee soon mounted his horse, seeing who it was, and met me. We had there between the lines, sitting on horseback, a very pleasant conversation of over half an hour, in the course of which Lee said to me that the South was a big country and that we might have to march over it three or four times before the war entirely ended, but that we would now be able to do it as they could no longer resist us. He expressed it as his earnest hope, however, that we would not be called upon to cause more loss and sacrifice of life, but he could not foretell the result. I then suggested to General Lee that there was not a man in the Confederacy whose influence with the soldiery and the whole people was as great as his, and that if he would now advise the surrender of all the armies I had no doubt his advice would be followed with alacrity. But Lee said, that he could not do that without consulting the President first. I knew there was no use to urge him to do anything against his ideas of what was right.

I was accompanied by my staff and other officers, some of whom seemed to have a great desire to go inside the Confederate lines. They finally asked permission of Lee to do so for the purpose of seeing some of their old army friends, and the permission was granted. They went over, had a very pleasant time with their old friends, and brought some of them back with them when they returned.

When Lee and I separated he went back to his lines and I returned to the house of Mr. McLean. Here the officers of both armies came in great numbers, and seemed to enjoy the meeting as much as though they had been friends separated for a long time while fighting battles under the same flag. For the time being it looked very much as if all thought of the war had escaped their minds. After an hour pleasantly passed in this way I set out on horseback, accompanied by my staff and a small escort, for Burkesville Junction, up to which point the railroad had by this time been repaired.

★   ★   ★   ★   ★

General Lee would give a farewell speech to his army the following day. Brigadier General Joshua Lawrence Chamberlain took charge of the formal surrender as Lee's 28,000 men laid down their arms. As news spread of Lee's surrender, other Confederate commanders realized that the Confederacy was all but dead, and followed Lee's example. Johnston's army in North Carolina surrendered to William T. Sherman on April 26. Edmund Kirby Smith surrendered the Confederate Trans-Mississippi Department in May, 1865.

Little Big Horn

CHIEF RED HORSE AND GEORGE HERENDON

The general who advances without coveting fame and retreats without fearing the disgrace, whose only thought is to protect his country and do good service to his sovereign, is the jewel of the kingdom.

—Sun Tzu

Custer's last stand at the Little Big Horn in June of 1876 is an event that has transcended history into legend. Few battles in American history have been studied and analyzed so repeatedly for each generation seeking new answers to old questions. Cut down to a man, his force of two hundred and ten men died fighting back to back against numbers three to five times their own. Today the small scattering of headstones marks where they fell atop the grassy hill, a quiet and peaceful place. Few would question the bravery on either side that day. Many would forever question the leadership that brought them to battle and their annihilation.

In 1876 the Northern Cheyenne and Lakota Sioux Indians gathered on the shores of the Rosebud River under the combined leadership of Chief Sitting Bull and Crazy Horse. They were outraged over the white man's incursion into the Black Hills country that was sacred to them. Their encampment numbered over nine hundred lodges with over a thousand warriors who came to follow Sitting Bull. Based on a report that the tribes gathered at the Little Big Horn were hostile, the U.S. Army sent the 7th Cavalry under the command of Lt. Colonel George Custer as part of a larger force under Brigadier General Alfred Terry to attack the Indian encampment.

Custer had a reputation for aggressive leadership and fearlessness in battle. On June 25 his regiment was in position within fifteen miles of the Indian encampment. His own Indian scouts warned him the encampment along the river was vast. Upon the discovery of a small band of Indian warriors, however, Custer divided his regiment into three columns. Major Marcus Reno would lead the attack with orders to move northward and bring the enemy to battle. A second group under Captain Fredrick Benteen would move laterally as a scouting force. Each had orders to support the other if the Indians stood their ground. With rolling hills and broken terrain before them, in the face of an opposing force of unknown size and disposition, Custer had without hesitation sent his smaller detachments forward to seek battle.

Reno's force of one hundred twenty five men crossed the river and attacked northward in the direction of the encampment. The Indians poured from their lodges to defend themselves and their families. Reno ordered his men to stand their ground and wait for reinforcements, yet neither Custer nor Benteen came to reinforce them. They were forced to retreat, taking cover in a nearby copse of woods. When this position stood in danger of being overrun, they fell back once again, in a near rout losing many men, across the river and up some bluffs to a more defensible position. Reno was wounded by gunfire in the head as his men fell around him. His force had taken casualties of more than 25 percent. Captain Benteen's column finally arrived and prevented Reno's command from being annihilated. In the direction of Custer's position to the north, they could hear gunfire. The wounded Reno, his men having suffered many casualties and protecting a slow-moving supply column that had joined them, would not order his troops to move toward Custer for over an hour. Within that time, Custer and his entire detachment were overrun by a group of warriors personally led by Crazy Horse.

The following chapter is taken from the eyewitness testimony of George Herendon, who served as a scout for the 7th Cavalry under Major Reno's command. He gave his account to a reporter from the *New York Herald Tribune* in July, 1876. The second account is from the Lakota Chief Red Horse, recorded at the Cheyenne River Reservation in 1881.

★ ★ ★ ★ ★

George Herendon

Reno took a steady gallop down the creek bottom three miles where it emptied into the Little Horn, and found a natural ford across the Little Horn River. He started to cross, when the scouts came back and called out to him to hold on, that the Sioux were coming in large numbers to meet him. He crossed over, however, formed his companies on the prairie in line of battle, and moved forward at a trot but soon took a gallop.

The Valley was about three fourth of a mile wide, on the left a line of low, round hills, and on the right the river bottom covered with a growth of cottonwood trees and bushes. After scattering shots were fired from the hills and a few from the river bottom, Reno's skirmishers returned the shots.

He advanced about a mile from the ford to a line of timber on the right and dismounted his men to fight on foot. The horses were sent into the timber, and the men forward on the prairie and advanced toward the Indians. The Indians, mounted on ponies, came across the prairie and opened a heavy fire on the soldiers. After skirmishing for a few minutes Reno fell back to his horses in the timber. The Indians moved to his left and rear, evidently with the intention of cutting him off from the ford.

Reno ordered his men to mount and move through the timber, but as his men got into the saddle the Sioux, who had advanced in the timber, fired at close range and killed one soldier. Colonel Reno then commanded the men to dismount, and they did so, but he soon ordered them to mount again, and moved out on to the open prairie.

The command headed for the ford, pressed closely by Indians in large numbers, and at every moment the rate of speed was increased, until it became a dead run for the ford. The Sioux, mounted on their swift ponies, dashed up by the side of the soldiers and fired at them, killing both men and horses. Little resistance was offered, and it was complete rout to the ford. I did not see the men at the ford, and do not know what took place further than a good many were killed when the command left the timber.

Just as I got out, my horse stumbled and fell and I was dismounted, the horse running away after Reno's command. I saw several soldiers who were dismounted, their horses having been killed or run away. There were also some soldiers mounted who had remained behind, I should think in all as many as thirteen soldiers, and seeing no chance of getting away, I called on them to come into the timber and we would stand off the Indians.

Three of the soldiers were wounded, and two of them so badly they could not use their arms. The soldiers wanted to go out, but I said no, we can't get to the ford, and besides, we have wounded men and must stand by them. The soldiers still wanted to go, but I told them I was an old frontiersman, understood the Indians, and if they would do as I said I would get them out of the scrape which was no worse than scrapes I had been in before. About half of the men were mounted, and they wanted to keep their horses with them, but I told them to let the horses go and fight on foot.

We stayed in the bush about three hours, and I could hear heavy firing below in the river, apparently about two miles distant. I did not know who it was, but knew the Indians were fighting some of our men, and learned afterward it was Custer's command. Nearly all the Indians in the upper part of the valley drew off down the river, and the fight with Custer lasted about one hour, when the heavy firing ceased. When the shooting below began to die away I said to the boys, 'come, now is the time to get out.' Most of them did not go, but waited for night. I told them the Indians would come back and we had better be off at once. Eleven of the thirteen said they would go, but two stayed behind.

I deployed the men as skirmishers and we moved forward on foot toward the river. When we had got nearly to the river we met five Indians on ponies, and they fired on us. I returned the fire and the Indians broke and we then forded the river, the water being heart deep. We finally got over, wounded men and all, and headed for Reno's command which I could see drawn up on the bluffs along the river about a mile off. We reached Reno in safety.

We had not been with Reno more than fifteen minutes when I saw the Indians coming up the valley from Custer's fight. Reno was then moving his whole command down the ridge toward Custer. The Indians crossed the river below Reno and swarmed up the bluff on all sides. After skirmishing with them Reno went back to his old position which was on one of the highest fronts along the bluffs. It was now about five o'clock, and the fight lasted until it was too dark to see to shoot.

As soon as it was dark Reno took the packs and saddles off the mules and horses and made breast works of them. He also dragged the dead horses and mules on the line and sheltered the men behind them. Some of the men dug rifle pits with their butcher knives and all slept on their arms.

At the peep of day the Indians opened a heavy fire and a desperate fight ensued, lasting until 10 o'clock. The Indians charged our position three or four times, coming up close enough to hit our men with stones, which they threw by hand. Captain Benteen saw a large mass of Indians gathered on his front to charge, and ordered his men to charge on foot and scatter them.

Benteen led the charge and was upon the Indians before they knew what they were about and killed a great many. They were evidently much surprised at this offensive movement, and I think in desperate fighting Benteen is one of the bravest men I ever saw in a fight. All the time he was going about through the bullets, encouraging the soldiers to stand up to their work and not let the Indians whip them; he went among the horses and pack mules and drove out the men who were skulking there, compelling them to go into the line and do their duty. He never sheltered his own person once during the battle, and I do not see how he escaped being killed. The desperate charging and fighting was over at about one o'clock, but firing was kept up on both sides until late in the afternoon.

Lakota Chief Red Horse

Five springs ago I, with many Sioux Indians, took down and packed up our tipis and moved from Cheyenne river to the Rosebud river, where we camped a few days; then took down and packed up our lodges and moved to the Little Bighorn river and pitched our lodges with the large camp of Sioux.

      The Sioux were camped on the Little Bighorn river as follows: The lodges of the Uncpapas were pitched highest up the river under a bluff. The Santee lodges were pitched next. The Oglala's lodges were pitched next. The Brule lodges were pitched next. The Minneconjou lodges were pitched next. The Sans Arcs' lodges were pitched next. The Blackfeet lodges were pitched next. The Cheyenne lodges were pitched next. A few Arikara Indians were among the Sioux (being without lodges of their own). Two-Kettles, among the other Sioux (without lodges).

      I was a Sioux chief in the council lodge. My lodge was pitched in the center of the camp. The day of the attack I and four women were a short distance from the camp digging wild turnips. Suddenly one of the women attracted my attention to a cloud of dust rising a short distance from camp. I soon saw that the soldiers were charging the camp. To the camp I and the women ran. When I arrived a person told me to hurry to the council lodge. The soldiers charged so quickly we could not talk (council). We came out of the council lodge and talked in all directions. The Sioux mount horses, take guns, and go fight the soldiers. Women and children mount horses and go, meaning to get out of the way.

      Among the soldiers was an officer who rode a horse with four white feet. [This officer was evidently Capt. French, Seventh Cavalry.] The Sioux have for a long time fought many brave men of different people, but the Sioux say this officer was the bravest man they had ever fought. I don't know whether this was Gen. Custer or not. Many of the Sioux men that I hear talking tell me it was. I saw this officer in the fight many times, but did not see his body. It has been told me that he was killed by a Santee Indian, who took his horse. This officer wore a large-brimmed hat and a deerskin coat. This officer saved the lives of many soldiers by turning his horse and covering the retreat. Sioux say this officer was the bravest man they ever fought. I saw two officers looking alike, both having long yellowish hair.

Before the attack the Sioux were camped on the Rosebud river. Sioux moved down a river running into the Little Bighorn river, crossed the Little Bighorn river, and camped on its west bank.

This day [day of attack] a Sioux man started to go to Red Cloud agency, but when he had gone a short distance from camp he saw a cloud of dust rising and turned back and said he thought a herd of buffalo was coming near the village.

The day was hot. In a short time the soldiers charged the camp. [This was Maj. Reno's battalion of the Seventh Cavalry.] The soldiers came on the trail made by the Sioux camp in moving, and crossed the Little Bighorn river above where the Sioux crossed, and attacked the lodges of the Uncpapas, farthest up the river. The women and children ran down the Little Bighorn river a short distance into a ravine. The soldiers set fire to the lodges. All the Sioux now charged the soldiers and drove them in confusion across the Little Bighorn river, which was very rapid, and several soldiers were drowned in it. On a hill the soldiers stopped and the Sioux surrounded them. A Sioux man came and said that a different party of soldiers had all the women and children prisoners. Like a whirlwind the word went around, and the Sioux all heard it and left the soldiers on the hill and went quickly to save the women and children.

From the hill that the soldiers were on to the place where the different soldiers [by this term Red-Horse always means the battalion immediately commanded by General Custer, his mode of distinction being that they were a different body from that first encountered] were seen was level ground with the exception of a creek. Sioux thought the soldiers on the hill [i.e., Reno's battalion] would charge them in rear, but when they did not the Sioux thought the soldiers on the hill were out of cartridges. As soon as we had killed all the different soldiers the Sioux all went back to kill the soldiers on the hill. All the Sioux watched around the hill on which were the soldiers until a Sioux man came and said many walking soldiers were coming near. The coming of the walking soldiers was the saving of the soldiers on the hill. Sioux can not fight the walking soldiers [infantry], being afraid of them, so the Sioux hurriedly left.

The soldiers charged the Sioux camp about noon. The soldiers were divided, one party charging right into the camp. After driving these soldiers across the river, the Sioux charged the different soldiers [i.e., Custer's] below, and drive them in confusion; these soldiers became foolish, many throwing away their guns and raising their hands, saying, "Sioux, pity us; take us prisoners." The Sioux did not take a single soldier prisoner, but killed all of them; none were left alive for even a few minutes. These different soldiers discharged their guns but little. I took a gun and two belts off two dead soldiers; out of one belt two cartridges were gone, out of the other five.

The Sioux took the guns and cartridges off the dead soldiers and went to the hill on which the soldiers were, surrounded and fought them with the guns and cartridges of the dead soldiers. Had the soldiers not divided I think they would have killed many Sioux. The different soldiers [i.e., Custer's battalion] that the Sioux killed made five brave stands. Once the Sioux charged right in the midst of the different soldiers and scattered them all, fighting among the soldiers hand to hand.

One band of soldiers was in rear of the Sioux. When this band of soldiers charged, the Sioux fell back, and the Sioux and the soldiers stood facing each other. Then all the Sioux became brave and charged the soldiers. The Sioux went but a short distance before they separated and surrounded the soldiers. I could see the officers riding in front of the soldiers and hear them shooting. Now the Sioux had many killed. The soldiers killed 136 and wounded 160 Sioux. The Sioux killed all these different soldiers in the ravine.

The soldiers charged the Sioux camp farthest up the river. A short time after the different soldiers charged the village below. While the different soldiers and Sioux were fighting together the Sioux chief said, "Sioux men, go watch soldiers on the hill and prevent their joining the different soldiers." The Sioux men took the clothing off the dead and dressed themselves in it. Among the soldiers were white men who were not soldiers. The Sioux dressed in the soldiers' and white men's clothing fought the soldiers on the hill.

The banks of the Little Bighorn river were high, and the Sioux killed many of the soldiers while crossing. The soldiers on the hill dug up the ground [i.e., made earth-works], and the soldiers and Sioux fought at long range, sometimes the Sioux charging close up. The fight continued at long range until a Sioux man saw the walking soldiers coming. When the walking soldiers came near the Sioux became afraid and ran away.

★   ★   ★   ★   ★

Fearing retribution, the Indians broke their camp and divided their numbers, fleeing from the scene of battle. Sitting Bull and Crazy Horse remained defiant of the American military power, yet their quest to preserve the Indian way of life would cost them their lives. The last tragic encounter between the Army and the Sioux would occur at Wounded Knee, South Dakota in December 1890. Major Reno was cleared of any charges for his conduct at the Little Big Horn at a court of inquiry in 1879.

The Battle of San Juan Hill

RICHARD HARDING DAVIS

> There are good men and bad men of all nationalities, creeds and colors; and if this world of ours is ever to become what we hope some day it may become, it must be by the general recognition that the man's heart and soul, the man's worth and actions, determine his standing.
>
> —Theodore Roosevelt

Richard Harding Davis was arguably the most influential reporter of his day. As a reporter for *The Sun* and managing editor for *Harper's Weekly*, Davis had become a well-known writer by the 1890s. In 1896, William Randolph Hearst, owner and editor of the *New York Journal*, commissioned Davis to cover the Cuban rebellion against Spanish rule. His work would lead him to cover the Spanish-American war in 1898 reporting for the *New York Herald, Times of London*, and *Scribner's Magazine*. Although regarded by his peers as a sensationalist writer, his work gave readers a vivid description of what he saw around him. His willingness to break the rules allowed him access to the front lines in time to witness the assault on Kettle Hill and San Juan heights as the American army fought its way past Spanish defenders to capture the city of Santiago on June 30, 1898. The following selection is the report of the battle filed by Davis for national coverage.

★ ★ ★ ★ ★

After the Guasimas fight on June 24, the army was advanced along the single trail which leads from Siboney on the coast to Santiago. Two streams of excellent water run parallel with this trail for short distances, and some eight miles from the coast crossed it in two places. Our outposts were stationed at the first of these fords, the Cuban outposts a mile and a half farther on at the ford nearer Santiago, where the stream made a sharp turn at a place called El Poso. Another mile and a half of trail extended from El Poso to the trenches of San Juan. The reader should remember El Poso, as it marked an important starting-point against San Juan on the eventful first of July.

For six days the army was encamped on either side of the trail for three miles back from the outposts. The regimental camps touched each other, and all day long the pack-trains carrying the day's rations passed up and down between them. The trail was a sunken wagon road, where it was possible, in a few places, for two wagons to pass at one time, but the greater distances were so narrow that there was but just room for a wagon, or a loaded mule-train, to make its way. The banks of the trail were three or four feet high, and when it rained it was converted into a huge gutter, with sides of mud, and with a liquid mud a foot deep between them. The camps were pitched along the trail as near the parallel stream as possible, and in the occasional places where there was rich, high grass. At night the men slept in dog tents, open at the front and back, and during the day spent their time under the shade of trees along the trail, or on the banks of the stream. Sentries were placed at every few feet along these streams to guard them from any possible pollution. For six days the army rested in this way, for as an army moves and acts only on its belly, and as the belly of this army was three miles long, it could advance but slowly.

This week of rest, after the cramped life of the troop-ship, was not ungrateful, although the rations were scarce and there was no tobacco, which was as necessary to the health of the men as their food.

During this week of waiting, the chief excitement was to walk out a mile and a half beyond the outposts to the hill of El Poso, and look across the basin that lay in the great valley which leads to Santiago. The left of the valley was the hills which hide the sea. The right of the valley was the hills in which nestle the village of El Caney. Below El Poso, in the basin, the dense green forest stretched a mile and a half to the hills of San Juan. These hills looked so quiet and sunny and well kept that they reminded one of a New England orchard. There was a blue bungalow on a hill to the right, a red bungalow higher up on the right, and in the centre the block-house of San Juan, which looked like a Chinese pagoda. Three-quarters of a mile behind them, with a dip between, were the long white walls of the hospital and barracks of Santiago, wearing thirteen Red Cross flags, and, as was pointed out to the foreign attaches later, two six-inch guns a hundred yards in advance of the Red Cross flags.

It was so quiet, so fair, and so prosperous looking that it breathed of peace. It seemed as though one might, without accident, walk in and take dinner at the Venus Restaurant, or loll on the benches in the Plaza, or rock in one of the great bent-wood chairs around the patio of the Don Carlos Club.

But, on the 27th of June, a long, yellow pit opened in the hill-side of San Juan, and in it we could see straw sombreros rising and bobbing up and down, and under the shade of the blockhouse, blue- coated Spaniards strolling leisurely about or riding forth on little white ponies to scamper over the hills. Officers of every regiment, attaches of foreign countries, correspondents, and staff officers daily reported the fact that the rifle-pits were growing in length and in number, and that in plain sight from the hill of El Poso the enemy was intrenching himself at San Juan, and at the little village of El Caney to the right, where he was marching through the streets. But no artillery was sent to El Poso hill to drop a shell among the busy men at work among the trenches, or to interrupt the street parades in El Caney. For four days before the American soldiers captured the same rifle-pits at El Caney and San Juan, with a loss of two thousand men, they watched these men diligently preparing for their coming, and wondered why there was no order to embarrass or to end these preparations.

On the afternoon of June 30, Captain Mills rode up to the tent of Colonel Wood, and told him that on account of illness, General Wheeler and General Young had relinquished their commands, and that General Sumner would take charge of the Cavalry Division; that he, Colonel Wood, would take command of General Young's brigade, and Colonel Carroll, of General Sumner's brigade.

"You will break camp and move forward at four o'clock," he said. It was then three o'clock, and apparently the order to move forward at four had been given to each regiment at nearly the same time, for they all struck their tents and stepped down into the trail together. It was as though fifteen regiments were encamped along the sidewalks of Fifth Avenue and were all ordered at the same moment to move into it and march downtown. If Fifth Avenue were ten feet wide, one can imagine the confusion.

General Chaffee was at General Lawton's head-quarters, and they stood apart whispering together about the march they were to take to El Caney. Just over their heads the balloon was ascending for the first time and its great glistening bulk hung just above the tree tops, and the men in different regiments, picking their way along the trail, gazed up at it open-mouthed. The head-quarters camp was crowded. After a week of inaction the army, at a moment's notice, was moving forward, and every one had ridden in haste to learn why.

There were attaches, in strange uniforms, self-important Cuban generals, officers from the flagship New York, and an army of photographers. At the side of the camp, double lines of soldiers passed slowly along the two paths of the muddy road, while, between them, aides dashed up and down, splashing them with dirty water, and shouting, "You will come up at once, sir." "You will not attempt to enter the trail yet, sir." "General Sumner's compliments, and why are you not in your place?"

Twelve thousand men, with their eyes fixed on a balloon, and treading on each other's heels in three inches of mud, move slowly, and after three hours, it seemed as though every man in the United States was under arms and stumbling and slipping down that trail. The lines passed until the moon rose. They seemed endless, interminable; there were cavalry mounted and dismounted, artillery with cracking whips and cursing drivers, Rough Riders in brown, and regulars, both black and white, in blue. Midnight came, and they were still stumbling and slipping forward.

General Sumner's head-quarters tent was pitched to the right of El Poso hill. Below us lay the basin a mile and a half in length, and a mile and a half wide, from which a white mist was rising. Near us, drowned under the mist, seven thousand men were sleeping, and, farther to the right, General Chaffee's five thousand were lying under the bushes along the trails to El Caney, waiting to march on it and eat it up before breakfast.

The place hardly needs a map to explain it. The trails were like a pitchfork, with its prongs touching the hills of San Juan. The long handle of the pitchfork was the trail over which we had just come, the joining of the handle and the prongs were El Poso. El Caney lay half-way along the right prong, the left one was the trail down which, in the morning, the troops were to be hurled upon San Juan. It was as yet an utterly undiscovered country. Three miles away, across the basin of mist, we could see the street lamps of Santiago shining over the San Juan hills. Above us, the tropical moon hung white and clear in the dark purple sky, pierced with millions of white stars. As we turned in, there was just a little something in the air which made saying "good-night" a gentle farce, for no one went to sleep immediately, but lay looking up at the stars, and after a long silence, and much restless turning on the blanket which we shared together, the second lieutenant said: "So, if anything happens to me, to-morrow, you'll see she gets them, won't you?" Before the moon rose again, every sixth man who had slept in the mist that night was either killed or wounded; but the second lieutenant was sitting on the edge of a Spanish rifle-pit, dirty, sweaty, and weak for food, but victorious, and the unknown she did not get them.

El Caney had not yet thrown off her blanket of mist before Capron's battery opened on it from a ridge two miles in the rear. The plan for the day was that El Caney should fall in an hour. The plan for the day is interesting chiefly because it is so different from what happened. According to the plan the army was to advance in two divisions along the two trails. Incidentally, General Lawton's division was to pick up El Caney, and when El Caney was eliminated, his division was to continue forward and join hands on the right with the divisions of General Sumner and General Kent. The army was then to rest for that night in the woods, half a mile from San Juan.

On the following morning it was to attack San Juan on the two flanks, under cover of artillery. The objection to this plan, which did not apparently suggest itself to General Shafter, was that an army of twelve thousand men, sleeping within five hundred yards of the enemy's rifle-pits, might not unreasonably be expected to pass a bad night. As we discovered the next day, not only the five hundred yards, but the whole basin was covered by the fire from the rifle-pits. Even by daylight, when it was possible to seek some slight shelter, the army could not remain in the woods, but according to the plan it was expected to bivouac for the night in those woods, and in the morning to manoeuvre and deploy and march through them to the two flanks of San Juan. How the enemy was to be hypnotized while this was going forward it is difficult to understand.

According to this programme, Capron's battery opened on El Caney and Grimes's battery opened on the pagoda-like block-house of San Juan. The range from El Poso was exactly 2,400 yards, and the firing, as was discovered later, was not very effective. The battery used black powder, and, as a result, after each explosion the curtain of smoke hung over the gun for fully a minute before the gunners could see the San Juan trenches, which was chiefly important because for a full minute it gave a mark to the enemy. The hill on which the battery stood was like a sugar-loaf. Behind it was the farm-house of El Poso, the only building in sight within a radius of a mile, and in it were Cuban soldiers and other non-combatants. The Rough Riders had been ordered to halt in the yard of the farm-house and the artillery horses were drawn up in it, under the lee of the hill. The First and Tenth dismounted Cavalry were encamped a hundred yards from the battery along the ridge. They might as sensibly have been ordered to paint the rings

in a target while a company was firing at the bull's-eye. To our first twenty
shots the enemy made no reply; when they did it was impossible, owing to
their using smokeless powder, to locate their guns. Their third shell fell in
among the Cubans in the block-house and among the Rough Riders and
the men of the First and Tenth Cavalry, killing some and wounding many.
These casualties were utterly unnecessary and were due to the stupidity of
whoever placed the men within fifty yards of guns in action.

A quarter of an hour after the firing began from El Poso one of
General Shafter's aides directed General Sumner to advance with his division down the Santiago trail, and to halt at the edge of the woods.

"What am I to do then?" asked General Sumner.

"You are to await further orders," the aide answered.

As a matter of fact and history this was probably the last order
General Sumner received from General Shafter, until the troops of his division had taken the San Juan hills, as it became impossible to get word to
General Shafter, the trail leading to his head-quarters tent, three miles in
the rear, being blocked by the soldiers of the First and Tenth dismounted
Cavalry, and later, by Lawton's division. General Sumner led the Sixth,
Third, and Ninth Cavalry and the Rough Riders down the trail, with instructions for the First and Tenth to follow. The trail, virgin as yet from the
foot of an American soldier, was as wide as its narrowest part, which was
some ten feet across. At places it was as wide as Broadway, but only for such
short distances that it was necessary for the men to advance in column, in
double file. A maze of underbrush and trees on either side was all but im-
penetrable, and when the officers and men had once assembled into the
basin, they could only guess as to what lay before them, or on either flank.
At the end of a mile the country became more open, and General Sumner
saw the Spaniards intrenched a half-mile away on the sloping hills. A
stream, called the San Juan River, ran across the trail at this point, and another stream crossed it again two hundred yards farther on. The troops
were halted at this first stream, some crossing it, and others deploying in
single file to the right. Some were on the banks of the stream, others at the
edge of the woods in the bushes. Others lay in the high grass which was so
high that it stopped the wind, and so hot that it almost choked and suffo-
cated those who lay in it.

The enemy saw the advance and began firing with pitiless accuracy
into the jammed and crowded trail and along the whole border of the
woods. There was not a single yard of ground for a mile to the rear which
was not inside the zone of fire. Our men were ordered not to return the fire

but to lie still and wait for further orders. Some of them could see the rifle-pits of the enemy quite clearly and the men in them, but many saw nothing but the bushes under which they lay, and the high grass which seemed to burn when they pressed against it. It was during this period of waiting that the greater number of our men were killed. For one hour they lay on their rifles staring at the waving green stuff around them, while the bullets drove past incessantly, with savage insistence, cutting the grass again and again in hundreds of fresh places. Men in line sprang from the ground and sank back again with a groan, or rolled to one side clinging silently to an arm or shoulder. Behind the lines hospital stewards passed continually, drawing the wounded back to the streams, where they laid them in long rows, their feet touching the water's edge and their bodies supported by the muddy bank. Up and down the lines, and through the fords of the streams, mounted aides drove their horses at a gallop, as conspicuous a target as the steeple on a church, and one after another paid the price of his position and fell from his horse wounded or dead. Captain Mills fell as he was giving an order, shot through the forehead behind both eyes; Captain O'Neill, of the Rough Riders, as he said, "There is no Spanish bullet made that can kill me." Steel, Swift, Henry, each of them was shot out of his saddle.

Hidden in the trees above the streams, and above the trail, sharp-shooters and guerillas added a fresh terror to the wounded. There was no hiding from them. Their bullets came from every side. Their invisible smoke helped to keep their hiding-places secret, and in the incessant shriek of shrapnel and the spit of the Mausers, it was difficult to locate the reports of their rifles. They spared neither the wounded nor recognized the Red Cross; they killed the surgeons and the stewards carrying the litters, and killed the wounded men on the litters. A guerilla in a tree above us shot one of the Rough Riders in the breast while I was helping him carry Captain Morton Henry to the dressing-station, the ball passing down through him, and a second shot, from the same tree, barely missed Henry as he lay on the ground where we had dropped him. He was already twice wounded and so covered with blood that no one could have mistaken his condition. The surgeons at work along the stream dressed the wounds with one eye cast aloft at the trees. It was not the Mauser bullets they feared, though they passed continuously, but too high to do their patients further harm, but the bullets of the sharp-shooters which struck fairly in among them, splashing in the water and scattering the pebbles. The sounds of the two bullets were as different as is the sharp pop of a soda-water bottle from the buzzing of an angry wasp.

For a time it seemed as though every second man was either killed or wounded; one came upon them lying behind the bush, under which they had crawled with some strange idea that it would protect them, or crouched under the bank of the stream, or lying on their stomachs and lapping up the water with the eagerness of thirsty dogs. As to their suffering, the wounded were magnificently silent, they neither complained nor groaned nor cursed.

"I've got a punctured tire," was their grim answer to inquiries. White men and colored men, veterans and recruits and volunteers, each lay waiting for the battle to begin or to end so that he might be carried away to safety, for the wounded were in as great danger after they were hit as though they were in the firing line, but none questioned nor complained.

I came across Lieutenant Roberts, of the Tenth Cavalry, lying under the roots of a tree beside the stream with three of his colored troopers stretched around him. He was shot through the intestines, and each of the three men with him was shot in the arm or leg. They had been overlooked or forgotten, and we stumbled upon them only by the accident of losing our way. They had no knowledge as to how the battle was going or where their comrades were or where the enemy was. At any moment, for all they knew, the Spaniards might break through the bushes about them. It was a most lonely picture, the young lieutenant, half naked, and wet with his own blood, sitting upright beside the empty stream, and his three followers crouching at his feet like three faithful watch-dogs, each wearing his red badge of courage, with his black skin tanned to a haggard gray, and with his eyes fixed patiently on the white lips of his officer. When the white soldiers with me offered to carry him back to the dressing-station, the negroes resented it stiffly. "If the Lieutenant had been able to move, we would have carried him away long ago," said the sergeant, quite overlooking the fact that his arm was shattered.

"Oh, don't bother the surgeons about me," Roberts added, cheerfully. "They must be very busy. I can wait."

As yet, with all these killed and wounded, we had accomplished nothing—except to obey orders—which was to await further orders. The observation balloon hastened the end. It came blundering down the trail, and stopped the advance of the First and Tenth Cavalry, and was sent up directly over the heads of our men to observe what should have been observed a week before by scouts and reconnoitring parties. A balloon, two miles to the rear, and high enough in the air to be out of range of the enemy's fire may some day prove itself to be of use and value. But a balloon on the advance line, and only fifty feet above the tops of the trees, was merely an invitation to the enemy to kill everything beneath it. And the enemy responded

to the invitation. A Spaniard might question if he could hit a man, or a number of men, hidden in the bushes, but had no doubt at all as to his ability to
hit a mammoth glistening ball only six hundred yards distant, and so all the
trenches fired at it at once, and the men of the First and Tenth, packed together directly behind it, received the full force of the bullets. The men lying
directly below it received the shrapnel which was timed to hit it, and which
at last, fortunately, did hit it. This was endured for an hour, an hour of such
hell of fire and heat, that the heat in itself, had there been no bullets, would
have been remembered for its cruelty. Men gasped on their backs, like fishes
in the bottom of a boat, their heads burning inside and out, their limbs too
heavy to move. They had been rushed here and rushed there wet with sweat
and wet with fording the streams, under a sun that would have made moving
a fan an effort, and they lay prostrate, gasping at the hot air, with faces aflame,
and their tongues sticking out, and their eyes rolling. All through this the
volleys from the rifle-pits sputtered and rattled, and the bullets sang continuously like the wind through the rigging in a gale, shrapnel whined and
broke, and still no order came from General Shafter.

Captain Howse, of General Sumner's staff, rode down the trail to
learn what had delayed the First and Tenth, and was hailed by Colonel
Derby, who was just descending from the shattered balloon.

"I saw men up there on those hills," Colonel Derby shouted; "they
are firing at our troops." That was part of the information contributed by
the balloon. Captain Howse's reply is lost to history.

General Kent's division, which, according to the plan, was to have
been held in reserve, had been rushed up in the rear of the First and Tenth,
and the Tenth had deployed in skirmish order to the right. The trail was
now completely blocked by Kent's division. Lawton's division, which was
to have re-enforced on the right, had not appeared, but incessant firing
from the direction of El Caney showed that he and Chaffee were fighting
mightily. The situation was desperate. Our troops could not retreat, as the
trail for two miles behind them was wedged with men. They could not remain where they were, for they were being shot to pieces. There was only
one thing they could do—go forward and take the San Juan hills by assault. It was as desperate as the situation itself. To charge earthworks held
by men with modern rifles, and using modern artillery, until after the
earthworks have been shaken by artillery, and to attack them in advance
and not in the flanks, are both impossible military propositions. But this
campaign had not been conducted according to military rules, and a series
of military blunders had brought seven thousand American soldiers into a
chute of death from which there was no escape except by taking the

enemy who held it by the throat and driving him out and beating him down. So the generals of divisions and brigades stepped back and relinquished their command to the regimental officers and the enlisted men.

"We can do nothing more," they virtually said. "There is the enemy."

Colonel Roosevelt, on horseback, broke from the woods behind the line of the Ninth, and finding its men lying in his way, shouted: "If you don't wish to go forward, let my men pass." The junior officers of the Ninth, with their negroes, instantly sprang into line with the Rough Riders, and charged at the blue block-house on the right.

I speak of Roosevelt first because, with General Hawkins, who led Kent's division, notably the Sixth and Sixteenth Regulars, he was, without doubt, the most conspicuous figure in the charge. General Hawkins, with hair as white as snow, and yet far in advance of men thirty years his junior, was so noble a sight that you felt inclined to pray for his safety; on the other hand, Roosevelt, mounted high on horseback, and charging the rifle-pits at a gallop and quite alone, made you feel that you would like to cheer. He wore on his sombrero a blue polka-dot handkerchief, a la Havelock, which, as he advanced, floated out straight behind his head, like a guidon. Afterward, the men of his regiment who followed this flag, adopted a polka-dot handkerchief as the badge of the Rough Riders. These two officers were notably conspicuous in the charge, but no one can claim that any two men, or any one man, was more brave or more daring, or showed greater courage in that slow, stubborn advance, than did any of the others. Some one asked one of the officers if he had any difficulty in making his men follow him. "No," he answered, "I had some difficulty in keeping up with them." As one of the brigade generals said: "San Juan was won by the regimental officers and men. We had as little to do as the referee at a prize-fight who calls 'time.' We called 'time' and they did the fighting."

I have seen many illustrations and pictures of this charge on the San Juan hills, but none of them seem to show it just as I remember it. In the picture-papers the men are running uphill swiftly and gallantly, in regular formation, rank after rank, with flags flying, their eyes aflame, and their hair streaming, their bayonets fixed, in long, brilliant lines, an invincible, overpowering weight of numbers. Instead of which I think the thing which impressed one the most, when our men started from cover, was that they were so few. It seemed as if some one had made an awful and terrible mistake. One's instinct was to call to them to come back. You felt that some one had blundered and that these few men were blindly following out some madman's mad order. It was not heroic then, it seemed merely absurdly pathetic. The pity of it, the folly of such a sacrifice was what held you.

They had no glittering bayonets, they were not massed in regular array. There were a few men in advance, bunched together, and creeping up a steep, sunny hill, the tops of which roared and flashed with flame. The men held their guns pressed across their chests and stepped heavily as they climbed. Behind these first few, spreading out like a fan, were single lines of men, slipping and scrambling in the smooth grass, moving forward with difficulty, as though they were wading waist high through water, moving slowly, carefully, with strenuous effort. It was much more wonderful than any swinging charge could have been. They walked to greet death at every step, many of them, as they advanced, sinking suddenly or pitching forward and disappearing in the high grass, but the others waded on, stubbornly, forming a thin blue line that kept creeping higher and higher up the hill. It was as inevitable as the rising tide. It was a miracle of self-sacrifice, a triumph of bull-dog courage, which one watched breathless with wonder. The fire of the Spanish riflemen, who still stuck bravely to their posts, doubled and trebled in fierceness, the crests of the hills crackled and burst in amazed roars, and rippled with waves of tiny flame. But the blue line crept steadily up and on, and then, near the top, the broken fragments gathered together with a sudden burst of speed, the Spaniards appeared for a moment outlined against the sky and poised for instant flight, fired a last volley, and fled before the swift-moving wave that leaped and sprang after them.

The men of the Ninth and the Rough Riders rushed to the block-house together, the men of the Sixth, of the Third, of the Tenth Cavalry, of the Sixth and Sixteenth Infantry, fell on their faces along the crest of the hills beyond, and opened upon the vanishing enemy. They drove the yellow silk flags of the cavalry and the flag of their country into the soft earth of the trenches, and then sank down and looked back at the road they had climbed and swung their hats in the air. And from far overhead, from these few figures perched on the Spanish rifle-pits, with their flags planted among the empty cartridges of the enemy, and overlooking the walls of Santiago, came, faintly, the sound of a tired, broken cheer.

★ ★ ★ ★ ★

Theodore Roosevelt would play up his command of the Rough Riders when he returned to politics after the war, which would help him win the vice presidency in 1900 with McKinley whom he would replace as president the following year. Davis would go on to write seven best-selling novels and twenty-five plays. He would also cover the First World War in France where he reached fame once again as he reported the German army's advance through Belgium.

Yanks: The Argonne

JOHN S. D. EISENHOWER

Over there, over there,
Send the word, send the word over there—
That the Yanks are coming,
The Yanks are coming,
The drums rum-tumming
Ev'rywhere.
So prepare, say a pray'r,
Send the word, send the word to beware.
We'll be over, we're coming over,
And we won't come back till it's over
Over there.

—George M. Cohan, 1917, "Over There"

The United States declared war on Germany on April 6, 1917. Unrestricted German submarine warfare and public indignation over the Zimmermann telegram had led to a final break of relations with the Central Powers. Further U-boat attacks on American merchant ships forced President Woodrow Wilson to abandon his policy of neutrality and request that Congress declare war on Germany. Wilson appointed General "Black Jack" Pershing, a West Point graduate of 1886 who had seen action in Cuba, to lead the American Expeditionary Force. Pershing insisted that the American force would not be used merely to fill gaps in the French and British armies. This attitude was resented by the Allied leaders who were short on troops. Yet Pershing stayed true to his course.

The Allies had already been at war since the summer of 1914. Millions of men had already died in the stalemate on the western front. Both sides had realized the war of manuever was not possible in the face of machine guns and artillery, and dug into the ground for protection. What followed was four years of pointless slaughter as each side attempted a break-through of the enemy's defenses. While the arrival of the "doughboys" was welcome by the exhausted armies of England and France, they remained an inexperienced and untested army. Their training and organization would take months before American units saw action in force. By June, 1917, the First Infantry Division would see action in the trenches at Nancy, France.

The first true American victory came at Cantigny in May, 1918. By September Pershing commanded the American First Army of seven divisions fighting in the Saint-Mihiel offensive. The German offensive that spring had been defeated. The time had come to assault the Hindenburg Line and defeat Germany. The Meuse-Argonne offensive, which would last from September 27 to October 6, was the largest and most costly military camapign in American history to that point. Pershing commanded over a million American and French troops that fought their way through the German defenses, forcing an armsistice in November 1918.

John S. D. Eisenhower published his acclaimed history of the American experience in the First World War, *Yanks*, in 2001. The following chapter describes the offensive in the final months of the war to sieze the Argonne forest from the German Army. Two legends are central to the story—the "Lost Battalion" of the eight units of the 77th Division led by Major Charles White Whittlesey and the story of Sgt. Alvin York of the 82nd Infantry Division.

★　★　★　★　★

Georges Clemenceau, the Tiger of France, was in the habit of taking an auto tour on Sunday afternoons. Moreover, as the Premier of his country, he was unaccustomed to being denied access to places he wanted to visit. So he thought it completely proper to appear unannounced at Pershing's Souilly headquarters on Sunday, September 29, intending to visit Montfaucon. He had heard that the Crown Prince's luxurious command post on that butte had survived intact and he wished to visit it.

Pershing attempted to dissuade Clemenceau. The roads, he protested, were in no condition for anyone to travel into the battle zone. But Clemenceau insisted. When the Premier threatened to go ahead on his own, Pershing reluctantly agreed to accompany him.

What Clemenceau saw dismayed him. As Pershing had predicted, the roads were jammed with trucks and animals, men struggling to maintain some sort of order and get men and matériel forward. Great 155mm guns, whose weight the roads could never carry, were tearing ruts into already torn-up ground. Part of the congestion was caused by elements of the 1st Division, en route from St. Mihiel. In many places, traffic was at a standstill.

As a result, Clemenceau never came close to seeing Montfaucon. For the moment, as long as he was with Pershing, he masked his fury behind a façade of geniality, but the Frenchman was now convinced that the Americans were unfit to operate as an independent command.

Clemenceau was overreacting to his disappointment. Pershing was all too aware of the chaos in his army's rear area, that the task before him and his men would be difficult and costly, the result of his having lost his race against time. Nevertheless, he had no intention of halting his offensive while he brought order out of chaos; his American superiors would never stand for that, and it would run counter to his own nature. On October 1, 1918, therefore, Pershing ordered the First U.S. Army to resume the attack northward to take the ridge of Romagne-sous-Montfaucon, which he had originally hoped to be assaulting on the first day in the Meuse-Argonne campaign.

Pershing had by now brought in some of his more experienced divisions. Those in Bullard's III Corps—the 4th, 80th, and 33d—were left in place. But Pershing removed all three of Cameron's divisions in V Corps. The 79th, so badly mauled in the attack on Montfaucon, he replaced with Beaumont Buck's 3d Division; the 37th was replaced by William Haan's 32d, the veterans of Fismes; and the 91st was pulled back into corps reserve. Those changes left V Corps with only two divisions, the 3d and 32d. At the same time Pershing relieved that corps of responsibility for taking Romagne Heights, specifically the Côte Dame Marie and the Côte de Châtillon. Those prime objectives could be approached indirectly from the southwest, by Liggett's I Corps.

To perform the gargantuan task of securing a foothold on the Romagne hill mass—or at least to initiate the effort—Pershing committed his Praetorian Guard, the 1st Division, in place of the 35th Division, which had been driven back from that position on September 29. That hill mass lay north of the Exermont Ravine, and the German trench line in that area was actually a switch position of the Kriemhilde Line itself. Gallwitz had counterattacked so fiercely on September 29 because an American success in that area would have exposed the Heights of Romagne, west of the Andon Creek. The town of Romagne itself, which lay in the valley of that creek, was unimportant.

To the east of Andon Creek stood the Heights of Cunel, hillocks that dominated the area from Romagne to the Meuse. The effort to take

Cunel was assigned to Bullard's III Corps. The objective of Cameron's V Corps was even more limited, the Bois de Chauvignon. To that end, First Army's Order No. 33, issued on October 1, set a boundary that gave Bullard the town of Nantillois as well as the road running from Nantillois to Cunel. Cameron was to have exclusive use of the road that ran from Montfaucon to Cierges, thence north toward the town of Romagne. In a situation where resupply and movement of artillery was at a premium, roads took precedence over high ground.

In the days between the halt and the resumption of the advance, the American high command had been conducting serious, even anguished reviews of what had gone wrong in the operation against Montfaucon. There were many factors, but prominent among them was the breakdown of liaison between the 79th Division of V Corps and the 4th Division of III Corps on its right. The 4th Division had driven on past Montfaucon without turning westward to assist its beleaguered sister division. Order No. 33 therefore included the following admonition:

> (X) (2) . . . Corps Commanders within their own corps and by mutual agreement with adjacent Corps Commanders will insure cooperative flanking maneuver between adjacent divisions and brigades. The personal attention of Corps Commanders will be given to this feature of the attack.

Other problems needed to be straightened out as well. One was the tendency of soldiers under fire to huddle together, to bunch up, a natural though dangerous human instinct. The other was the coordination between infantry and artillery:

> (3) Division commanders will give their personal attention to the formation of their infantry in depth and to insure that this depth is employed, not to thicken advanced lines but to pass through advanced lines or for maneuver to the flanks. The mixing of units by the constant reinforcing of the advance lines will be provided against.
>
> (4) Special step[s] will be taken by Corps and Division Commanders to insure close liaison between the advance infantry line and its supporting artillery. Artillery information officers will accompany the advance infantry line for this purpose.

H-Hour was set for 5:30 a.m., on October 4, 1918.

The results of the renewed attack were again disappointing, especially in the eastern portion of the American line. The 4th Division of III Corps took three days to capture the Bois de Fays, only one mile ahead of the line of departure. In V Corps the 3d Division pushed forward but was unable to take the Bois de Cunel. The 32d took Cierges. These were all minimal gains by some of Pershing's best divisions, local successes only.

Once more staffs at all levels began analyzing the problems. The major fault, they concluded, lay not with ineptness on the part of the divisions themselves but in the volume of enemy artillery fire that was raining down from the Heights of the Meuse. Up to that time Pershing had limited the mission of the French XVII Corps, on the Heights of the Meuse, to keeping the enemy "busy by demonstrations." He now reconsidered, and on October 5, 1918, he ordered the French corps to attack along a five-mile front with five divisions, four French and one American. German artillery east of the Meuse would now have a new preoccupation, to protect the front on their own side of the Meuse. If Pershing ever had second thoughts about his original orders, he did not express them.

The advance east of the Meuse would be slow, but more immediate action could be taken against the Argonne, to the west, the area of Hunter Liggett's I Corps. Action in that area was dramatic; in fact, the operations there between October 2 and October 7 have left the two most vivid stories of the campaign, the ones by which it will be remembered. They are the stories of the "Lost Battalion" and of Alvin York.

Pershing's order of September 29 to suspend operations had not applied to the attack in the Argonne Forest; the 77th Division was ordered to keep pushing ahead to silence the German guns located in the Argonne at the first possible moment. German artillery there was having such an effect on the Americans in the Aire Valley that one officer at First Army feared that their effect would force the Americans to pull back south of Montfaucon, even back to the original jump-off point. The guns had to be eliminated, and efforts to reduce their hiding places in the Argonne Forest by attack up both sides of the forest were not working. So General Robert Alexander's 77th had to keep pushing.

The conditions in the Argonne were different from those anywhere else on the front. The forest was as thick as Belleau Wood, but many times larger. If, as Liggett thought, the forest resembled Manhattan in size and shape, the Americans were beginning on 14th Street. The density of the forest meant that cohesive action between units was impossible; even most of the infantry's supporting weapons were of little use. The Argonne battle therefore degenerated into a series of small unit actions, in which each battalion fought its own little war. No ground, once taken, could be given up. As General Evan Johnson, commander of the 154th Brigade, put it: "Any ground gained must be held. . . . If I find anybody ordering a withdrawal from ground once held, I will see that he leaves the Service."

Such admonitions, while not ignored, were taken with a grain of salt by most officers. One officer who took Johnson at his word, however, was Major Charles W. Whittlesey, commanding the 1st Battalion of the 308th Infantry in Johnson's brigade. Whittlesey had already demonstrated his determination to abide by them. During the advance to the regiment's present position, the 1st Battalion had been cut off by a German infiltration from the west; the regiment of the 92d Division, attached to French units on his left, had failed to keep up. In that "first trap" his men had gone for three days with little or no food, and they were already tired by the time the rest of the regiment had caught up with them. Nevertheless, since some resupply had been possible, Whittlesey's battalion had not been relieved when friendly troops made contact; instead it was ordered to keep its place in the line.

The advance of the 77th was resumed on October 2, two days before the rest of the First Army was scheduled to jump off. Whittlesey's 1st Battalion was in the vanguard, despite his protests. His direction of attack led his battalion up a valley in the direction of Charlevaux, north of Binarville. Soon General Johnson, realizing that Whittlesey's battalion was lacking a company, sent three companies from the 2d Battalion, under Captain George G. McMurtry, to reinforce him. Somehow a company from the 307th Infantry also joined him. Whittlesey therefore commanded a force of seven depleted rifle companies and parts of two machine gun companies. His total at the start was about 670 men.

As Whittlesey's composite battalion moved north, it found a gap in the German line caused by the temporary movement of enemy troops elsewhere. Whittlesey pushed forward and reached his assigned objective on the road leading from Binarville on the west to Apremont on the east. The day was drawing to a close, and he had lost about ninety men pushing through the gap. He placed his command in a ravine south of the road, on the east side of the gully he had been following, where his men would be relatively safe from incoming artillery during the night. He was out of contact with the units on his flank, but that was common in that tangled forest.

Early the next morning, Whittlesey's men began receiving heavy German mortar fire. Becoming uneasy about his open flanks, he sent Company E, now down to about fifty men, back toward the rear with a request that Johnson send his two remaining companies up to join him. A little over an hour later, eighteen men struggled back into his perimeter; they had been ambushed. The Germans had strung wire defenses between Whittlesey and the rest of the 77th Division, and the 1st Battalion was now cut off. Whittlesey sent off the first of his six carrier pigeons reporting his whereabouts.

The second pigeon, released the following morning, October 4, carried a report that Whittlesey had lost 222 men, eighty-two of them killed. His machine gun crews were down to five, manned at half strength. He had only three enlisted medics with him, and they were running out of bandages. Based on that report, General Alexander sent the two companies that Whittlesey lacked; they failed after two tries, each reduced to the size of a platoon.

October 5, the third day of the ordeal, would be the worst. Becoming desperate to silence the mortars and machine guns hitting his position, Whittlesey sent a pigeon requesting artillery support. The shells came in—right on top of his battalion. One platoon was wiped out from the "friendly" fire, and after a couple of hours, Whittlesey had become desperate. He sent his fourth pigeon, pleading, "Our own artillery is dropping a barrage directly on us. For heaven's sake stop it!" Unfortunately the soldier tending the pigeons was nervous, and he allowed a bird to get away without the message. The next pigeon was Whittlesey's next to last, affectionately named Cher Ami. Cher Ami, it turned out, was as frightened as were the soldiers. It flew straight up and perched shivering on a branch of a tree. Whittlesey and the pigeon keeper were therefore forced to expose themselves by throwing stones at the bird. Finally it left for home through the incoming artillery fire.

The next day American artillery fire began to come in on the enemy. The prospect of an immediate German attack was diminishing, and the chief threats to the men of the battalion would now be fatigue, hunger, and thirst. Efforts to combat those enemies were futile. American airplanes spotted Whittlesey's position and attempted to drop supplies. The food, ammunition, water and medicines fell into German hands, and the Americans were forced to hear the Germans enjoying the bonanza while they continued to suffer.

The worst cause of suffering was the thirst. A clear brook flowed only fifty yards from Whittlesey's elongated position, in which the troops were huddled against the hill. Some men tried to make it down the precipitous hill to fill canteens. Few if any survived. Whittlesey then took a drastic step; he posted guards to shoot anyone attempting to sneak down and fill canteens.

Through it all, the men of the 1st Battalion, 308th Infantry, held on, partly out of numbness and resignation to death but also because of the inspiration given them by their two leaders, Whittlesey and McMurtry.

Both officers were wounded—McMurtry's swollen knee had been festering for days from a shrapnel wound—but both defied danger by limping and staggering among the men, from foxhole to foxhole, assuring them that help was on the way. After four whole days of siege, they were down to 245 effectives and one pigeon.

While Whittlesey's beleaguered men were enduring their ordeal, events were taking place seven miles to the east that would eventually bring about their rescue. It was not to come from the efforts of their own division in the Argonne Forest but from their comrades across the Aire.

On the night of September 30–October 1, the 1st Division had moved into the lines formerly occupied by the 35th Division. The Big Red One had suffered heavy casualties at Cantigny and Soissons, and had lost a few men at St. Mihiel, but their spirit remained high, thanks to their professional leadership, and they had worked out procedures to develop mutual confidence between units. The 6th Field Artillery, for example, had always supported the 1st Brigade (16th and 18th Infantry Regiments). The 7th Field Artillery had teamed up with the 2d Brigade (26th and 28th Infantry Regiments). The 5th Field Artillery was kept in general support of the whole division.

In the distribution of machine gun companies also, unit association had become routine. Each infantry battalion had its own machine gun company through attachment of companies from the divisional machine gun battalions.

The frontage the division occupied extended about four kilometers, from the Aire River eastward to Eclisefontaine. The eastern portion of the divisional area extended along the Apremont–Eclisefontaine road, but the west part slanted southwestward to Baulny. Almost immediately upon taking over this sector the 1st Division pushed the west portion of the line forward to occupy the Apremont road for its entire length. The 1st Brigade was on the left (west) and the 2d on the right (east).

During the night of October 2, as Charles Whittlesey was first settling into his position, the 1st Division sent out combat patrols to learn the nature of the enemy. What they found was not encouraging. The enemy was obviously there in force, and many patrols were ambushed or caught in machine gun fire. The front of the 1st Brigade was occupied by the German 5th Guards Division, and prisoners taken from that unit reported that they had orders to fight to the last man. The 2d Brigade was facing the 52d German Division. Both, according to 1st Division intelligence, were "fresh, first-class divisions."

The terrain over which the 1st Division was to attack was about as difficult as it could get. The left flank of the 1st Brigade sector ran along high ground above the north–south Apremont–Fléville road, which ran along the Aire, and was open to the raking fire of German guns in the Argonne Forest.

First the troops were to seize a hill mass called the Montrebeau, on which the Chaudron Farm hillock occupied about a mile square. Beyond that hill about a mile was the more formidable Montrefagne, the point of a nose leading northeast to an even more formidable position. Hill 272. To get from Montrebeau to Montrefagne, the troops would be forced to cross a steep cross-compartment, the Exermont Valley, along which ran the east–west Exermont road. General Summerall's plans for the first day called for seizing both Montrebeau and Montrefagne, plus most of the distance to Hill 272. Nobody would have assigned such a mission to any division but Pershing's best.

First Day, October 4

The attack of the 1st Division jumped off on schedule, at 5:25 a.m. The tanks, which had been held back to prevent signaling the imminence of the attack, immediately joined the lead ranks. The 1st Brigade, following their rolling artillery barrage and utilizing what swales they could to protect them from fire from the Argonne, attacked over the ground that had once been occupied temporarily by the 35th Division. The sight of American corpses, wounds bandaged, left out to die by the Germans, enraged the Americans, inspiring them to take additional revenge. There was also evidence of the carnage that had befallen the various patrols sent out two nights earlier. Despite heavy fire from all directions, the 1st Brigade took its first objective, the northern edge of the Montrebeau, by 7:00 a.m. A half hour later the 2d Brigade was on its first objective also, despite heavy resistance.

After a half hour to pause and regroup, the 1st Brigade continued its attack across the Exermont Ravine, headed for the heights beyond. Elements of the 16th Infantry, along the main road, entered the town of Fléville. The cost was high. The 3d Battalion, 16th Infantry, had crossed the line of departure that morning with twenty officers and eight hundred men. By the time it had secured its second objective it was down to two officers and 240 men. And fire continued from the west. The nearest friendly troops on the left were two kilometers to the rear.

To the right of the 16th Infantry, other regiments had made less progress. But orders were for each infantry unit to push forward on its own, and artillery support had decentralized to create four independent regimental combat teams of infantry and artillery. Despite the fact that the 18th was halted at Beauregard Farm just across the Exermont Ravine, and the 28th at La Neuville-le-Compte Farm to its right, the front remained continuous.

The tanks proved to be a great help in reducing German machine gun nests. Forty-seven of them had started the day with the division, one company with the 1st Brigade, two companies with the 2d Brigade, and one company in reserve. Yet so fierce was hostile fire that only three tanks remained at the end of the day; 84 percent of the tankers were casualties.

The soldiers on the ground saw the operation from a different perspective. Lieutenant Maury Maverick, of the 28th Infantry, for one, has left a vivid account of the Exermont attack.

After his easy capture of twenty-six frightened Germans at St. Mihiel, Maverick had undergone a sobering baptism of fire as his regiment, part of the 2d Brigade, had pulled into line at Exermont four days earlier. While Maverick was conferring with his company commander, Captain Frank Felbel, they heard a shrieking noise, then a dull explosion. Suspecting gas, they quickly donned their masks. Groping in the dark, Maverick stumbled over the body of a dead American. When he removed his mask, Maverick winced; the man stank. He was probably one of those men of the 35th Division who had been killed three days earlier. The next morning, in position, Maverick was jarred by the burst of a shell close by. One man was dead; another lost a leg and both arms. Maverick was buried in dirt. He was afraid to move for fear that he would "fall to pieces." But he was unhurt.

As Maverick's company was preparing to jump off at 5:30 a.m. four days later, on October 4, he could hear the various lieutenants shouting at their men. "God damn it, don't you know we're going over the top at five thirty-five?" On the German side there was only silence, a vacuum. Maverick began to hope that the enemy had retreated. When they jumped off on schedule, however, they discovered that the Germans, at least a rear guard of machine gunners, were still there. Forewarned by the American shouting, they could not have been surprised at the timing of the attack.

The Germans were veterans; most of the Americans were not. But the Yanks advanced bravely into the barrage of steel and fire, and their ranks dwindled fast. Of a company of two hundred, half were dead or wounded within a few minutes. Captain Felbel was one of the dead.

Maverick took command. When he counted the survivors, he found that the company had not a single sergeant left. Three of the four platoons were commanded by corporals; the fourth was commanded by Private Quinn, recently reduced for being absent without leave, but a veteran soldier. Maverick recorded his confusion:

> At this moment of five-thirty-five, everything happened that never happens in the story books of war. We literally lost each other. There were no bugles, no flags, no drums, and as far as we knew, no heroes. The great noise was like a great stillness, everything seemed blotted out. We hardly knew where the Germans were. We were simply in a big black spot with streaks of screaming red and yellow, with roaring giants in the sky tearing and whirling and roaring.

Still Maverick and his men—what was left of them—pushed ahead. His walking stick did him no good; when he came to a ditch, he fell in it. Still there was nothing to do but keep going. Maverick later recalled holding his head down so that any shell fragments would hit his steel helmet, only to discover that he was not wearing a helmet at all. He borrowed one from "a poor fellow who had no further use for it." It was too small, but there was no shortage of dead Americans who had no further use for their helmets.

On they went. Then a shell burst over Maverick's head, and a piece of it tore out part of his shoulder blade and collarbone. On the ground but still conscious, Maverick was amazed that it seemed less than five seconds before a Medical Corps man was dressing his wound. He looked for the runners who had been with him a minute before. "The two in the middle had been cut down to a pile of horrible red guts and blood and meat, while the two men on the outside had been cut up somewhat less badly but no less fatally."

Still Maury Maverick stayed with his company, for the simple reason that there was nobody else to take over. He found four more runners and kept going. After an hour, however, he had lost so much blood that he was getting weak. He could carry on no longer—though he could still walk. He turned the company over to Private Quinn and headed for the rear.

Second Day, October 5, 1918

In the course of the first day's fighting, only the 16th Infantry, on the left of the 1st Division zone, had attained its objective, crossing the Exermont Ravine and gaining a foothold on the hill mass across. Elsewhere the division had crossed the Exermont Ravine from Montrebeau and Eclise-fontaine and secured footholds on the long, thin hill mass beyond but had fallen short of taking Montrefagne, which was simply the nose of the ridge line running northeast up to Hill 272.

On the second day, therefore, the division's first object was to bring the other three regiments, to the east of the 16th, into line with the 16th. The second objective was to take Montrefagne, and then Hill 272. After that it would continue another mile to seize the Côte Maldah.

As it turned out, only the first objective for the day was accomplished, plus the seizure of Montrefagne, which had nearly been accomplished the day before. At tremendous cost, the 18th, 28th, and 26th Regiments, from west to east, fought ahead about a mile so that the line, as of the end of the day, ran (west to east) from Fléville–Ariétal Farm, into the Bois de Moncy. Only the barest of footholds had been taken on the Hill 272 mass. But the Argonne Forest, to the west, had been flanked.

At his headquarters in Floriment, Major General Hunter Liggett, in whose I Corps the 1st Division had been fighting, saw an opportunity to exploit the division's gains. In spite of the fact that the division had not attained all the ambitious goals set for it, its advance from Apremont to Fléville had opened the enemy's east flank in the Argonne. Between those two towns the Americans held the right bank of the Aire and the Germans the left. But the Americans held the initiative.

On the evening of October 5 Liggett blocked out a plan that he submitted to First Army for approval. He would commit his reserve, the 82d Division, from the area just taken by the 1st Division, to attack westward across the Aire, behind the German troops in the Argonne. If successful, the attack would force the enemy to evacuate the Argonne Forest. It would save Whittlesey's Lost Battalion and relieve the 1st Division of the heavy shelling it was still receiving from German artillery west of the Aire.

Liggett's plan was not without risk. By hitting the German rear in the Argonne, he was also opening his own right flank to possible German counterattack from the north. The crossing points of the Aire were problematical; no Americans knew exactly where they were. So Liggett ran into resistance from fainter hearts. At his own headquarters, only his chief of staff, Malin Craig, supported his plan. The French officers attached to his headquarters were unanimously opposed to it. But after Liggett secured the approval of Hugh Drum, chief of staff of the First Army, and then of General McAndrew, chief of staff at Chaumont, Liggett considered it authorized, and he was willing to take the chance. The plight of Whittlesey and of the 1st Division made it all worth the risk.

The attack of the 82d Division lacked the full weight that Liggett would have liked. The bulk of the division was in corps reserve, a considerable distance from the action, and it could not be ready, as a whole division, for some time.

Fortunately for the Americans, one regiment of the 82d, the 328th Infantry, under Colonel Frank Ely, had been attached to the 28th. Liggett immediately sent it to the rear of the 1st Division, on the right bank of the Aire, south of Fléville. Some guides, though not nearly enough, were available.

Early in the morning of Monday, the 7th of October, several companies of the 328th Infantry forded the frigid waters of the Aire River and deployed to cut the north–south road running through the Argonne through Cornay. To secure that town they were forced to scale the steep sides of Hill 180 and, further south, Hill 233. At the same time a brigade of the 28th stormed Hill 244 and took the adjacent one-street town of Châtel Chéhéry. The Americans had turned the German flank in the Argonne.

With the loss of that road and the prospect of reinforcing troops from the 82d cutting off their rear, the German command realized that their position in the Argonne had become untenable. They began a hasty withdrawal, and between the morning of the 7th and the 9th they evacuated as much as five miles along the western reaches of the forest. In the south, the 77th Division resumed its attack to the north.

On that same morning of October 7, Charles Whittlesey's Lost Battalion was entering its fifth day isolated in the Argonne Forest. All efforts to resupply by air had failed, as had all the attacks launched in his direction by the rest of the division. Like many others of Whittlesey's men, Private Lowell B. Hollingshead had given up all hope of surviving this ordeal. He was slightly wounded and weak with hunger. Above all his other desires, even survival, was a yearning for rest and food.

At about 10:00 a.m. an unfamiliar sergeant crept over to the foxhole where Hollingshead and several of his buddies were huddled. Major Whittlesey, the sergeant said, had called for eight volunteers to infiltrate out through the German lines and report the situation of the battalion to their comrades a few miles south. Hollingshead volunteered immediately. He did not know the sergeant, nor did he know what company he was from, but he was impelled by one driving thought, the "desire for food and anything that would help me secure it."

Soon the small patrol was heading south, protected by a light fog and mist. The men crossed the small Charlevaux Creek, some stepping, some wading. In such a dangerous situation none dared stop to drink, thirsty though they were. Stopping to rest for a moment in the protection of a thicket, the men hoped they had broken free. To add to their hope, they had one man, a full-blooded Indian, to act as their guide. They placed their trust in him.

The Indian managed his charges well, stopping periodically to allow them to rest in their weakened condition. Finally, however, he stopped and raised his hand; danger lay ahead.

Then it happened. The patrol found themselves right in the middle of a spate of machine gun fire, and Hollingshead saw little spurts of dirt kicking around them. He lost consciousness and sometime later awoke to find himself looking down the long barrel of a German Luger. The officer holding the weapon was half smiling, half sneering. Hollingshead threw his hands up and muttered "Kamerad." The German, a handsome fellow, then broke into a broad smile. Looking around, Hollingshead discovered the fate of his comrades; four of them, including the Indian scout, were dead. The rest were wounded. Hollingshead's wound in the leg was the least serious.

The next few hours were a relief for the famished doughboy. In the tent of an interrogation officer he refused to talk, but the officer appeared to accept his reluctance. Hollingshead was generously fed and allowed to rest. He identified the officer as Lieutenant Heinrich Prinz, a German who had lived for some time in the United States.

Soon Prinz gave up on interrogating Hollingshead and went across the tent to a typewriter and began typing out a message. He asked Hollingshead if he would take the message back to his commanding officer. The soldier agreed if he could be given time for a little rest. He then dozed off.

Eventually Hollingshead felt a tap on the shoulder. "If you are going to get the message back before dark you must start now." Hollingshead indicated that he was ready. One of the German captors gave him a cane; another tied a white cloth to the end of it. Conducted out of the German position blindfolded, Hollingshead was suddenly alone with a single guide. The guide led him down a road and removed the blindfold. Both men smiled and shook hands. A few minutes later Hollingshead was in the presence of Whittlesey, who immediately began reading the message.

The message was courteous. It described Hollingshead's conduct in glowing terms, calling him "quite an honorable fellow, doing honor to his Fatherland in the strictest sense of the word." Conceding rather generously that Hollingshead was carrying the message "very much against his will," the message got to the point. It urged the American commander to "surrender with his forces, as it would be quite useless to resist any more, in view of the present conditions." Then:

The suffering of your wounded men can be heard over here in the German lines, and we are appealing to your humane sentiments to stop. A white flag shown by one of your men will tell us that you agree with these conditions.

Whittlesey never bothered to reply. It was not worth the effort. He deduced from the tone of the message that the Germans were finished and that the note was an act of desperation.

That evening elements of the 77th Division broke through the German lines and relieved the Lost Battalion, or what remained of it. Only 191 of Whittlesey's original 670 men were able to walk out of their position.

The saga of the lost battalion was one of the stories that have become legend as the result of the actions in the Argonne in early October 1918. The other was the unbelievable exploit of Corporal, later Sergeant, Alvin C. York. The two incidents were related indirectly, because York's feat was part of the envelopment of the German position in the Argonne, which in turn contributed to the relief of Whittlesey and his men. Neither man was a member of what might be considered the elite formations of the AEF.

Ironically, York had registered for the draft as a conscientious objector to war, for although he was an expert hunter and woodsman from Wolf Valley, Tennessee, he was also an elder in the Church of Christ, which subscribed to the words in the Bible forbidding killing. His mother and the congregation of the church protested his going into uniform when he was called by the draft. At Camp Gordon, Georgia, however, his company commander convinced him of the righteousness of the American cause by quoting scripture. York entered the Army as an infantryman, assigned to the 82d Division. He had no ambition for advancement, and despite his obvious leadership abilities, he had been promoted only to the grade of corporal when the division was committed in the Argonne.

By the morning of October 8, the 328th Infantry, on the left of the 82d Division, had penetrated the Argonne only about 1,500 yards, holding Hill 223. That morning it was ordered to continue the attack westward to seize the Decauville Railroad a little over a mile away, thus cutting a major German line of retreat. York's platoon, on the extreme left of the attack, was commanded by Lieutenant Harry M. Parsons, a former New York vaudeville actor. The platoon having run up against a machine gun nest, Parsons sent Sergeant Bernard Early, with fifteen men, to reduce it. York was one of them.

Under the cover of a heavy morning mist, Early and his men made their way undetected to the rear of the machine gun nest. They fixed bayonets and were preparing to charge the German position when they stumbled on a battalion field headquarters, where three German officers were studying a map and various other soldiers were resting. At one volley, the entire group threw their hands in the air in surrender.

Immediately the German machine gun crew, realizing what had happened, turned around and began spraying both Early and his prisoners, all of whom hit the ground. That burst wounded Early and two others, killing six. York, untouched, immediately assumed command of the seven remaining Americans.

At this point, Alvin York began his own private little war. Ordering the other doughboys to guard the prisoners, he hid a secluded position and began picking off the Germans, one by one. An expert rifleman, and firing at close range, he missed only one; the rest he killed. Always hoping to end the killing, he shouted "Come down" between shots. At one point a German lieutenant and six men charged York's position. Now down to using a service pistol (so he later claimed), he killed every one.

Seeing what had happened, York's prisoner, the German major, offered to arrange the surrender of all the gun positions, even though York was still vastly outnumbered. The German suggested a route that he said led to the American lines but York's backwoods sense of direction said otherwise. He placed the major up front, and, his service pistol in the small of the major's back, he pointed him in the other direction. As the strange group approached each machine gun position, the German officer would call out and the gun crew would join York's group of prisoners. By the time they reached the lines of the 2d Battalion, the number had grown to 132 enemy. The number that York had actually killed was never determined, but was probably around twenty.

The heroism of Alvin York, subsequently promoted to Sergeant York, was of course only one incident in a large battle. However, the American Battle Monuments Commission *Guidebook* gives the incident much credit: "Largely on account of York's exceptional coolness, skill with firearms, bravery, and leadership his regiment was able to continue its advance on this day."

The episode carries another aspect, however. Alvin York's astonishing feat was made possible in part by growing German demoralization. German soldiers, no matter how professional, knew at last that their cause in the First World War was lost.

By October 10, only three days after the 82d Division crossed the Aire River, the German Army had evacuated the Argonne.

★   ★   ★   ★   ★

By the time Germany signed the Armistice on November 11, 1918, the American Expeditionary Force had evolved into a modern, combat-tested army. The United States had sustained an estimated 360,000 casualties in the First World War. General Pershing was regarded as a mentor by the generation of American generals who led the United States army forces in Europe during World War II, including George C. Marshall, Dwight D. Eisenhower, Omar Bradley, and George S. Patton, Jr. Sgt. Alvin C. York would receive the medal of Honor in April, 1919, and return home a national hero. Major Whittlesey, along with several other officers, received the Medal of Honor for their valiant actions, yet Whittlesey was weighed by depression and guilt over the loss of so many men under his command and took his own life in 1921.

My War—Normandy

ANDY ROONEY

> You will bring about the destruction of the German war ma-
> chine, the elimination of Nazi tyranny over the oppressed peo-
> ples of Europe, and security for ourselves in a free world. . . .We
> will accept nothing less than full victory.
> —General Dwight D. Eisenhower,
> Message to the troops, D-Day, June 6, 1944

Andy Rooney is known to almost everyone as the affable and witty com-
mentator who appears every week at the end of *60 Minutes*. It is hard to
imagine he was once a soldier, but in the summer of 1941 Rooney reported for duty in the U.S. Army. His wit and penchant for wisecrackery
got him into all kinds of trouble, but he managed to graduate from basic
training. For the good fortune of us all, he was assigned to the "Writing
69th" covering the war in Europe for *Stars and Stripes*. He would go on to
take part in the air war over Europe, the D-Day invasion of Normandy,
and the Allied drive into Germany.

In 2002 Rooney published his memoir of those experiences in
My War. His writing brings with it a lifetime of reflection on the war years
and the experiences of a young man trying to write about events too big
to comprehend. In doing so he brought those overwhelming events into
focus, and detailed the everyday fears, tribulations, and adventures he encountered while scouring Normandy for good copy in 1944. With his
easygoing style, he also reminds us that the landings of D-Day were just
the beginning. Behind the beaches lay the fields and fortresslike hedgerows
where German defenses waited in ambush for the American army. For
those of us who were not there, or for whom time has faded the memories, Andy Rooney brings back for us what it was like to be young, and
scared, in the greatest invasion of all time.

★ ★ ★ ★ ★

Thead have been only a handful of days since the beginning of time on which the direction the world was taking has been changed for the better in one twenty-four-hour period by an act of man. June 6, 1944, was one of them.

What the Americans, the British, and the Canadians were trying to do was get back a whole continent that had been taken from its rightful owners and whose citizens had been taken captive by Adolf Hitler's German army. It was one of the most monumentally unselfish things one group of people ever did for another.

In answer to the standard questions, do I know where I was when John F. Kennedy was shot or do I know where I was when I heard that Franklin D. Roosevelt had died, the answers are yes. But, for some reason, I can't remember where I was or when I heard that the Allied Invasion of France had finally taken place.

It seems most likely that when the announcement of the Invasion was made, Charley Kiley and I were already onboard the small ship that was to take us around the end of England, past Cornwall, which Mother's father had left when he was sixteen, and across the Channel to France. I looked forward to getting to France because I hoped to determine, once and for all, whether Mr. Sharp was right when he failed me for two successive years in the French course he taught at The Academy.

The whole world knew that the Invasion was taking place about the time we were midway between Bristol and the French coast alongside the Cotentin Peninsula, but we didn't know. Not knowing was a familiar condition that soldiers found themselves in all the time during the process of fighting a war—theirs not to reason why, theirs but to do or die or, in my case, try to find out. They were always the last to know what they were doing and the last to know what they had done when it was over. There had been rumors of television before the war but it was not yet a fact. Radio was not part of our lives once we were shipped out of the United States and they weren't delivering newspapers to us onboard our invasion craft. We were part of a vast armada moving toward the action along those narrow strips of beach that the first waves had already landed on.

There were ships and smaller vessels everywhere. The operation was more than I could think about and I didn't do much on the trip across except hope I wouldn't be seasick. Some of the guys played cards or wrote letters but I didn't feel like doing anything but stare at the Channel waters.

Someone had organized this great seaborne movement of men—built the ships that managed to float and not tip over after being crammed with men and materiel. They had arranged to clothe everyone, to put weapons in their hands, to supply them with food, to put toilet paper in their backpacks, and I was staring out at the rough waters of the Channel and idly considering that Gertrude Ederle had once swum across it. Far from thoughts of the magnitude of the adventure was I. It's hard to see the big picture and especially hard if you're in the picture.

We all have days of our lives that stand out from the blur of days that have gone by, and the day I came ashore on Utah Beach is one of mine.

As we approached the French coast, there were small clouds of smoke and sudden eruptions behind the small, weed-covered hills bordering Utah Beach. German artillery was lobbing shells, blindly now, hoping to hit U.S. troops or some of the massive amount of equipment piled up on the shore.

The French call D-Day "J-Jour" and I don't have a lot of complaints with the French but it was our day and I think they ought to call it by our name, D-Day.

If you're young, and not really clear what D-Day was, let me tell you, it was a day unlike any other.

I landed on Utah Beach several days after the first assault waves went in on the morning of June 6. I am uncertain of the day. When I came in, row on row of dead American soldiers were laid out on the sand just above the high-tide mark where the beach turned into weedy clumps of grass. They were covered with olive-drab blankets, just their feet sticking out at the bottom, their GI boots sticking out. I remember their boots—all the same on such different boys.

They had been dead several days and some of them had been killed, not on the beaches, but inland.

No one can tell the whole story of D-Day because no one knows it. Each of the 60,000 men who waded ashore that day knew a little part of the story too well.

To them, the landing looked like a catastrophe. Each knew a friend shot through the throat, shot through the knee. Each knew the names of five hanging dead on the barbed wire in the water twenty yards offshore, three who lay unattended on the stony beach as the blood drained from holes in their bodies.

They saw whole tank crews drowned when the tanks rumbled off the ramps of their landing craft and dropped into twenty feet of water.

There were heroes here no one will ever know because they're dead. The heroism of others is known only to themselves.

Across the Channel in Allied headquarters in England, the war directors, remote from the details of tragedy, were exultant. They saw no blood, no dead, no dying. From the statisticians' point of view, the invasion was a great success. The statisticians were right. They always are—that's the damned thing about it.

It's not possible for anyone who's been in a war to describe the terror of it to anyone who hasn't. I wrote a poem the day I came ashore, writing in my jeep with a pad on my knee. I thought it was a poem.

> *"Here" the battleground guide will say when the tourists come,*
> *"They fought the bloody battle for the beach."*
> *They'll talk on with pointers in their hands*
> *To a bus-load of people*
> *About events that never happened*
> *In a place they never were.*
> *How would anyone know that John Lacey died*
> *In that clump of weeds by the wagon path*
> *As he looked to the left toward Simpson . . .*
> *And caught a bullet behind the ear?*
> *And if there had been a picture of it*
> *It wouldn't show the snapshot in his breast pocket*
> *Of his girlfriend with his mom and dad*
> *At Christmas.*

I sound young and I didn't have any experience punctuating poetry but on five subsequent visits to the beaches over the years, I've been pleased to find how accurate I was with the observations about the battleground guides. The buses dump crowds on the bluffs above the beaches and twenty-five-year-old French guides, speaking a variety of languages, tell the tourists what happened down there on the sand.

On each visit, I've wept. It's almost impossible to keep back the tears as you look across the rows of crosses and think of the boys under them who died that day.

Even if you didn't know anyone who died, the heart knows something the brain does not—and you weep. If you think the world is selfish and rotten go to the cemetery at Colleville overlooking Omaha Beach. See what one group of men did for another on D-Day, June 6, 1944.

My tears dried up on the fiftieth anniversary visit to Omaha when I got thinking of how presumptuous it was of some Army authority to have put nothing but crosses or Stars of David over the graves, as though there was no room in the cemetery for anyone who held beliefs other than those represented by two religious symbols.

Normandy after our landing was a crash course in land warfare for me. It didn't have any relationship to what we'd been taught on maneuvers with the Seventeenth Field Artillery in North Carolina. One of the things I was learning was that the reason everyone in a war doesn't get killed is that most bullets, most artillery shells, and most bombs don't hit anything. The world would be out of trouble if it had all the money to spend on poverty that it has spent during its history on ammunition that failed to serve its purpose—to kill. How slow does a bullet go before it falls? It's strange that, for all the millions of rounds of ammunition that came toward U.S. forces from the Germans, I never saw a bullet fall, spent. Uncle Bill used to take me to the Saratoga battlefield where the British general Burgoyne had enlisted Indian troops to help fight American soldiers, and in the 1930s, 150 years after the battle, we used to find arrowheads. I should think French farmers would be tilling metal bullet fragments from their soil for a thousand years.

I landed in France near the inner elbow of the Cotentin Peninsula at the end of which, twenty-five miles out, is the port of Cherbourg. It had not been as rough for the men who came in at Utah as it had been at Juno, Gold, Sword, or Omaha. Omaha was closest to Utah and the worst. The two beaches were separated by several miles and the promontory known as Pointe-du-Hoc.

The war was still close to the beaches when I came ashore and I waited to be raked with machine-gun fire but there were no German soldiers within two miles of where I was. There were none because the areas immediately behind Utah had been cleared out by paratroopers. The Eighty-second and 101st Airborne Divisions had cut off the only main road leading from the mainland out the thick, thumblike Cotentin Peninsula to Cherbourg. Their mission was to interrupt German supply columns feeding their tank and infantry divisions that were isolated from the main body of their troops but were still ferociously defending the port. The Fourth Infantry Division had sliced clear across to the other side of the peninsula before turning and heading out toward Cherbourg, away from the main lines of the war behind the beaches. When I came in, the Fourth, Ninth, and Seventy-ninth Divisions, a formidable force of about 50,000 men, were stretched across the peninsula from one side to the other and moving on Cherbourg in a solid phalanx.

The German lines were intact on the mainland behind Omaha Beach, twenty miles away, around the elbow formed by the peninsula. The

Germans, under do-or-die orders from Hitler, were desperately trying to push the British, Canadians, and Americans back into the Channel where bodies still floated facedown in the water lapping the shore. Bodies always floated facedown.

The major German forces defending the Cotentin Peninsula had all run toward Cherbourg to form a defensive line in front of it, so the area behind our beaches, leading out to the peninsula itself, was relatively safe. The enemy meant to save the port for themselves, or destroy it so we couldn't use it.

In Bristol, I had spent some of the time waterproofing my jeep with the help of mechanics who supervised those of us who didn't know how. I covered all the electrical connectors, the generator, and the ignition with a thick, greasy coating to enable the jeep to wade, in two or three feet of water, without stalling. When Army rifles were shipped in boxes, they were coated with something called Cosmoline to prevent rust. One of the things first sergeants liked to do best was supervise the removal of Cosmoline from a private's rifle. The stuff I put on my jeep was not Cosmoline, but Not Cosmoline is as close as I can come to a name for it.

The exhaust pipe had been disconnected, and in its place I attached an L-shaped pipe to the manifold that came up alongside the driver's seat and stuck a foot above the top of the jeep's windshield. The theory was that the jeep would actually have to run a short distance from the ramp of the landing craft, through several feet of water offshore, and to dry sand on the beach without having its engine sputter to a stop.

When I came ashore, I was wearing an Army olive-green wool uniform that had been impregnated with some kind of greasy wax intended to protect the skin in case of a mustard-gas attack by the Germans. Just the threat of gas had cost Allied forces thousands of hours of time and millions of dollars. The uniforms were very uncomfortable and the jeeps didn't like what had been done to them any better than we liked our uniforms. Our orders were to get the coating off the jeep engine as soon after landing as possible.

I got the waterproofing off my jeep and headed out to the peninsula toward Cherbourg, trying to make heads or tails of a battle I didn't understand. The geography of Normandy on a map is easy for me to understand now, but I didn't comprehend it at the time. By the time you're familiar enough with territory to understand a map, you no longer need it.

There were two large towns on the peninsula before Cherbourg, Montebourg and Valognes. It would be more accurate to say, they *had been* towns. I've seen hundreds since, but then I had never seen a town that had been leveled. Our bombers must have destroyed the towns in an effort to cut the German supply lines to Cherbourg and it was the first time it had occurred to me that the French people of Normandy must have felt some ambivalence about the Invasion. It was true they were being freed but at the cost of the total destruction of everything they had. And there's no question that many of the people of Normandy were sullen in their attitude toward the Americans.

There have been half a dozen times in my life that I'd like to live over so that I could improve on my performance and the next few weeks are foremost in my memory among those times. My output as a reporter was small and the stories I wrote for the paper were petty. I was not experienced enough to understand that everything I saw was a story. I was witness to one of the most monumental operations ever staged by man, and I was writing pieces about a Fourth Division infantryman from Texas who adopted a lost and bewildered Morgan stallion and rode the horse for several days as the division moved on Cherbourg. It was a good feature piece but it seemed to me I should have been providing readers who weren't there details of how our effort to capture the port was going. The problem was, I didn't know how it was going. I was too close to the battle to see the war. That was the first of a lot of times that was true in the following months.

Within a few days after the invasion, a *Stars and Stripes* headquarters had been established at a small printing plant in Carentan, not far from Omaha Beach. The infantry was still unable to break out of that narrow strip of coast where it was being contained by German forces behind a low range of hills running parallel to the beach. The landing infantry had forced its way ashore in the face of terrible fire from the bluffs above the beaches but had been able to push inland and break through the main line of German resistance containing them.

Night and day German artillery poured shells into the thin strip of land we held. Ships offshore were dumping supplies on the beaches and it got so the area we'd taken was so constricted that there was no place to pile them. Carentan and *The Stars and Stripes* printing plant were part of that narrow strip. The paper was printed there for just two days before being forced to move back up the Contentin Peninsula and eventually to Sainte-Mère-Église.

At some point, date unknown to me, I left the Cherbourg area and drove back down the peninsula to *The Stars and Stripes* headquarters that had been established in Sainte-Mère-Église. The staff had taken over two attached stone houses to live in on the main street. Most war buffs know the town because it was from the church steeple there that the American paratrooper, John Steele, hung all night from the cords of his parachute, wounded but not daring to make a sound. There were German soldiers in the streets below when he first drifted down and they would have riddled his body with bullets.

One paratrooper who made it told me about his commander.

"Colonel Wolverton got hung up in a tree," he said. "He was killed in his parachute."

"The Germans shot him as he hung there?" I asked.

"Everyone come along shot him," he said.

Every trooper had a story if he was lucky enough to have lived through the night. Months later when the men from one battalion of the Eighty-second Airborne reassembled in England, there were only 114 of the original 800 left.

Several *Stars and Stripes* editors were living in an old stone house on the main street in Sainte-Mère-Église. Two Frenchwomen lived in adjoining houses and someone on the newspaper struck a great deal with them. It was my first exposure to the genius of French cooking.

The basic Army field ration was called ten-in-one. It came in a heavy, waxed cardboard carton weighing about forty-five pounds. I think ten-in-one meant it served ten men for one day. *Stars and Stripes* people roamed freely, and all it took was a stop at a quartermaster depot to pick up as many ten-in-ones as a jeep would carry. There were no tight controls so soon after the Invasion. The newspaper staff people in Sainte-Mère (we dropped the *Église* soon after we got there) simply gave the ten-in-one boxes to the two women and they worked their French magic on them.

Sainte-Mère was surrounded by the lush Norman countryside and, while many of the farmers had fled, and the bloated carcasses of dead cows were everywhere, there were still chickens laying eggs and cows giving milk. The ten-in-one contained, among other things, a two-pound tin of bacon.

The following morning I headed back out the Contentin Peninsula toward Cherbourg and again drove through Montebourg and Valognes. On the fiftieth anniversary of D-Day, I arrived in Cherbourg on the *Queen Mary* and drove down the peninsula, through those restored towns, to where I'd come ashore on Utah Beach. It's hard to describe how I felt. I kept looking at the people living there in 1994, young people mostly, and I wanted to stop every one of them and tell them what their town looked like in June of 1944. I suppose it interested me more than it would have interested them. They'd read about it and seen pictures and anyway, they had cows to milk or chores to do.

It was my real first look at war on the ground. The closest I'd been previously was 25,000 feet above Germany in a B-17 or 12,000 in a B-26 and I realize, in retrospect, that I was more a tourist than a reporter.

The three infantry divisions were too late reaching Cherbourg. The port had been totally destroyed and rendered unusable as a landing place for Allied ships carrying men and equipment. I suppose it had taken thirty years to construct the port facilities because they were among the best in Europe, but the Germans had made them useless with demolition charges in three days. A masterful job of deconstruction.

Just outside Cherbourg, railroad tracks disappeared into a hillside and, although the railroad was no longer operative, I saw a small group of American soldiers crowding into the tunnel. I thought perhaps some German soldiers who'd been hiding in there had come out to surrender. As I came up to the mouth of the tunnel, I saw that the point of interest was not the enemy. The German officers had used the tunnel as what was, at that time, probably the world's greatest wine cellar. The cavernous interior was stacked with thousands of cases of the best wines they could appropriate in France. There was cognac, champagne, port, and sherry enough for, literally, an army. German officers apparently lived better than our own.

Soldiers and several reporters who got there ahead of me were going in and then reappearing at the mouth of the tunnel a few minutes later, carrying cases of wine of an excellence far beyond their beer-trained taste buds' ability to appreciate. It was my first exposure to the spoils of war and to the word "loot" used as a noun. They put the loot in jeeps and trucks and drove off. It gave me a new view of looting, too.

In school I'd read how Hannibal's troops looted and plundered as they moved across the Alps and then into Rome. It was something out of the ancient past but as I watched this anthill of activity at the mouth of the tunnel, as Americans helped themselves to this great stock of wine and liquor, I realized the standards of what's right and wrong change in a war. These soldiers and the newsmen helping themselves didn't have any sense that they were stealing. Stealing suggests taking property away from someone else. They weren't taking from anyone, and it didn't seem wrong to them. It wasn't wrong, I guess. They were taking something that wasn't theirs but it wasn't anyone else's, either.

These were second-generation spoils, of course. They'd already been spoils once when the Germans took them from the French. Now they were spoils again as American soldiers helped themselves. I remember the feeling I had that I should get in on this good thing going on and take several cases back to Sainte-Mère myself. Here was something valuable absolutely free. Mine for the taking.

I didn't take any wine that day. It wasn't so much that I had any inhibitions about taking it because it wasn't mine. At that time in my life, I didn't drink wine or liquor of any kind—a personal shortcoming that I was to correct after the war when I learned what a good, wholesome, American drink bourbon is.

Cherbourg was of vital importance to the success of the Allied drive toward Germany because without a port it was difficult to bring ashore the vast quantity of supplies that a million soldiers already ashore needed. They had to be fed, moved, and stocked with ammunition, a monumental supply job.

Without Cherbourg, supply ships were coming into Mulberry, the huge code-named docking area off the landing beaches. The Mulberries had been constructed in England and then towed across the Channel and sunk to form a pier for landings. This man-made harbor was built in a top-secret operation by 19,000 British construction workers, and when they got it over to the coast of France it looked like a six-story building lying on its side. It was one of the most inventive things the Allies did in planning the Invasion. One of the good things about war is, people come up with a lot of good ideas. The bad thing about those good ideas is, half of them are ideas about how to kill people.

Two Mulberries, one off the British beach, Gold, and one off the American, Omaha, had been put in place shortly after the Invasion. The one off Omaha was destroyed a few days later by the worst storm to hit the area in fifty years and it could never be used. You can still see parts of its sticking up out of the water at low tide now, fifty years later. The one off Gold, the British beach, stood up and was an important factor in the success the Allies had in shoveling millions of tons of supplies into France.

Those Mulberries are not the only evidence left of the landing on the coast of Normandy. The French have been casual about removing or paying much attention at all to the vestiges of D-Day that are everywhere. Schoolchildren play tag amid the ruins of a massive German fortress on top of Pointe-du-Hoc. They haven't preserved it but they haven't removed it. It's just there and it's going to be there for the 100th anniversary of the landings, too.

A few French people have summer cottages just behind the beaches, and many of them live with six-foot-thick German bunkers in their front yard. They'll be there in the year 3000—if there is one.

I was wide-eyed in those first days ashore as I gaped at the land war. Everything was so different. The only similarity to a bomber base was the imminence of death. There were so many things to feel bad about that it was hard to feel as bad about all of them as you knew you should. We seem to have some built-in governor that limits our capacity for sadness.

Many French farmers, who had looked forward with great hope to the invasion, had been killed by the U.S. bombs. Families had lost fathers, mothers, brothers, sisters. Every family had lost someone. Surviving farmers in Normandy often had to flee their homes and fields as they were surrounded or overrun by both German and American soldiers spraying machine-gun bullets everywhere. They returned to their homes days or weeks later to find them ruined and ransacked. Their cows were dead in the fields and, as the sun beat down on the animal carcasses, they had begun to rot. Their bellies swelled with gases trapped inside and turned them on their backs. With bodies bloated, their four feet stuck straight up, pointing to the sky in a grotesque death pose. The cows that had survived often wandered the fields in pain, their udders unmilked, distended to the bursting point.

Think of taking a drive on a maze of narrow country roads where every farmhouse is an armed fortress, every church steeple a sniper's observation post, where every stone wall conceals infantry with rifles and machine guns and where, at every curve in a road, there may be a tank with an 88mm gun trained on the curve you're coming around. That's the way it was in Normandy in June and July of 1944.

There were good stories in Cherbourg and I stayed there for several days, talking with American soldiers during the day and sleeping at night in a three-story French house whose flat stone façade was separated from the cobblestone street by nothing but four feet of flagstone sidewalk.

Joe Liebling was staying in the same house, and if you don't know who Joe Liebling was I can only say you don't know much about reporting, because he is one of the patron saints of the art and one of the very best who ever lived. He and Homer Bigart would be at the top of any reporter's ten-best list. I didn't know that at the time. All I knew was that Joe had a big reputation as an eater and a writer and I was impressed that he wrote for so literary a publication as *The New Yorker* magazine.

I didn't learn as much as I should have from Joe. He had such a strange and flawed personality that it didn't occur to me at the time that he was as good as he was. We talked at night as if we were equals.

★ ★ ★ ★ ★

Andy Rooney's postwar career in journalism would earn him three Emmy awards and a nationally-syndicated column. In late July of 1944, American forces of the army's VII Corps under the command of General Omar Bradley would break out of the hedgerow country with an awesome display of firepower during Operation Cobra. The result was the encirclement of German forces in the Falaise pocket where many were destroyed. Allied forces would liberate Paris on August 25 as German forces retreated to the east.

And Yet We Got On

> The war will be won or lost on the beaches. We'll have only
> one chance to stop the enemy and that's while he's in the water
> . . . struggling to get ashore. Reserves will never get up to the
> point of attack and it's foolish even to consider them . . . every-
> thing we have must be on the coast.
> —Field Marshal Erwin Rommel, April 22, 1944.

Ernie Pyle was America's most beloved war correspondent of the Second
World War. Already well-known as the first aviation columnist for the
Washington Daily News and as a roving columnist for Scripps-Howard, he
became a war correspondent when he traveled to England to cover the
Battle of Britain. Within a year he was covering the American entry into
the war in Africa, where he devoted himself to covering stories of the
common soldier. "I love the infantry because they are the underdogs," he
wrote. "They are the mud-rain-frost and wind boys. They have no com-
forts, and they even learn to live without the necessities. And in the end
they are the guys that wars can't be won without."

In an era of heavy censorship, when the printed word was still the
main source of news, Pyle's writing brought the plight of the soldiers
home to the American people. His folksy style never failed to mention an
individual's name, the hometown he hailed from, or the everyday details
of life in the front line that were so often overlooked by the average press.
His friend John Steinbeck would later say of him, "There are really two
wars and they haven't got much to do with each other. There is the war of
maps and logistics, of campaigns, of ballistics, armies, divisions and regiments—and that is General Marshall's war. Then there is the war of the
homesick, weary, funny, violent, common men who wash their socks in
helmets, complain about the food, whistle at Arab girls, or any girls for

that matter, and bring themselves through as dirty a business as the world has ever seen and do it with humor and dignity and courage—and that is Ernie Pyle's war."

In the spring of 1944 Pyle received the Pulitzer Prize while he awaited the invasion of Normandy in England. By then his work was syndicated in over 200 newspapers and collected into a best-selling volume entitled *Brave Men*. Some of his most evocative writing was still to come. On June 7th, the morning after the invasion, Pyle walked through the detritus of war along Omaha Beach and filed what would become a masterpiece of wartime journalism describing the overwhelming odds, the vast effort of men and machines to capture the beach, and the personal cost of hundreds as they were slaughtered at the shore's edge. His writing stands as a timeless reminder for the generations that followed of the sacrifices made to win the Second World War.

★　　★　　★　　★　　★

NORMANDY BEACHHEAD—(by wireless)—Due to a last-minute alteration in the arrangements, I didn't arrive on the beachhead until the morning after D-day, after our first wave of assault troops had hit the shore.

By the time we got here the beaches had been taken and the fighting had moved a couple of miles inland. All that remained on the beach was some sniping and artillery fire, and the occasional startling blast of a mine geysering brown sand into the air. That plus a gigantic and pitiful litter of wreckage along miles of shoreline.

Submerged tanks and overturned boats and burned trucks and shell-shattered jeeps and sad little personal belongings were strewn all over these bitter sands. That plus the bodies of soldiers lying in rows covered with blankets, the toes of their shoes sticking up in a line as though on drill. And other bodies, uncollected, still sprawling grotesquely in the sand or half hidden by the high grass beyond the beach.

That plus an intense, grim determination of work-weary men to get this chaotic beach organized and get all the vital supplies and the reinforcements moving more rapidly over it from the stacked-up ships standing in droves out to sea.

Now that it is over it seems to me a pure miracle that we ever took the beach at all. For some of our units it was easy, but in this special sector where I am now our troops faced such odds that our getting ashore was like my whipping Joe Louis down to a pulp.

In this column I want to tell you what the opening of the second front in this one sector entailed, so that you can know and appreciate and forever be humbly grateful to those both dead and alive who did it for you.

Ashore, facing us, were more enemy troops than we had in our assault waves. The advantages were all theirs, the disadvantages all ours. The Germans were dug into positions that they had been working on for months, although these were not yet all complete. A 100-foot bluff a couple of hundred yards back from the beach had great concrete gun emplacements built right into the hilltop. These opened to the sides instead of to the front, thus making it very hard for naval fire from the sea to reach them. They could shoot parallel with the beach and cover every foot of it for miles with artillery fire.

Then they had hidden machine-gun nests on the forward slopes, with crossfire taking in every inch of the beach. These nests were connected by networks of trenches, so that the German gunners could move about without exposing themselves.

Throughout the length of the beach, running zigzag a couple of hundred yards back from the shoreline, was an immense V-shaped ditch 15 feet deep. Nothing could cross it, not even men on foot, until fills had been made. And in other places at the far end of the beach, where the ground is flatter, they had great concrete walls. These were blasted by our naval gunfire or by explosives set by hand after we got ashore.

Our only exits from the beach were several swales or valleys, each about 100 yards wide. The Germans made the most of these funnel-like traps, sowing them with buried mines. They contained, also, barbed-wire entanglements with mines attached, hidden ditches, and machine guns firing from the slopes.

This is what was on the shore. But our men had to go through a maze nearly as deadly as this before they even got ashore. Underwater obstacles were terrific. The Germans had whole fields of evil devices under the water to catch our boats. Even now, several days after the landing, we have cleared only channels through them and cannot yet approach the whole length of the beach with our ships. Even now some ship or boat hits one of these mines every day and is knocked out of commission.

The Germans had masses of those great six-pronged spiders, made of railroad iron and standing shoulder-high, just beneath the surface of the water for our landing craft to run into. They also had huge logs buried in the sand, pointing upward and outward, their tops just below the water. Attached to these logs were mines.

In addition to these obstacles they had floating mines offshore, land mines buried in the sand of the beach, and more mines in checkerboard rows in the tall grass beyond the sand. And the enemy had four men on shore for every three men we had approaching the shore.

And yet we got on.

Beach landings are planned to a schedule that is set far ahead of time. They all have to be timed, in order for everything to mesh and for the following waves of troops to be standing off the beach and ready to land at the right moment.

As the landings are planned, some elements of the assault force are to break through quickly, push on inland, and attack the most obvious enemy strong points. It is usually the plan for units to be inland, attacking gun positions from behind, within a matter of minutes after the first men hit the beach.

I have always been amazed at the speed called for in these plans. You'll have schedules calling for engineers to land at H-hour plus two minutes, and service troops at H-hour plus 30 minutes, and even for press censors to land at H-hour plus 75 minutes. But in the attack on this special portion of the beach where I am—the worst we had, incidentally—the schedule didn't hold.

Our men simply could not get past the beach. They were pinned down right on the water's edge by an inhuman wall of fire from the bluff. Our first waves were on that beach for hours, instead of a few minutes, before they could begin working inland.

You can still see the foxholes they dug at the very edge of the water, in the sand and the small, jumbled rocks that form parts of the beach.

Medical corpsmen attended the wounded as best they could. Men were killed as they stepped out of landing craft. An officer whom I knew got a bullet through the head just as the door of his landing craft was let down. Some men were drowned.

The first crack in the beach defenses was finally accomplished by terrific and wonderful naval gunfire, which knocked out the big emplacements. They tell epic stories of destroyers that ran right up into shallow water and had it out point-blank with the big guns in those concrete emplacements ashore.

When the heavy fire stopped, our men were organized by their officers and pushed on inland, circling machine-gun nests and taking them from the rear.

As one officer said, the only way to take a beach is to face it and keep going. It is costly at first, but it's the only way. If the men are pinned down on the beach, dug in and out of action, they might as well not be there at all. They hold up the waves behind them, and nothing is being gained.

Our men were pinned down for a while, but finally they stood up and went through, and so we took that beach and accomplished our landing. We did it with every advantage on the enemy's side and every disadvantage on ours. In the light of a couple of days of retrospection, we sit and talk and call it a miracle that our men ever got on at all or were able to stay on.

Before long it will be permitted to name the units that did it. Then you will know to whom this glory should go. They suffered casualties. And yet if you take the entire beachhead assault, including other units that had a much easier time, our total casualties in driving this wedge into the continent of Europe were remarkably low—only a fraction, in fact, of what our commanders had been prepared to accept.

And these units that were so battered and went through such hell are still, right at this moment, pushing on inland without rest, their spirits high, their egotism in victory almost reaching the smart-alecky stage.

Their tails are up. "We've done it again," they say. They figure that the rest of the army isn't needed at all. Which proves that, while their judgment in this regard is bad, they certainly have the spirit that wins battles and eventually wars.

Scripps-Howard wire copy, June 12, 1944

"The Wreckage Was Vast and Startling"

NORMANDY BEACHHEAD, D DAY PLUS TWO—(by wireless, delayed)—I took a walk along the historic coast of Normandy in the country of France.

It was a lovely day for strolling along the seashore. Men were sleeping on the sand, some of them sleeping forever. Men were floating in the water, but they didn't know they were in the water, for they were dead.

The water was full of squishy little jellyfish about the size of your hand. Millions of them. In the center each of them had a green design exactly like a four-leaf clover. The good-luck emblem. Sure. Hell yes.

I walked for a mile and a half along the water's edge of our many-miled invasion beach. You wanted to walk slowly, for the detail on that beach was infinite.

The wreckage was vast and startling. The awful waste and destruction of war, even aside from the loss of human life, has always been one of its outstanding features to those who are in it. Anything and everything is expendable. And we did expend on our beachhead in Normandy during those first few hours.

For a mile out from the beach there were scores of tanks and trucks and boats that you could no longer see, for they were at the bottom of the water—swamped by overloading, or hit by shells, or sunk by mines. Most of their crews were lost.

You could see trucks tipped half over and swamped. You could see partly sunken barges, and the angled-up corners of jeeps, and small landing craft half submerged. And at low tide you could still see those vicious six-pronged iron snares that helped snag and wreck them.

On the beach itself, high and dry, were all kinds of wrecked vehicles. There were tanks that had only just made the beach before being knocked out. There were jeeps that had burned to a dull gray. There were big derricks on caterpillar treads that didn't quite make it. There were half-tracks carrying office equipment that had been made into a shambles by a single shell hit, their interiors still holding their useless equipage of smashed typewriters, telephones, office files.

There were LCT's turned completely upside down, and lying on their backs, and how they got that way I don't know.

There were boats stacked on top of each other, their sides caved in, their suspension doors knocked off.

In this shoreline museum of carnage there were abandoned rolls of barbed wire and smashed bulldozers and big stacks of thrown-away lifebelts and piles of shells still waiting to be moved.

In the water floated empty life rafts and soldiers' packs and ration boxes, and mysterious oranges.

On the beach lay snarled rolls of telephone wire and big rolls of steel matting and stacks of broken, rusting rifles.

On the beach lay, expended, sufficient men and mechanism for a small war. They were gone forever now. And yet we could afford it.

We could afford it because we were on, we had our toehold, and behind us there were such enormous replacements for this wreckage on the beach that you could hardly conceive of their sum total. Men and equipment were flowing from England in such a gigantic stream that it made the waste on the beachhead seem like nothing at all, really nothing at all.

A few hundred yards back on the beach is a high bluff. Up there we had a tent hospital, and a barbed-wire enclosure for prisoners of war. From up there you could see far up and down the beach, in a spectacular crow's-nest view, and far out to sea.

And standing out there on the water beyond all this wreckage was the greatest armada man has ever seen. You simply could not believe the gigantic collection of ships that lay out there waiting to unload.

Looking from the bluff, it lay thick and clear to the far horizon of the sea and on beyond, and it spread out to the sides and was miles wide. Its utter enormity would move the hardest man.

As I stood up there I noticed a group of freshly taken German prisoners standing nearby. They had not yet been put in the prison cage. They were just standing there, a couple of doughboys leisurely guarding them with Tommy guns.

The prisoners too were looking out to sea—the same bit of sea that for months and years had been so safely empty before their gaze. Now they stood staring almost as if in a trance.

They didn't say a word to each other. They didn't need to. The expression on their faces was something forever unforgettable. In it was the final horrified acceptance of their doom.

If only all Germany could have had the rich experience of standing on the bluff and looking out across the water and seeing what their compatriots saw.

Scripps-Howard wire copy, June 16, 1944

"This Long Thin Line of Personal Anguish"

NORMANDY BEACHHEAD—(by wireless)—In the preceding column we told about the D-Day wreckage among our machines of war that were expended in taking one of the Normandy beaches.

But there is another and more human litter. It extends in a thin little line, just like a high-water mark, for miles along the beach. This is the strewn personal gear, gear that will never be needed again, of those who fought and died to give us our entrance into Europe.

Here in a jumbled row for mile on mile are soldiers' packs. Here are socks and shoe polish, sewing kits, diaries, Bibles and hand grenades. Here are the latest letters from home, with the address on each one neatly razored out—one of the security precautions enforced before the boys embarked.

Here are toothbrushes and razors, and snapshots of families back home staring up at you from the sand. Here are pocketbooks, metal mirrors, extra trousers, and bloody, abandoned shoes. Here are broken-handled shovels, and portable radios smashed almost beyond recognition, and mine detectors twisted and ruined.

Here are torn pistol belts and canvas water buckets, first-aid kits and jumbled heaps of lifebelts. I picked up a pocket Bible with a soldier's name in it, and put it in my jacket. I carried it half a mile or so and then put it back down on the beach. I don't know why I picked it up, or why I put it back down.

Soldiers carry strange things ashore with them. In every invasion you'll find at least one soldier hitting the beach at H-Hour with a banjo slung over his shoulder. The most ironic piece of equipment marking our beach—this beach of first despair, then victory—is a tennis racket that some soldier had brought along. It lies lonesomely on the sand, clamped in its rack, not a string broken.

Two of the most dominant items in the beach refuse are cigarets and writing paper. Each soldier was issued a carton of cigarets just before he started. Today these cartons by the thousand, watersoaked and spilled out, mark the line of our first savage blow.

Writing paper and air-mail envelopes come second. The boys had intended to do a lot of writing in France. Letters that would have filled those blank, abandoned pages.

Always there are dogs in every invasion. There is a dog still on the beach today, still pitifully looking for his masters.

He stays at the water's edge, near a boat that lies twisted and half sunk at the waterline. He barks appealingly to every soldier who approaches, trots eagerly along with him for a few feet, and then, sensing himself unwanted in all this haste, runs back to wait in vain for his own people at his own empty boat.

Over and around this long thin line of personal anguish, fresh men today are rushing vast supplies to keep our armies pushing on into France. Other squads of men pick amidst the wreckage to salvage ammunition and equipment that are still usable.

Men worked and slept on the beach for days before the last D-Day victim was taken away for burial.

I stepped over the form of one youngster whom I thought dead. But when I looked down I saw he was only sleeping. He was very young, and very tired. He lay on one elbow, his hand suspended in the air about six inches from the ground. And in the palm of his hand he held a large, smooth rock.

I stood and looked at him a long time. He seemed in his sleep to hold that rock lovingly, as though it were his last link with a vanishing world. I have no idea at all why he went to sleep with the rock in his hand, or what kept him from dropping it once he was asleep. It was just one of those little things without explanation, that a person remembers for a long time.

The strong, swirling tides of the Normandy coastline shift the contours of the sandy beach as they move in and out. They carry soldiers' bodies out to sea, and later they return them. They cover the corpses of heroes with sand, and then in their whims they uncover them.

As I plowed out over the wet sand of the beach on that first day ashore, I walked around what seemed to be a couple of pieces of driftwood sticking out of the sand. But they weren't driftwood.

They were a soldier's two feet. He was completely covered by the shifting sands except for his feet. The toes of his G.I. shoes pointed toward the land he had come so far to see, and which he saw so briefly.

Scripps-Howard wire copy, June 17, 1944

★   ★   ★   ★   ★

Ernie Pyle would go to the war in the Pacific to cover the invasion of Okinawa. While on a patrol with infantry he was killed by enemy fire. The soldiers paid tribute to him by placing a plaque that read simply, "At this spot, the 77th Infantry Division lost a buddy, Ernie Pyle, 18 April 1945."

The Longest Day

CORNELIUS RYAN

> Two kinds of people are staying on this beach, the dead and
> those who are going to die—now let's get the hell out of here!
> —Col. George A. Taylor, 16th RCT,
> Omaha Beach, D-Day, June 6, 1944

June 6, 1944 was a day when the fate of the world hung in the balance. The vast might of the Allied nations was poised to attempt the long-awaited invasion of France, the liberation of Western Europe, and the end of Hitler's Third Reich. Operation Overlord was the genesis of years of planning and preparation, all with a single goal—to gain a foothold on the shores of Normandy and hold it so reinforcements could be put ashore and move inland. General Dwight D. Eisenhower was named the Supreme Commander of the Allied Expeditionary Force. British General Sir Bernard Montgomery was the operational commander for the invasion ground forces. They had under their command the largest invasion force ever assembled—thousands of ships, 12,000 aircraft, and forty-seven divisions of Allied soldiers, of which eight were scheduled to make the initial assault.

Opposing them along the shoreline in Normandy were twelve divisions of the German Army, including the elite 21st Panzer Division backed by ten more armor and mechanized infantry divisions further inland. To lead them Hitler had appointed two of his greatest generals: Gerd von Rundstedt, who commanded all of the Axis forces in Western Europe; and Erwin Rommel, who was appointed Inspector of Coastal Defenses in November, 1943. Rommel believed their only chance to stop the Allies would be on the coast and at the moment of attack. To accomplish this he ordered the construction of a vast network of defensive positions that became the "Atlantic Wall." German engineers enveloped the coastline of

France with thousands of steel reinforced concrete bunkers, artillery positions, beach obstacles, and minefields.

The Allied plan was direct, simple, and audacious. The night before the landings along the Cotentin Peninsula, the American 101st and 82nd and 6th British airborne divisions would drop behind the beaches to seize key junctions, destroy enemy artillery, and cut off the Germans from reinforcement. The following morning, after a naval and air bombardment, the U.S. VII Corps would attack Utah Beach while the U.S. V Corps would attack Omaha Beach. The U.S. 2nd and 5th Ranger Battalion would scale the cliffs at Pointe du Hoc between Utah and Omaha beaches to destroy the German guns deployed there. The British 3rd Infantry Division and 27th armored brigade would land at Sword Beach. The Canadian 3rd Infantry Division, 2nd Armored Brigade and No. 48 (RM) Commando would land on Juno Beach. Lastly the British 50th British Division and 8th Armored would hit Gold Beach.

The mission was fraught with risks. Two years earlier in August 1942, the British, Canadians, and a small group of American Rangers had attempted a raid in force against the port of Dieppe to test German defenses. The loss of surprise cost the attacking force over half its men in a single day before the survivors who could be reached were withdrawn. Operation Overlord would face those same dangers in a similar all-or-nothing gamble. If anyone had betrayed the Allied plan at any point, the invaders risked the same fate as the raid on Dieppe. Estimates for airborne losses began at fifty percent. In his coat pocket on June 6th, General Eisenhower carried a handwritten note:

> Our landings in the Cherbourg-Havre area have failed to gain a satisfactory foothold and I have withdrawn the troops. My decision to attack at this time and place was based upon the best information available. The troops, the air and the Navy did all that Bravery and devotion to duty could do. If any blame or fault attaches to the attempt it is mine alone.

The original plan was to make the assault on the morning of June 5th. Poor weather conditions forced the invasion fleet to turn back in the night. If the weather didn't improve, it would be another two weeks for the right tides to attempt another landing. In two weeks the Germans could discover the Allied armada and the game would be up. A small break in the high seas and rain was forecast for the morning of June 6th. Eisenhower, with the full weight of command squarely on his shoulders, made the fateful decision and set the invasion for the morning of June 6th.

It would prove to be one of the greatest strokes of luck for the Allied cause. The German meteorologists had informed Field Marshall Rommel the weather for the following weeks would be too poor for an Allied invasion attempt. He returned to Germany for his wife's 50th birthday on June 6th. His field commanders traveled to southern France to conduct war games. On the morning of the invasion, the Allies achieved total surprise.

Cornelius Ryan was one of the preeminent writers of the history of World War II. He was born in Dublin in 1920 and worked as a reporter covering the battles in Europe for Reuters and the *London Daily Telegraph* from 1941 to 1945, and then the final months of the Pacific campaign. His first book, *The Longest Day,* was published in 1959. In the chapter *H-Hour* he described the American assault on Omaha and Utah beaches. On Utah, the attack went mostly according to plan. On Omaha, where the German 352nd Regiment held the high bluffs overlooking the beaches in prepared defenses, everything would go tragically wrong.

★   ★   ★   ★   ★

By now the long, bobbing lines of assault craft were less than a mile from Omaha and Utah beaches. For the three thousand Americans in the first wave H-Hour was just fifteen minutes away.

The noise was deafening as the boats, long white wakes streaming out behind them, churned steadily for the shore. In the slopping, bouncing craft the men had to shout to be heard over the roar of the diesels. Overhead, like a great steel umbrella, the shells of the fleet still thundered. And rolling out from the coast came the booming explosions of the Allied air forces' carpet bombing. Strangely, the guns of the Atlantic Wall were silent. Troops saw the coastline stretching ahead and wondered about the absence of enemy fire. Maybe, many thought, it would be an easy landing after all.

The great square-faced ramps of the assault craft butted into every wave, and chilling, frothing green water sloshed over everyone. There were no heroes in these boats—just cold, miserable, anxious men, so jam-packed together, so weighed down by equipment that often there was no place to be seasick except over one another. *Newsweek's* Kenneth Crawford, in the first Utah wave, saw a young 4th Division soldier, covered in his own vomit, slowly shaking his head in abject misery and disgust. 'That guy Higgins,' he said, 'ain't got nothin' to be proud of about inventin' this goddamned boat.'

Some men had no time to think about their miseries—they were bailing for their lives. Almost from the moment the assault craft left the mother ships, many boats had begun to fill with water. At first men had paid little attention to the sea slopping about their legs; it was just another misery to be endured. Lieutenant George Kerchner of the Rangers watched the water slowly rise in his craft and wondered if it was serious. He had been told that the LCA was unsinkable. But then over the radio Kerchner's soldiers heard a call for help: 'This is LCA 860! . . . LCA 860! . . . We're sinking! . . . We're sinking!' There was a final exclamation: 'My God, we're sunk!' Immediately Kerchner and his men began bailing.

Directly behind Kerchner's boat, Sergeant Regis McCloskey, also of the Rangers, had his own troubles. McCloskey and his men had been bailing for more than an hour. Their boat carried ammunition for the Pointe du Hoc attack and all the Rangers' packs. The boat was so water-logged McCloskey was sure it would sink. His only hope lay in lightening the wallowing craft. McCloskey ordered his men to toss all unnecessary equipment overboard. Rations, extra clothing and packs went over the side. McCloskey heaved them all into the swell. In one pack was $1,200 which Private Chuck Vella had won in a crap game; in another was First Sergeant Charles Frederick's false teeth.

Landing-craft began to sink in both the Omaha and Utah areas—ten off Omaha, seven off Utah. Some men were picked up by rescue boats coming up behind, others would float around for hours before being rescued. And some soldiers, their yells and screams unheard, were dragged down by their equipment and ammunition. They drowned within sight of the beaches, without having fired a shot.

In an instant the war had become personal. Troops heading for Utah Beach saw a control boat leading one of the waves suddenly rear up out of the water and explode. Seconds later heads bobbed up and survivors tried to save themselves by clinging to the wreckage. Another explosion followed almost immediately. The crew of a landing-barge trying to launch four of the thirty-two amphibious tanks bound for Utah had dropped the ramp right on to a submerged sea mine. The front of the craft shot up and Sergeant Orris Johnson on a nearby LCT watched in frozen horror as a tank 'soared more than a hundred feet into the air, tumbled slowly end over end, plunged back into the water and disappeared.' Among the many dead, Johnson learned later, was his buddy. Tanker Don Neill.

Scores of Utah-bound men saw the dead bodies and heard the yells and screams of the drowning. One man, Lieutenant Francis X. Riley of the Coast Guard, remembers the scene vividly. The twenty-four-year-old officer, commanding an LCI, could only listen 'to the anguished cries for help from wounded and shocked soldiers and sailors as they pleaded with us to pull them out of the water.' But Riley's orders were to 'disembark the troops on time regardless of casualties.' Trying to close his mind to the screams, Riley ordered his craft on past the drowning men. There was nothing else he could do. The assault waves sped by, and as one boat carrying Lieutenant-Colonel James Batte and the 4th Division's 8th Infantry Regiment troops threaded its way through the dead bodies, Batte heard one of his grey-faced men say, 'Them lucky bastards—they ain't seasick no more.'

The sight of the bodies in the water, the strain of the long trip in from the transport ships and now the ominous nearness of the flat sands and the dunes of Utah Beach jerked men out of their lethargy. Corporal Lee Cason, who had just turned twenty, suddenly found himself 'cursing to high heaven against Hitler and Mussolini for getting us into this mess.' His companions were startled at his vehemence—Cason had never before been known to swear. In many boats now soldiers nervously checked and rechecked their weapons. Men became so possessive of their ammunition that Colonel Eugene Caffey could not get a single man in his boat to give him a clip of bullets for his rifle. Caffey, who was not supposed to land until 9 a.m., had smuggled himself aboard an 8th Infantry craft in an effort to catch up with his veteran 1st Engineer Brigade. He had no equipment and although all the men in the boat were overloaded with ammunition, they were 'hanging on to it for dear life.' Caffey was finally able to load the rifle by taking up a collection of one bullet from each of eight men.

In the waters off Omaha Beach there had been a disaster. Nearly half the amphibious tank force scheduled to support the assault troops had foundered. The plan was for sixty-four of these tanks to be launched two to three miles offshore. From there they were to swim in to the beach. Thirty-two of them had been allotted to the 1st Division's area—Easy Red, Fox Green and Fox Red. The landing-barges carrying them reached their positions, the ramps were dropped and twenty-nine tanks were launched into the heaving swell. The weird-looking amphibious vehicles, their great balloon-like canvas skirts supporting them in the water, began breasting the waves, driving towards the shore. Then tragedy overtook the men of the 741st Tank Battalion. Under the pounding of the waves the canvas water-wings ripped, supports broke, engines were flooded—and, one after another, twenty-seven tanks foundered and sank. Men came clawing up out of the hatches, inflating their lifebelts, plunging into the sea. Some succeeded in launching survival rafts. Others went down in the steel coffins.

Two tanks, battered and almost awash, were still heading for the shore. The crews of three others had the good fortune to be on a landing-barge whose ramp jammed. They were put ashore later. The remaining thirty-two tanks—for the 29th Division's half of the beach—were safe. Officers in charge of the craft carrying them, overwhelmed by the disaster they had seen, wisely decided to take their force directly on to the beach. But the loss of the 1st Division tanks would cost hundreds of casualties within the next few minutes.

From two miles out the assault troops began to see the living and the dead in the water. The dead floated gently, moving with the tide towards the beach, as though determined to join their fellow Americans. The living bobbed up and down in the swells, savagely pleading for the help the assault boats could not tender. Sergeant Regis McCloskey, his ammunition boat again safely under way, saw the screaming men in the water, 'yelling for help, begging us to stop—and we couldn't. Not for anything or anyone.' Gritting his teeth, McCloskey looked away as his boat sped past, and then, seconds later, he vomited over the side. Captain Robert Cunningham and his men saw survivors struggling, too. Instinctively their Navy crew swung the boat towards the men in the water. A fast launch cut them off. Over its loudspeaker came the grim words, 'You are not a rescue ship! Get on shore!' In another boat near by, Sergeant Noel Dube of an engineer battalion said the Act of Contrition.

Now the deadly martial music of the bombardment seemed to grow and swell as the thin wavy lines of assault craft closed in on Omaha Beach. Landing-ships lying about one thousand yards offshore joined in the shelling; and then thousands of flashing rockets whooshed over the heads of the men. To the troops it seemed inconceivable that anything could survive the massive weight of fire-power that flayed the German defences. The beach was wreathed in haze, and plumes of smoke from grass fires drifted lazily down from the bluffs. Still the German guns remained silent. The boats bored in. In the thrashing surf and running back up the beach men could now see the lethal jungles of steel-and-concrete obstacles. They were strewn everywhere, draped with barbed wire and capped with mines. They were as cruel and ugly as the men had expected. Behind the defences the beach itself was deserted; nothing and no one moved upon it. Closer and closer the boats pressed in . . . five hundred yards . . . four hundred and fifty yards. Still no enemy fire. Through waves that were four to five feet high the assault craft surged forward, and now the great bombardment began to lift, shifting to targets farther inland. The first boats were barely four hundred yards from the shore when the German guns—the guns that few believed could have survived the raging Allied air and sea bombardment—opened up.

Through the din and clamour one sound was nearer, deadlier than all the rest—the sound of machine-gun bullets clanging across the steel, snoutlike noses of the boats. Artillery roared. Mortar shells rained down. All along the four miles of Omaha Beach German guns flayed the assault craft.

It was H-Hour.

They came ashore on Omaha Beach, the slogging, unglamorous men that no one envied. No battle ensigns flew for them, no horn or bugles sounded. But they had history on their side. They came from regiments that had bivouacked at places like Valley Forge, Stoney Creek, Antietam, Gettysburg, that had fought in the Argonne. They had crossed the beaches of North Africa, Sicily and Salerno. Now they had one more beach to cross. They would call this one 'Bloody Omaha.'

The most intense fire came from the cliffs and high bluffs at either end of the crescent-shaped beach—in the 29th Division's Dog Green area to the west and the 1st Division's Fox Green sector to the east. Here the Germans had concentrated their heaviest defences to hold two of the principal exits leading off the beach at Vierville and towards Colleville. Everywhere along the beach men encountered heavy fire as their boats came in, but the troops landing at Dog Green and Fox Green hadn't a chance. German gunners on the cliffs looked almost directly down on the waterlogged assault craft that heaved and pitched towards these sectors of the beach. Awkward and slow, the assault boats were nearly stationary in the water. They were sitting ducks. Coxswains at the tillers, trying desperately to manoeuver their unwieldy craft through the forest of mined obstacles, now had to run the gauntlet of fire from the cliffs.

Some boats, unable to find a way through the maze of obstacles and the withering cliff fire, were driven off and wandered aimlessly along the beach seeking a less heavily defended spot to land. Others, doggedly trying to come in at their assigned sectors, were shelled so badly that men plunged over the sides into deep water, where they were immediately picked off by machine-gun fire. Some landing craft were blown apart as they came in. Second Lieutenant Edward Gearing's assault boat, filled with thirty men of the 29th Division, disintegrated in one blinding moment three hundred yards from the Vierville exit at Dog Green. Gearing and his men were blown out of the boat and strewn over the water. Shocked and half-drowned, the nineteen-year-old lieutenant came to the surface yards away from where his boat had gone down. Other survivors began to bob up, too. Their weapons, helmets and equipment were gone. The coxswain had disappeared and near by one of Gearing's men, struggling beneath the weight of a heavy radio set strapped to his back, screamed out, 'For God's sake, I'm drowning!' Nobody could get to the radioman before he went under. For Gearing and the remnants of his section the ordeal was just beginning. It would be three hours before they got on the beach. Then Gearing would learn that he was the only surviving officer of his company. The others were dead or seriously wounded.

All along Omaha Beach, the dropping of the ramps seemed to be the signal for renewed, more concentrated machine-gun fire, and again the most murderous fire was in the Dog Green and Fox Green sectors. Boats of the 29th Division, coming into Dog Green, grounded on the sand-bars. The ramps came down and men stepped out into water three to six feet deep. They had but one object in mind—to get through the water, cross two hundred yards of the obstacle-strewn sand, climb the gradually rising shingle and then take cover in the doubtful shelter of a sea wall. But, weighed down by their equipment, unable to run in the deep water and without cover of any kind, men were caught in criss-crossing machine-gun and small-arms fire.

Seasick men, already exhausted by the long hours spent on the transports and in the assault boats, found themselves fighting for their lives in water which was often over their heads. Private David Silva saw the men in front of him being mowed down as they stepped off the ramp. When his turn came, he jumped into chest-high water and, bogged down by his equipment, watched spellbound as bullets flicked the surface all around him. Within seconds machine-gun fire had riddled his pack, his clothing, and his canteen. Silva felt like a 'pigeon at a trap shoot.' He though he spotted the German machine-gunner who was firing at him, but he could not fire back. His rifle was clogged with sand. Silva waded on, determined to make the sands ahead. He finally pulled himself up on the beach and dashed for the shelter of the sea wall, completely unaware that he had been wounded twice—once in the back, and one in the right leg.

Men fell all along the water's edge. Some were killed instantly, others called pitifully for help as the incoming tide slowly engulfed them. Among the dead was Captain Sherman Burroughs. His friend, Captain Charles Cawthon, saw the body washing back and forth in the surf. Cawthon wondered if Burroughs had recited 'The Shooting of Dan

McGrew' to his men on the run-in as he had planned. And when Captain Carroll Smith passed by, he could not help but think that Burroughs 'would no longer suffer from his constant migraine headaches.' Burroughs had been shot through the head.

Within the first few minutes of the carnage at Dog Green one entire company was put out of action. Less than a third of the men survived the bloody walk from the boats to the edge of the beach. Their officers were killed, severely wounded or missing, and the men, weaponless and shocked, huddled at the base of the cliffs all day. Another company in the same sector suffered even higher casualties. Company C of the 2nd Ranger Battalion had been ordered to knock out enemy strongpoints at Pointe de la Percée, slightly west of Vierville. The Rangers landed in two assault craft with the first wave on Dog Green. They were decimated. The leading craft was sunk almost immediately by artillery fire, and twelve men were killed outright. The moment the ramp of the second craft dropped down machine-gun fire sprayed the disembarking Rangers, killing and wounding fifteen. The remainder set out for the cliffs. Men fell one after another. PFC Nelson Noyes, staggering under the weight of a bazooka, made a hundred yards before he was forced to hit the ground. A few moments later he got up and ran forward again. When he reached the shingle he was machine-gunned in the leg. As he lay there Noyes saw the two Germans who had fired looking down on him from the cliff. Propping himself on his elbows he opened up with his Tommy gun and brought both of them down. By the time Captain Ralph E. Goranson, the company commander, reached the base of the cliff, he had only thirty-five Rangers left out of his seventy-man team. By nightfall these thirty-five would be cut down to twelve.

Misfortune piled upon misfortune for the men of Omaha Beach. Soldiers now discovered that they had been landed in the wrong sectors. Some came in almost two miles away from their original landing areas. Boat sections from the 29th Division found themselves intermingled with men of the 1st Division. For example, units scheduled to land on Easy Green and fight towards an exit at Les Moulins discovered themselves at the eastern end of the beach in the hell of Fox Green. Nearly all the landing-craft came in slightly east of their touch-down points. A control boat drifting off-station, a strong current running eastward along the beach, the haze and smoke from grass fires which obscured landmarks—all these contributed to the wrong landings. Companies that had been trained to capture certain objectives never got near them. Small groups found themselves pinned down by German fire and isolated in unrecognisable terrain, often without officers or communications.

The special Army-Navy demolition engineers who had the job of blowing paths through the beach obstacles were not only widely scattered, they were brought in crucial minutes behind schedule. These frustrated men set to work wherever they found themselves. But they fought a losing battle. In the few minutes they had before the following waves of troops bore down on the beaches, the engineers cleared only five and a half paths instead of the sixteen planned. Working with desperate haste, the demolition parties were impeded at every turn—infantrymen waded in among them, soldiers took shelter behind the obstacles they were about to blow, and landing-craft, buffeted by the swells, came in almost on top of them. Sergeant Barton A. Davis of the 299th Engineer Combat Battalion saw an assault boat bearing down on him. It was filled with 1st Division men and was coming straight in through the obstacles. There was a tremendous explosion and the boat disintegrated. It seemed to Davis that everyone in it was thrown into the air all at once. Bodies and parts of bodies landed all around the flaming wreckage. 'I saw black dots of men trying to swim through the gasoline that had spread on the water and as we wondered what to do a headless torso flew a good fifty feet through the air and landed with a sickening thud near us.' Davis did not see how anyone could have lived through the explosion, but two men did. They were pulled out of the water, badly burned but alive.

But the disaster that Davis had seen was no greater than that which had overtaken the heroic men of his own unit, the Army-Navy Special Engineer Task Force. The landing-boats carrying their explosives had been shelled, and the hulks of these craft lay blazing at the edge of the beach. Engineers with small rubber boats loaded with plastic charges and detonators were blown apart in the water when enemy fire touched off the explosives. The Germans, seeing the engineers working among the obstacles, seemed to single them out for special attention. As the teams tied on their charges, snipers took careful aim at the mines on the obstacles. At other times they seemed to wait until the engineers had prepared whole lines of steel trestles and tetrahedral obstacles for blowing. Then the Germans themselves would detonate the obstacles with mortar fire—before the engineers could get out of the area. By the end of the day casualties would be almost fifty per cent. Sergeant Davis himself would be one. Nightfall would find him aboard a hospital ship with a wounded leg, heading back for England.

It was 7 a.m. The second wave of troops arrived on the shambles that was Omaha Beach. Men splashed ashore under the saturating fire of the enemy. Landing-craft joined the ever-growing graveyard of the wrecked, blazing hulks. Each wave of boats gave up its own bloody contribution to the incoming tide, and all along the crescent-shaped strip of beach dead Americans gently nudged each other in the water.

Piling up along the shore was the flotsam and jetsam of the invasion. Heavy equipment and supplies, boxes of ammunition, smashed radios, field telephones, gas masks, entrenching tools, canteens, steel helmets and life-preservers were strewn everywhere. Great reels of wire, ropes, ration boxes, mine detectors and scores of weapons, from broken rifles to stove-in bazookas littered the sand. The twisted wrecks of landing craft canted up crazily out of the water. Burning tanks threw great spirals of black smoke into the air. Bulldozers lay on their sides among the obstacles. Off Easy Red, floating in and out among all the cast-off materials of war, men saw a guitar.

Small islands of wounded men dotted the sand. Passing troops noticed that those who could sat bolt upright as though now immune to any further hurt. They were quiet men, seemingly oblivious to the sights and sounds around them. Staff Sergeant Alfred Eigenberg, a medical orderly attached to the 6th Engineers Special Brigade, remembers 'a terrible politeness among the more seriously injured.' In his first few minutes on the beach, Eigenberg found so many wounded that he did not know 'where to start or with whom.' On Dog Red he came across a young soldier sitting in the sand with his leg 'laid open from the knee to the pelvis as neatly as though a surgeon had done it with a scalpel.' The wound was so deep that Eigenberg could clearly see the femoral artery pulsing. The soldier was in deep shock. Calmly he informed Eigenberg, 'I've taken all my sulphur pills and I've shaken all my sulphur powder into the wound. I'll be all right, won't I?' The nineteen-year-old Eigenberg didn't know quite what to say. He gave the soldier a shot of morphine and told him, 'Sure, you'll be all right.' Then folding the neatly sliced halves of the man's leg together, Eigenberg did the only thing he could think of—he carefully closed the wound with safety pins.

Into the chaos, confusion and death on the beach poured the men of the third wave—and stopped. Minutes later the fourth wave came in—and they stopped. Men lay shoulder to shoulder on the sands, stones and shale. They crouched down behind obstacles; they sheltered among the bodies of the dead. Pinned down by the enemy fire which they had expected to be neutralised, confused by their landings in the wrong sectors, bewildered by the absence of the sheltering craters they had expected from the air force bombing, and shocked by the devastation and death all around them, the men froze on the beaches. They seemed in the grip of a strange paralysis. Overwhelmed by it all, some men believed the day was lost. Technical Sergeant William McClintock of the 741st Tank Battalion came upon a man sitting at the edge of the water, seemingly unaware of the machine-gun fire which rippled all over the area. He sat there 'throwing stones into the water and softly crying as if his heart would break.'

The shock would not last long. Even now a few men here and there, realising that to stay on the beach meant certain death, were on their feet and moving.

Ten miles away on Utah Beach the men of the 4th Division were swarming ashore and driving inland fast. The third wave of assault boats were coming in and still there was virtually no opposition. A few shells fell on the beach, some scattered machine-gun and rifle fire rattled along it, but there was none of the fierce infighting that the tense, keyed-up men of the 4th had expected. To many of the men the landing was almost routine. PFC Donald N. Jones in the second wave felt as though it was 'just another practice invasion.' Other men thought the assault was an anticlimax; the long months of training at Slapton Sands in England had been tougher. PFC Ray Mann felt a little 'let down' because 'the landing just wasn't a big deal after all.' Even the obstacles were not as bad as everyone had feared. Only a few concrete cones and triangles and hedgehogs of steel cluttered the beach. Few of these were mined and all of them were lying exposed, easy for the engineers to get at. Demolition teams were already at work. They had blown one fifty-yard gap through the defences and had breached the sea wall, and within the hour they would have the entire beach cleared.

Strung out along the mile of beach, their canvas skirts hanging limply down, were the amphibious tanks—one of the big reasons why the assault had been so successful. Lumbering out of the water with the first waves, they had given a roaring support to the troops as they dashed across the beach. The tanks and the pre-assault bombardment seemed to have shattered and demoralised the German troops holding positions behind this beach. Still, the assault had not been without its share of misery and death. Almost as soon as he got ashore, PFC Rudolph Mozgo saw his first dead man. A tank had received a direct hit and Mozgo found 'one of the crew lying half in and half out of the hatch.' Second Lieutenant Herbert Taylor of the 1st Engineer Special Brigade was numbed by the sight of a man 'decapitated by an artillery burst just twenty feet away.' and PFC Edward Wolfe passed a dead American 'who was sitting on the beach, his back resting against a post, as though asleep.' So natural and peaceful did he seem that Wolfe had an urge to reach over and shake him awake.'

Stomping up and down the sands, occasionally massaging his arthritic shoulder, was Brigadier-General Theodore Roosevelt. The fifty-seven-year-old officer—the only general to land with first-wave troops—had insisted on this assignment. His first request had been turned down, but Roosevelt had promptly countered with another. In a hand-written note to the 4th's commanding officer, Major-General Raymond O. Barton, Roosevelt pleaded his case on the ground that 'it will steady the boys to know I am with them.' Barton reluctantly agreed, but the decision preyed on his mind. 'When I said good-bye to Ted in England,' he recalls, 'I never expected to see him alive again.' The determined Roosevelt was very much alive. Sergeant Harry Brown of the 8th Infantry saw him 'with a cane in one hand, a map in the other, walking around as if he was looking over some real estate.' Every now and then a mortar burst on the beach, sending showers of sand into the air. It seemed to annoy Roosevelt; impatiently he would brush himself off.

As the third-wave boats beached and men began to wade ashore, there was the sudden whine of German 88 fire and shells burst among the incoming troops. A dozen men went down. Seconds later, a lone figure emerged from the smoke of the artillery burst. His face was black, his helmet and equipment were gone. He came walking up the beach in complete shock, eyes staring. Yelling for an orderly, Roosevelt ran over to the man. He put his arm round the soldier. 'Son,' he said gently, 'I think we'll get you back on a boat.'

As yet only Roosevelt and a few of his officers knew that the Utah landings had been made in the wrong place. It had been a fortunate error; heavy batteries that could have decimated the troops were still intact, sited along the planned assault area. There had been a number of reasons for the mistake. Confused by smoke from the naval bombardment which had obscured landmarks, caught by a strong current moving down the coast, a solitary control boat had guided the first wave into a landing more than a mile south of the original beach. Instead of invading the beach opposite Exits 3 and 4—two of the vital five causeways towards which the 101st Airborne was driving—the entire beach-head had slipped almost two thousand yards and was now astride Exit 2. Ironically, at this moment Lieutenant-Colonel Robert G. Cole and a miscellaneous band of seventy-five 101st and 82nd troopers had just reached the western end of Exit 3. They were the first paratroopers to get to a causeway. Cole and his men concealed themselves in the swamps and settled down to wait; he expected the men of the 4th Division along at any moment.

On the beach, near the approach to Exit 2, Roosevelt was about to make an important decision. Every few minutes from now on wave after wave of men and vehicles were due to land—thirty thousand men and 3,500 vehicles. Roosevelt had to decide whether to bring succeeding waves into this new, relatively quiet area with only one causeway, or to divert all assault troops and take their equipment to the original Utah Beach with its two causeways. If the single exit could not be opened and held, a nightmarish jumble of men and vehicles would be trapped on the beach. The General huddled with his battalion commanders. The decision was made. Instead of fighting for the planned objectives which lay back on the original beach, the 4th would drive inland on the single causeway and engage German positions when and where they found them. Everything now depended on moving as fast as possible before the enemy recovered from the initial shock of the landings. Resistance was light and the men of the 4th were moving off the beach fast. Roosevelt turned to Colonel Eugene Caffey of the 1st Engineer Special Brigade. 'I'm going ahead with the troops,' he told Caffey. 'You get word to the Navy to bring them in. We're going to start the war from here.'

★   ★   ★   ★   ★

Backed by naval gunfire, small groups of soldiers secured Omaha Beach by midday on June 6. They fought past the murderous enemy fire and worked their way up the bluffs and took 2,400 casualties. Utah beach would suffer the fewest casualties of any landing point on D-Day. Brigadier General Theodore Roosevelt would receive the Medal of Honor for his leadership that day. A few weeks later, the fifty-seven year old Roosevelt would fall to a heart attack. By the evening of June 6, the Allies had achieved the bridgehead they needed to land the armies waiting offshore. The liberation of France was under way.

Dachau

MARTHA GELLHORN

"Dachau—the significance of this name will never be erased from German history. It stands for all concentration camps which the Nazis established in their territory."
—Eugen Kogon

Adolf Hitler came to power in 1933 with the stated goal of restoring Germany to a world power, establishing "living space" in the form of German colonies in Eastern Europe, the destruction of Bolshevism, and the elimination of Jewish people from Europe. To achieve these aims the Nazi regime would spare no effort to eliminate political resistance in Germany and other "enemies of the state." The Nazis established Dachau, near Munich, as the first concentration camp in 1933 for the political enemies of the Third Reich. In 1938, following "Kristallnacht" and the increased persecution of Jews, the population of the camp expanded to include a large number of Jewish inmates. It was a training camp for SS guards and became a model for other Nazi concentration camps where prisoners were used for slave labor and medical experiments.

When war came to Europe in 1939, the Nazis expanded their war against the Jews and other "untermenschen," or subhuman peoples. Roving groups of military death squads terrorized the conquered territories. The SS and German military rounded up the Jews and forced them into ghettos in the major cities to await transportation to the camps. Once there, the Jews and other prisoners were forced to work for the Nazi war effort as slaves. The Germans immediately executed anyone who was too weak, too young, or too old for work. Conditions in the camps ensured those selected for labor would not last long. The SS constructed gas chambers as the most efficient way of killing people. The victims' bodies were then burned in huge ovens built expressly for that purpose. Hundreds of camps such as Dachau were built in Germany, Poland, and Russia. The largest camps were Auschwitz and Buchenwald, where tens of thousands of people worked under impossible conditions of backbreaking labor, starvation, and disease. In all, it is estimated that eight million people were victims of the Holocaust, including six million Jews.

As the Allied armies entered Germany in 1945 they encountered Hitler's war against the Jews for the first time. The United States Army liberated Dachau on April 26, 1945. At the time there were over 67,000 prisoners at the prison and its subcamps. Approximately 7,000 more had gone on a death march led by SS guards toward Tegernsee to the south. Those who survived this ordeal were later saved as well. What the Americans found defied belief—tens of thousands of starving, sick prisoners, more than thirty rail cars filled with bodies left by the Germans, and thousands of dead heaped by the crematorium. The experience was overwhelming for the hardened combat veterans, as some were moved to tears, others to stunned silence.

Martha Gellhorn witnessed the horrors at Dachau following the liberation and interviewed survivors. Writing for *Collier's*, she became a witness for the American people. It was a story Allied soldiers wanted the world to hear. Few American veterans thought the public at home would even believe them. It was an experience that would stay with them as an indelible reminder why the war had been fought. As the war came to a close, the full reckoning of the Holocaust showed the true nature of the Nazi regime. Army General C. Eaker, commander of the 8th Air Force stated, "Let any doubter, in all the generations to come, contemplate what it would be like to live in a world dominated by Hitler, the Japanese warlords, or any other cruel dictator or despot."

★　★　★　★　★

We came out of Germany in a C-47 carrying American prisoners of war. The planes were lined up on the grass field at Regensburg, and the passengers waited sitting in the shade under the wings. They would not leave the planes: this was a trip no one was going to miss. When the crew chief said "All aboard," we got in as if we were escaping from a fire.

No one looked out the windows as we flew over Germany. No one ever wanted to see Germany again. They turned away from it with hatred and sickness; everything about it was evil. At first they did not talk but when it became real that Germany was behind forever they began talking of their prisons. We did not comment on the Germans: they are past words.

"No one will believe us," a soldier said.

They agreed on that: No one would believe them.

"Where were you captured, miss?" a soldier asked.

"I am only bumming a ride; I've been down to see Dachau."

One of the men said suddenly, "We got to talk about it, see? We got to talk about it if anyone believes us or not." . . .

Behind the barbed wire and the electric fence, the skeletons sat in the sun and searched themselves for lice. They have no age and no faces; they all look alike and like nothing you will ever see if you are lucky. We crossed the wide, crowded, dusty compound between the prison barracks and went to the hospital. In the hall sat more of the skeletons and from them came the smell of disease and death. They watched us but did not move: No expression shows on a face that is only yellowish stubbly skin stretched across bone.

What had been a man dragged himself into the doctor's office; he was a Pole and he was about six feet tall and he weighed less than a hundred pounds and he wore a striped prison shirt, a pair of unlaced boots and a blanket which he tried to hold around his legs. His eyes were large and strange and stood out from his face, and his jawbone seemed to be cutting through his skin. He had come to Dachau from Buchenwald on the last death transport.

There were fifty boxcars of his dead traveling companions still on the siding outside the camp, and for the last three days the American Army had forced Dachau civilians to bury these dead.

When this transport arrived, the German guards locked the men, women and children in the cars and there they slowly died of hunger and thirst. They screamed and they tried to fight their way out; from time to time the guards fired into the cars to stop the noise.

This man had survived; he was found under a pile of dead. Now he stood on the bones that were his legs and talked, and then suddenly he wept. "Everyone is dead," he said, and the face that was not a face twisted with pain or sorrow or horror. "No one is left. Everyone is dead. I cannot help myself," he said "Here I am and I am finished and cannot help myself. Everyone is dead."

The Polish doctor who had been a prisoner here for five years said, "In four weeks, you will be a young man again. You will be fine."

Perhaps his body will live and take strength, but one cannot believe that his eyes will ever be like other people's eyes.

The doctor spoke with great detachment about the things he had watched in this hospital. He had watched them, and there was nothing he could do to stop them. All the prisoners talked in the same way—quietly, with a strange little smile as if they apologized for talking of such loathsome things to someone who lived in a real world and could hardly be expected to understand Dachau.

"The Germans made here some unusual experiments," he said. "They wished to see how long an aviator could go without oxygen; how high in the sky he could go. So they had a closed car from which they pumped the oxygen. It is a quick death," he said. "It does not take more than fifteen minutes. But it is a hard death. They killed not so many people, only eight hundred, in that experiment. It was found that no one can live above 36,000 feet altitude without oxygen."

"Whom did they choose for this experiment?" I asked.

"Any prisoner," he said, "so long as he was healthy. They picked the strongest. The mortality was one hundred per cent, of course."

"It is very interesting, is it not?" said another doctor. We did not look at one another. I do not know how to explain it, but aside from the terrible anger you feel, you are ashamed. You are ashamed for mankind.

"There was also the experiment of the water," said the first doctor. "This was to see how long pilots could survive when they were shot down over water like the Channel, let us say. For that, the German doctors put the prisoners in great vats of sea water, and they stood in water up to their necks. It was found that the human body can resist for two hours and a half in water eight degrees below zero. They killed six hundred people on this experiment. Though sometimes a man had to suffer three times, for he fainted early in the experiment and then he was revived, and a few days later the experiment was again undertaken."

"Didn't they scream? Didn't they cry out?" I said.

He smiled at that question. "There was no use in this place for a man to scream or cry out. It was no use for any man ever."

A colleague of the doctor's came in. He was the one who knew about the malaria experiment. The German doctor who was chief of the army tropical medicine research used Dachau as an experimental station. He was attempting to find a way to immunize German soldiers against malaria. To that end, he inoculated 11,000 Dachau prisoners with tertiary malaria. The death rate from the malaria was not too heavy; it simply meant that these prisoners weakened by fever died more quickly afterward from hunger. However, in one day three men died of overdoses of pyramidon with which, for some unknown reason, the Germans were then experimenting. No immunization for malaria was ever found.

Down the hall in the surgery, the Polish surgeon got out the record book to look up some data on operations performed by the SS doctors. These were castration and sterilization operations. The prisoner was forced to sign a paper beforehand saying that he willingly undertook this self-destruction. Jews and gypsies were castrated; any foreigner who had had relations with a German woman was sterilized. The woman was sent to a concentration camp.

The surgeon mentioned another experiment, really a very bad one, he said, and obviously quite useless. The guinea pigs were Polish priests. (Over two thousand Catholic priests passed through Dachau, but only one thousand are alive.) The German doctors injected streptococcus germs in the upper leg of the prisoners between the muscle and the bone. An extensive abscess formed, accompanied by fever and extreme pain.

The Polish doctor knew of more than a hundred cases who had been treated this way; there may have been more. He had a record of thirty-one deaths, but it took usually from two to three months of ceaseless pain before the patient died, and all of them died after several operations performed during the last few days of their lives. The operations were a further experiment to see if a dying man could be saved, but the answer was that he could not. Some prisoners recovered entirely because they were treated with the already known and proved antidote, but there were others who were now moving around the camp as best they could, crippled for life.

And then because very simply I could listen to no more, my guide who had been in Dachau for ten and a half years took me across the compound to the jail. In Dachau if you want to rest from one horror you go and see another.

The jail was a long clean building with small white cells in it. Here lived the people whom the prisoners called the N.N. men. N.N. stands for *nacht und nebel*, which means "night and mist." Translated into less romantic terms, this means that the prisoners in these cells never saw a human being; were never allowed to speak to anyone; were never taken out into the sun and the air. They lived in solitary confinement on the watery soup and a slice of bread which was the camp diet.

There was, of course, the danger of going mad. But no one ever knew what happened to them in the years of their silence. And on Friday before the Sunday when the Americans entered Dachau, eight thousand men were removed by the SS on a final death transport. Amongst these were all the prisoners from the solitary cells. None of these men have been heard of since.

In Dachau if a man was found with a cigarette butt in his pocket he received twenty-five to fifty lashes with a bull whip. If he failed to stand at attention with his hat off six feet away from any SS trooper who happened to pass, he had his hands tied behind his back and he was hung by his bound hands from a hook on the wall for an hour. If he did any other little thing which displeased the jailers he was put in the box. "The box" is a room the size of a telephone booth. It is so constructed that being in it alone, a man cannot sit down nor kneel down nor, of course, lie down. It was usual to put four men in it together. Here they stood for three days and nights without food or water or any form of sanitation. Afterward they went back to the sixteen-hour day of labor and the diet of watery soup and a slice of bread like soft gray cement.

It is not known how many people died in this camp in the twelve years of its existence but at least 45,000 are known to have died in the last three years. And last February and March, 2,000 were killed in the gas chamber because, though they were too weak to work, they did not have the grace to die, so it was arranged for them.

The gas chamber is part of the crematorium. The crematorium is a brick building outside the camp compound standing in a grove of pine trees. A Polish priest had attached himself to us and, as we walked there, he said, "I started to die twice of starvation but I was very lucky. I got a job as a mason when we were building this crematorium, so I received a little more food and that way I did not die."

I said nothing and I would like to know what there is to say.

Then he said, "Have you seen our chapel, Madam?"

I said I had not, and my guide said I could not; it was within the zone where the 2,000 typhus cases were more or less isolated.

"It is a pity," the priest said. "We finally got a chapel and we had Holy Mass there almost every Sunday. There are very beautiful murals. The man who painted them died of hunger two months ago."

Now we were at the crematorium, and there suddenly but never to be believed were the bodies of the dead. They were everywhere. There were piles of them inside the oven room, outside the door and alongside the building. They were all naked and behind the crematorium the ragged clothing of the dead was neatly stacked—shirts, jackets, trousers and shoes awaiting sterilization and further use. The clothing was handled with order but the bodies were dumped like garbage rotting in the sun.

We have all seen the dead like bundles lying on all the roads of half the earth, but nowhere was there anything like this. Nothing about war was ever as insanely wicked as these starved and outraged naked, nameless dead. Behind one pile of dead lay the clothed healthy bodies of the German guards who had been found in this camp. They were killed at once by the prisoners when the American Army entered. And for the first time anywhere, one could look at a dead man with gladness.

Just behind the crematorium stood the hothouses and they were fine big modern hothouses. Here the prisoners grew the flowers that the SS officers loved. Next to the hothouses were the vegetable gardens and very rich ones, too, where the starving prisoners cultivated the vitamin foods that kept the SS strong. But if a man dying of hunger furtively pulled up and gorged himself on a head of lettuce he would be beaten until he was unconscious. And in front of the crematorium separated from it by a stretch of garden stood a long row of well-built commodious homes. The families of the SS officers lived here; their wives and children lived here quite happily while the chimneys of the crematorium spewed out the unending human ashes.

The American soldier in the plane said, "We got to talk about it."

You cannot talk about it very well, because there is a kind of shock that sets in and makes it almost unbearable to go back and remember what you have seen.

I have not talked about the women who were moved to Dachau three weeks ago from their own concentration camps. Their crime was that they were Jews. There was the lovely girl from Budapest who somehow was still lovely, and the woman with mad eyes who had watched her sister walk into the gas chamber at Auschwitz and been held back, and the Austrian woman who pointed out quite calmly that they all had the dresses they wore on their backs, and they had never had anything more, and that they worked sixteen hours a day, too, in the long winters and that they, too, were "corrected," as the Germans say, for any offense, real or imaginary.

I have not talked about how it was the day the American Army arrived, though the prisoners told me. In their joy to be free and longing to see the friends who had come at last, the prisoners rushed to the fence and died—electrocuted. There were those who died cheering, because that effort of happiness was more than their bodies could endure. There were those who died because at last they had food and they ate before they could be stopped and it killed them. I do not know words fine enough to talk of the men who have lived in this horror for years—three years, five years, ten years—and whose minds are as clear and unafraid as the day they entered.

I was in Dachau when the German armies surrendered unconditionally to the Allies. It was a suitable place to be. For surely this war was made to abolish Dachau and all the other places like Dachau and everything that Dachau stands for. To abolish it forever. That these cemetery prisons existed is the crime and shame of the German people.

We are not entirely guiltless, we the Allies, because it took us twelve years to open the gates of Dachau. We were blind and unbelieving and slow, and that we can never be again. We must know now that there can never be peace if there is cruelty like this in the world.

And if ever again we tolerate such cruelty we have no right to peace.

★   ★   ★   ★   ★

In the aftermath of World War II, many of the survivors from Nazi concentration camps found refuge and treatment at displaced persons camps organized by the Allies. Between 1948 and 1951 almost 700,000 Jews emigrated to Israel. Others would move to the United States and other countries. Martha Gellhorn returned to the United States in 1947 but covered events all over the world including the Arab-Israeli war, the trial of Adolf Eichman, and the war in Vietnam. Even at the age of eighty-one she reported on the American invasion of Panama. She passed away in February, 1998.

The Story of the Bulge

JOHN TOLAND

> At the core, the American citizen soldiers knew the difference
> between right and wrong, and they didn't want to live in a
> world in which wrong prevailed. So they fought, and won, and
> we all of us, living and yet to be born, must be forever pro-
> foundly grateful.
>
> —Stephen E. Ambrose, *Citizen Soldiers*

By the fall of 1944, the German army had been pushed back to the
Siegfried Line along their frontier border. The Allies were advancing on a
broad front towards the Rhineland as the Russians approached Germany
from the East through Poland. Hitler realized his armies needed to strike
in order to buy time against his Russian enemies. A surprise attack through
the thinly-defended American lines in the Ardennes forest and a defeat of a
major Allied force might split the American and British armies, possibly
forcing a separate peace with Britain. If Hitler could take the vital port of
Antwerp, the Allied advance into Germany would be set back indefinitely,
giving Germany time to face the Russian onslaught in the east.

Hitler's plans centered the opening attacks against American
forces, due largely to his view that Americans were incapable of fighting
effectively, and his belief that the American home front was likely to crack
after a military loss. He thought that America was a decadent and racially
impure culture that would never withstand the assault of Germany's finest
soldiers. When his armies broke out of the Ardennes in a blinding snowstorm on December 16 and crashed into the American lines, his predic-
tions came undone as American soldiers, with their backs to the wall, put
up a tenacious defense.

At no place was this American spirit of defiance more prevalent
than at the Belgian town of Bastogne, a vital road junction directly in the

path of the German advance. Even before the end of the first day's fighting, Eisenhower realized the German attack was a full-scale effort, and rushed the 101st Airborne Division under General Anthony McAuliffe to defend Bastogne, along with a combat team from the U.S. 10th Armored Division. By December 21, they were surrounded by enemy units who were desperate to sieze their objective—clearing the way for more German divisions. Conditions inside the perimeter were tough—most of the medical supplies and personnel had been captured. The weather continued to worsen in the coldest winter on record for fifty years, cutting off any hope of resupply or fire support from the air. Ammunition was running low and the casualties were mounting. The German army attacked with everything they had, day after day, yet the Americans held on.

Pulitzer Prize–winning author John Toland wrote about the battle for Bastogne in the following chapter from his superb work *Battle: The Story of the Bulge*, published in 1959.

★   ★   ★   ★   ★

On December 22, the Battle of the Bulge was one week old. In Washington at his press conference, President Roosevelt refused to make any comments about the great German offensive. He did state that the "end was not in sight," and those on the home front should exert every effort at this critical time to back up the fighters.

In Paris, civilians were more than ever alarmed over Skorzeny's "trained assassins." Parachutists had been seen in Mayenne. The convergence of Skorzeny men on the Café le la Paix was expected momentarily.

In Versailles, Eisenhower was still a prisoner of his own guards. But the new reports of German parachutists only irritated him. "Hell's fire," he told his secretary, Lieutenant Kay Summersby, "I'm going for a walk. If anyone wants to shoot me, he can go right ahead. I've got to get out."

He strode into the courtyard, and under the anxious eyes of guards, enjoyed his forbidden walk. When he returned he was feeling better. He sat down and wrote one of his rare "orders of the day." It was defiant and confident:

> By rushing out from his fixed defenses the enemy may give us the chance to turn his great gamble into the worst defeat. So I call upon every man, of all the Allies, to rise now to new heights of resolution and of effort. Let everyone hold before him a single thought—to destroy the enemy on the ground, in the air, everywhere—destroy him! United in

this determination and with unshakable faith in the cause for which we fight, we will, with God's help, go forward to our greatest victory.

In Luxembourg City the daily target conference was in session at the Ninth Air Force Advanced Headquarters War Room. Major Stuart Fuller was reading his weather forecast. A front had settled east of the Ardennes in the Rhine Valley and showed no signs of leaving.

"For the next few days," he concluded, "there will be unrelieved gloom. No break can be expected until about 26 December."

The gloom in the war room was as heavy as the forecast. Lieutenant General Hoyt Vandenberg, commandant of the Ninth Air Force, and Fuller mulled over the most remote possibility of a break. There were stagnant high areas to the east and west but it was extremely unlikely that they would move.

"That means no ops," said Vandenberg grimly. From the cobblestone streets the rumble of a passing Patton armored column deepened his frustration. What help could he give these men in their coming fight?

A few blocks away George Patton was reading a sheaf of reports. At six o'clock that morning tanks and infantry of his III Corps had jumped off in the first American counteroffensive of the Bulge.

Through thick swirls of fog, and gusts of snow, three divisions had flung themselves up against the great Ardennes salient. On the west flank was the 4th Armored, its goal Bastogne; in the center the 26th was aimed at Wiltz; and on the east, or right flank, the veteran 80th Division, led by the hard-driving "Hairless Horace" McBride, expected to recapture Ettelbruck in a day and drive up to St. Vith.

Patton was delighted. His critics had been confounded. The three divisions had moved one hundred miles over strange roads, under icy conditions, in less than forty-eight hours. As predicted, his attack was on schedule.

Now he gave an even more startling prediction. "We'll be in St. Vith," he said, "by December 26."

The week before, Patton had ordered his chaplain to publish a prayer for good weather for his Saar attack. "See if we can't get God to work on our side."

"Sir," replied Chaplain O'Neill, "it's going to take a pretty thick rug for that kind of praying."

"I don't care if it takes a flying carpet."

"Yes, sir," replied O'Neill reluctantly. "But it usually isn't customary among men of my profession to pray for clear weather to kill fellow men."

"Chaplain, are you teaching me theology or are you the chaplain of the Third Army? I want a prayer."

The prayer was written:

> Almighty and merciful Father, we humbly beseech Thee of Thy great goodness, to restrain these immoderate rains with which we have had to contend. Grant us fair weather for battle.

Patton, delighted with O'Neill's prayer, ordered thousands of copies printed. But before they could be distributed, the Saar attack was canceled and the entire Third Army pivoted ninety degrees toward the Ardennes.

Now, as Patton's III Corps headed north to bite into the great German offensive, the prayer was being passed out, even though Patton's chief of staff, General Gay, had reminded him that it had been printed for an earlier attack.

"Oh, the Lord won't mind," was Patton's answer. "He knows we're too busy right now killing Germans to print another prayer."

That morning it was being read by men of three divisions in a driving snowstorm.

In German-occupied Wiltz only a few civilians dared to walk the streets that morning. One was an elderly woman, climbing up the steep hill, over rubble and wreckage, to the hospital. Mme. Balthasar-Wagener was trembling, but not from age or cold. She and her husband, Jean-Pierre, had a wounded GI hidden in their attic. Why had they had the misfortune to find him? Ironically many of their neighbors considered them collaborators, for their daughter, Mariette, had married a German officer, Fritz Schultheiss. Already a dozen German soldiers were billeted in their home on the Rue Plank. And what if Fritz should suddenly come home on leave?

She walked into the big modern hospital which looked over the valley, wandering a few minutes in the sterile hallways, not knowing what to do.

"I'm a volunteer nurse," said a young fragile-looking woman. "They call me Mlle. Anna. Can I help you?"

Her sympathetic face encouraged Mme. Balthasar-Wagener. "I have an American soldier named Georges," she blurted out. "He's wounded!"

Mlle. Anna took the old woman's arm and led her to an empty room. "First we'll get some medicine for your American," she said. "Then we'll go to your house."

Half a mile away, several trucks marked with big red crosses were pulling into the courtyard of the ancient castle. A few days ago the

castle had housed an American field hospital. Now it was German. Aid-
men of both sides were carrying wounded American prisoners into the
castle.

Directing the operations from one of the German trucks was an
unwounded GI, Sergeant Lester Koritz, formerly of the 28th Division
Order of Battle team.

Koritz, self-styled "interpreter" for wounded Americans, looked
around. It seemed incredible, but he was back where he had started four
days before. He looked through the ancient archway to Grand' Rue. A
hundred yards up the street was the tobacco shop of his good friends the
Goebel sisters. He wondered if they were still alive.

Three days previously the sisters had fled south to Boulaide. But
when the Germans took this town, all refugees were ordered to return to
their homes. Now the Goebels and hundreds of other citizens of Wiltz
were walking, through a driving snowstorm, past Café Schumann. Their
arduous round-trip flight was almost over.

That morning, a thick white mantle covered the somber buildings of Bastogne, giving the town an air of peace and security. In the northwestern outskirts, at McAuliffe's command post, there was an atmosphere of confidence.

Two encouraging messages had just arrived. One read, "Hugh is
coming." This meant that General Hugh Gaffey's 4th Armored Division
was driving up toward the beleaguered town on the left flank of Patton's
III Corps attack. The other message was from VIII Corps: "Resupply by air
will start coming at 2000."

The men in the foxholes and in lonely company command posts
on the edges of the defense circle felt a growing confidence too, but for a
different reason. When word spread that they were surrounded, rivalry
among the various units was suddenly forgotten. The paratroopers now
grudgingly admitted that the 10th Armored Division teams had put up
one hell of a fight and had saved the bacon during the first two days.

The sharp rivalry among the regiments of the 101st also ceased.
Of course no self-respecting 501st man would want to be in the Five-O-
Deuce, the 504th, or the 327th Glider. But those were pretty good outfits
to have at your side.

Negro artillerymen of the Long Tom outfit which had wandered
into town were stuffing the bottoms of their trousers into their boots.
"What the devil kind of uniform is that?" a 101st officer asked curiously.
"Man," was the answer, "we're airborne!" So was their spirit.

Even the stragglers, Team Snafu, had finally caught the spirit. They had stumbled into town exhausted, shocked in mind and body, but several days of sleep and food had revived them.

Three miles south of Bastogne, Sergeant Oswald Butler, of the 327th Glider Infantry Regiment, was standing in the basement of a lonely farmhouse overlooking the highway to Arlon.

At exactly 11:30 a.m. he saw four figures coming up the road from the south carrying what looked like a bedspread on a pole. They were Germans. He picked up a phone and called his commanding officer, Captain Adams. "There're four Krauts coming up the road. They're carrying a white flag. It looks like they want to surrender."

Butler, followed by two of his men, went out to meet the Germans. A short stocky captain, with medical insignia, stepped up to him. "We are parlementaires," he said in careful English, "and we want to talk to your officers."

An artillery major, wearing Panzer Lehr markings, said something in German to the captain. "We want to talk to your commanding general," said the captain.

Butler tore off several strips from the white flag and blindfolded the two officers. He told Private Gommell to stay there with the two German enlisted men, and then led the officers up the hill toward the rear.

Half an hour later Colonel Joseph Harper, commander of the 327th, was talking on the phone to Lieutenant Colonel Ned Moore, McAuliffe's acting chief of staff.

"I have some Germans," said Harper. "They have a request for surrender. I'll bring them up to the command post."

"Good," said Moore. Then he opened the door to a small room where McAuliffe was sleeping. He shook the General awake and told him Harper was on the way with a surrender request.

A few minutes later Colonel Harper walked down the steep steps to the division command post and handed Moore two typewritten sheets of paper—one in German, one in English.

Moore read the English translation:

To the U.S.A. Commander of the encircled town of Bastogne.
The fortune of war is changing. This time the U.S.A. forces in and near Bastogne have been encircled by strong German armored units . . .
There is only one possibility to save the encircled U.S.A. troops from total annihilation: that is the honorable surrender of the encircled town . . .

If this proposal should be rejected one German Artillery Corps and six heavy A.A. Battalions are ready to annihilate the U.S.A. troops in and near Bastogne . . .

All the serious civilian losses caused by this artillery fire would not correspond with the well-known American humanity.

The German Commander

McAuliffe, yawning, came out of his room. "What's on the paper, Ned?" he asked.

"They want us to surrender."

McAuliffe, after glancing carelessly at the papers, laughed and said, "Aw, nuts." He let the two papers fall to the floor and drove out to the front to personally congratulate some men who had just wiped out a German roadblock.

When McAuliffe returned to his command post, Colonel Harper was there. "Say, Tony," he said, "those two Kraut envoys are still at my command post. They say they brought a formal military communication and they're entitled to an answer."

"What the hell should I tell them?" McAuliffe sat down, thoughtfully fingering a pencil.

"That first remark of yours would be hard to beat, General," suggested Colonel Kinnard, the youthful operations officer.

"What'd I say?"

"You said, 'Nuts.'"

Everyone in the room, officers and enlisted men, liked this answer.

McAuliffe wrote and then handed the paper to Harper. "Here's the answer."

Harper read:

To the German Commander:
Nuts!
—The American Commander

"Will you see that it's delivered?" said McAuliffe.

Harper grinned. "I'll deliver it myself. It will be a lot of fun."

At 1:30 p.m. Sergeant Butler, who had just finished checking his lines, walked into the farmhouse overlooking the Arlon highway. He was amazed to see the two German privates of the surrender team sitting on the basement floor, machine pistols propped against the wall. Private Gommell, their guard, was proudly fingering a P-38 pistol.

"What the hell's going on?" asked Butler.

"They just surrendered to me," said Gommell innocently.

"Give them back their guns."

Reluctantly Gommell handed the P-38 to one of the privates, a frightened youngster who looked less than sixteen. The boy was just as reluctant to take it.

Butler heard a jeep approaching. Followed by the others, he hurried outside. In the jeep were Colonel Harper and the two German officers.

"But what does it mean?" the medical officer was asking in bewilderment.

"If you don't understand what 'Nuts' means," said Harper, losing his temper, "in plain English it's the same as 'Go to Hell.' And I'll tell you something else. If you continue to attack we'll kill every goddam German that tries to break into this city!"

The Germans saluted sharply.

"We will kill many Americans," said the medical captain regretfully.

"On your way, Bud," said Harper. Then, without thinking, he added, "And good luck to you."

About ten miles southwest of Bastogne, comrades of the German surrender team had made almost no western progress that day. At an advance command post of the Panzer Lehr Division, Baron von Manteuffel, who had personally taken a tank all the way to the approaches of St. Hubert the day before, was berating General Bayerlein.

"There's nothing out west," he stormed. "Get your damned people moving!" Manteuffel was also angry with his corps commander, Lüttwitz. For the Baron had learned of the surrender note to Bastogne too late to stop the envoys. Besides being in poor military taste, it contained hollow threats. The artillery battalions which were to lay waste the town existed only in Lüttwitz's mind.

Now the hollow threats had to be made good. Manteuffel picked up a phone.

It was midnight in Bastogne. In McAuliffe's command post the mood had suddenly changed. The air drop promised for 10:00 p.m. had been called off because of bad weather.

McAuliffe and his staff again reviewed their situation. So far three things had kept the Germans from overwhelming Bastogne: lack of artillery, uncoordinated attacks, and the stubbornness of the defenders. As yet the Germans had hit only one sector at a time, giving the defenders time to rush reserves to the threatened spot.

McAuliffe studied the latest "sitrep"—situation report. There was bitter fighting at Marvie; reports of rumbling traffic at other points presaged other attacks. When these came he would have little to stop them. Infantry commanders all around the perimeter were calling for artillery and getting almost none. Ammunition was rationed to ten rounds a day per gun.

To one commander who continued to plead for artillery, McAuliffe drily replied, "If you see 400 Germans in a hundred-yard area, and they have their heads up, you can fire artillery at them. But not more than two rounds."

Colonel Robert's big 105s, the heavy punch of the town's defense, were so low on ammunition that three of his tanks and two half-tracks were now making a break for the south. This desperate force, led by Captain McCloskey, hoped to fight its way back to Bastogne with an ammunition train. But before McCloskey had gone a mile all five vehicles were knocked out.

As news of this reached Bastogne, the unfamiliar hum of German bombers could be heard. Their roar grew louder, then deafening. There were shrill whistles, followed by explosions. Manteuffel was carrying out von Lüttwitz's threat to devastate the town.

The men in the foxholes around Bastogne were bitter. If Germans could fly over, why not the Allies? The confidence of that morning was waning. This bombing was an indication that the end was near.

★   ★   ★   ★   ★

On 23 December the weather conditions started improving, allowing the Allied air forces to attack. They launched devastating bombing raids on the German supply points at the rear, and P-47s destroyed German troops at will on the roads. The Allied air forces also helped the defenders of Bastogne, dropping much-needed supplies—medicine, food, blankets and ammunition. A team of volunteer surgeons flew in by glider and began operating. By December 24 the German advance was effectively stalled short of the Meuse River. General McAuliffe sent a Christmas message to his men:

> What's merry about all this, you ask? We're fighting—it's cold—we aren't home. All true, but what has the proud Eagle Division accomplished with its worthy comrades of the 10th Armored Division, the 705th Tank Destroyer Battalion and all the rest? Just this: We have stopped cold everything that has been thrown at us from the north, east, south and

west. We have identifications from four German panzer divisions, two German infantry divisions and one German parachute division. These units, spearheading the last desperate German lunge, were heading straight west for key points when the Eagle Division was hurriedly ordered to stem the advance. How effectively this was done will be written in history; not alone in our Division's glorious history but in world history. The Germans actually did surround us, their radios blared our doom. Allied troops are counterattacking in force. We continue to hold Bastogne. By holding Bastogne we assure the success of the Allied armies. We know that our Division commander, General Taylor, will say: "Well done!" We are giving our country and our loved ones at home a worthy Christmas present and being privileged to take part in this gallant feat of arms are truly making for ourselves a merry Christmas.

★ ★ ★ ★ ★

General Patton's Third Army would break the siege the following day.

Merrill's Marauders

DAVE RICHARDSON

Cry "Havoc!" and let slip the dogs of war.
—William Shakespeare, *Julius Caesar*

On December 11, 1941, the Japanese army invaded Burma with 35,000 men. By May the British and American forces and their Chinese allies were forced to retreat back to India. The vital Burma Road, by which supplies were transported to China from India, was severed. The British theater commander General A. Wavell and Major General Ord Wingate, organized long range raiding groups known as Chindits (Stone Lions) to operate deep behind enemy lines attacking Japan's supply routes and communications. They were to prove highly successful, forcing the Japanese to go on the defensive and abandon any plans for invading India.

The Americans wished to create their own long range striking force. In the Quebec Conference in August 1943, Allied leaders decided to form a U.S. raiding force partially modeled on the Chindits that would attack Japanese troops in Burma. A call for volunteers attracted about 2,900 from the United States. The unit was officially designated as 5307th Composite Unit (provisional) with a code name GALAHAD. They were sent to India, arriving in Bombay on October 31, 1943 to train and were reinforced with Air Corps and Signal Corps personnel.

The new unit was set to be under the command of Wingate. American General Joseph Stilwell did not wish to see American soldiers fighting under the command of British officers. He convinced Admiral Lord Mountbatten, the supreme Allied commander of the South East Asia Command, that the American raider forces should serve under an American. Stilwell assigned Brigadier General Frank Merrill to lead them. American correspondents were quick to dub the new unit "Merrill's Marauders."

The men were organized into two combat teams per battalion. In February 1944 six combat teams—coded Blue, Green, Khaki, Orange, Red, and White—began a 1000-mile march over the Himalayas and through jungle to Burma. Deep behind enemy lines they would take the fight to the Japanese where they least expected it.

Dave Richardson accompanied the Marauders into action in June, 1944, on assignment for *Yank* magazine and wrote the following account of the first engagement between Merrill's Marauders and men from the veteran Japanese 18th Division.

★　★　★　★　★

Behind Japanese Lines in Northern Burma

The crackle of a couple of Nambu light machine guns and the whipsnap of Ariska rifles stopped the single-file column of Merril's Marauders and sent the men scrambling for cover on both sides of the narrow jungle trail.

They had trudged nearly 250 miles in the last four weeks. After marching up 116 miles of the Ledo Road, they had swung wide around the Jap positions that were holding up the Chinese drive in the Hukawng Valley of Northern Burma. They had followed narrow native paths and elephant trails through dense undergrowth and high elephant grass and across dozens of rivers and streams.

This was to be the first of their missions as a volunteer raiding outfit behind Jap lines—attacking the enemy rear supply base of Walawbum to force a Jap withdrawal 30 miles northward so the Chinese could push through. The Marauders led by Brig. Gen. Frank D. Merrill, who had walked out of Burma with Stilwell two years before, were this afternoon only three miles from their goal.

The CO of the unit that had bumped into Jap resistance sent for 1st Lt. Logan E. Weston of Youngstown, Ohio. A slim, quiet poker-faced young officer, Weston edged his way through the bush to the CO's side.

"Weston," said the CO, "take your intelligence and reconnaissance platoon across the river and move south to a position near the riverbank that will cover us from the Walawbum area when we drive through this village of Langag Ga on the east bank."

Lt. Weston, like most of the others in this Marauder unit, had fought Japs before. Quitting Transylvania Bible School in Freeport, Pa., midway through his study for the ministry, he had joined the Army. He went to the South Pacific as a squad leader in the 37th Division, he was graduated from OCS in the Fiji's, and then he fought in New Georgia as a platoon leader in the 37th. That's where he picked up a nickname.

"Fightin' Preacher," his men called him. As one of his original platoon explained it, "Lt. Weston continued his Bible study in spare moments, but when we got into a scrap with the Japs he was one of the fightingest platoon leaders in the outfit."

In New Georgia the Fightin' Preacher had always made one point clear to his men: he did not like to kill. After each action he got his men aside and said, half-apologetically: "I'm sorry I had to kill those Japs, fellas, but today it was a case of either my getting them or their getting me."

Lt. Weston's tough, swaggering platoon was a marked contrast to its gentle, mild-mannered leader. Among his men were such veterans as Cpl. Werner Katz of New York, N.Y., who fought with the International Brigade in the Spanish Civil War and with the American Division on Guadacanal. Katz, a burly first scout, became the first American Infantryman to kill a Jap on the continent of Asia when the platoon had a fleeting brush with a Jap patrol the week before.

Then there was Pfc. Norman J. (Chief) Janis, a full-blooded Sioux Indian and former rodeo rider from Deadwood, S. Dak., who thought it was a bad day during the Buna battle in New Guinea if he had to use more than one bullet to kill a Jap. And Sgt. William L. Grimmes of Lonaconing, Md., who won the Silver Star for knocking off 25 Japs at Guadalcanal. And a couple of dozen others who had battled Japs in the jungles and swamps of the South and Southwest Pacific. They had all volunteered for this "dangerous and hazardous" jungle-fighting mission.

The Fightin' Preacher's men got to their feet and slung on their 60-pound horseshoe-type packs. They moved through the dark jungle undergrowth down to the muddy little river and crossed it Indian file wading 40 feet to the other side through crotch-deep water. Then, rifles cradled in their arms, they climbed the bank.

They rustled their way through the brush alongside the riverbank all afternoon, cautiously covering a few hundred yards. Once or twice the scouts spotted Jap sentries and traded a few bullets with them, but the Japs got away. Just before dusk the platoon halted and dug in a perimeter of fox holes to spend the night. They could hear the main body of Marauders pushing through the Jap resistance across the river, using lots of tommy guns and BAR's.

The men ate no supper; they had run out of K-rations two days before. (While the Marauders were behind the Jap lines, they were supplied entirely by airdrop and there were never any drops when the men were sneaking close to their objective, because this might reveal their position and strength.) There was nothing for the men to do but decide on the hours of perimeter guard and then curl up in blanket and poncho and go to sleep.

By dawn the next morning the Fightin' Preacher's platoon was on the move again. The scouts had located a bend in the river from which the platoon could command a wide field of fire to the south. From here they could cover the main Marauder unit as it pushed down the trail along the opposite bank.

The river bend was only 150 yards away from the night perimeter, and the platoon reached it in half an hour in the early-morning fog. They started to dig in at 0700 hours. Half an hour later Pvt. Pete Leitner, a scout from Okeechobee, Fla., was out in front of the perimeter collecting green branches to camouflage his fox hole when a Nambu light machine gun opened up.

Leitner was hit in the middle and crumpled to the ground, severely wounded. Before anyone could get his sights on the Jap machine gunner, he ran away through the brush. Sgt. Paul Mathis of Grey Eagle, Minn., platoon guide and Lt. Weston went out and dragged Leitner back to the perimeter. The rest of the men in the platoon got down in their holes and braced themselves for a Jap attack.

They didn't have long to wait. Through the brush they spotted tan-uniformed Japs walking toward them at a crouch, some with twigs camouflaging their helmets. The platoon opened up. The Japs hit the ground and fanned out, crawling closer and shooting furiously. The Japs chattered among themselves; some seemed to be giving commands.

Then came the hollow snap of knee mortars being discharged behind the Japs. Seconds later the mortar shells exploded in the trees over the Fightin' Preacher's men. After that the mortars were fired in salvoes.

"Five Japs on the right flank!" somebody yelled. Sgt. John Gately of Woburn, Mass., spotted the first one and killed him. Pfc. Harold Hudson of Bristol, Conn., glimpsed the other four and mowed them all down, starting his tommy gun at the rear of the quartet and working forward.

The main Jap attack was coming in the center of the platoon's defense. A squad of Japs moved in closer, crawling and shooting. Grimmes, the Silver Star winner from Guadalcanal, now added to his record of 25

Japs by pumping bullets into each one that lifted his head. T-5 Raymond F. Harris of Pekin, Ill., sprayed the squad with his BAR as some of the Japs managed to creep within 30 feet of his position. One Jap shot at Harris just as he ducked his head to put a magazine in his BAR. The bullet dented his helmet.

Inside the perimeter, Lt. Weston and his platoon sergeant, T/Sgt. Alfred M. Greer of Malden, Mass., got a message from Pfc. Benny Silverman of New York, N.Y., walkie-talkie radioman, that the main body of the Marauders had chased the remaining Japs from the opposite bank of the river and had taken up position there.

"Fine," the Fightin' Preacher told Greer. "Let's get them to help us with their mortars." Acting as mortar observer, Greer got Silverman to radio back a rough estimate of positions based on his map. Soon the crack of a mortar discharge answered from across the river. An 81-mm mortar shell burst with a hollow explosion behind the Japs. Greer gave Silverman new elevation and azimuth figures. Another mortar shell lobbed over. It burst a little closer to the Japs but over to one side.

"Anybody got a compass with mils on it instead of degrees?" asked Greer. Near him Cpl. Joe Gomez, aid man from Gallup, N. Mex., had just finished working on Sgt. Lionel Parquette of Calumet, Mich., who was mortally wounded in the head. Gomez opened a pouch at his belt and handed his compass over to Greer. "We medics got everything," he grinned.

Greer told the mortars to lay in a smoke shell and he took an azimuth reading on it. Then he gave Silverman a new set of figures to radio the mortar crew.

Across the river, the mortar chief—1st Lt. William F. Woomer of State Collage, Pa., called "Woomer the Boomer" in New Guinea—shouted the figure to the mortar crew. Sgt. Edwin Kopec of Lowell, Mass.; Pvt. James McGowan of West Newton, Mass., and Pvt. Wise Alderman of Floyd, Va., set the figures on the scales and lobbed over another one. Theirs was the only mortar in position to fire across the river. Another mortar crew was changing its position to clear some trees with its trajectory.

Soon with Greer's observation, the mortars were right on their target. Greer then varied the figures every few rounds to cover the Japs from the flank.

"Nice going boys," he yelled after a series of six bursts. "We just saw a couple of Japs blown out of their holes 40 yards from our point man." As fast as the mortarmen could rip open shell cases, they poured fire across the river.

The Japs kept coming. They edged into position on three sides of the perimeter and were even trying to get between the river and the Fightin' Preacher's platoon. Their machine-gun and rifle fire increased in intensity and volume. Lt. Weston estimated about a company of Japs was opposing him.

Then Silverman at the walkie-talkie got an order for the platoon to withdraw to the other side of the river. Its mission had been accomplished. There was no use staying to fight the Japs with such a small force when the main body of Marauders was moving south to make a direct attack on Walawbum.

Greer, Siverman and a couple of others made litters out of bamboo poles and buttoned-up fatigue jackets to carry the few wounded who could not walk. Then, under cover of Lt. Woomer's mortar fire, the platoon withdrew to the river and prepared to cross. The Japs followed, figuring on catching them in the riverbed.

Across the river four BAR's opened up to cover the crossing. The bullets whined over the platoon's heads. Lt. Weston told Silverman to radio back that the Japs were on the flanks waiting to knock off some men crossing the river. Then two of the platoons peeled off their white undershirts and put one in a tree on each flank of the platoon to serve as firing guides for the BAR's. Just before crossing, Lt. Weston ordered the mortars to throw smoke shells to the rear and flanks of the withdrawing platoon to screen the move.

One by one the men of the platoon splashed back across the river as BAR's stuttered away and mortar burst echoed down the riverbed. After Chief Janis, the Indian crack shot, had crossed, he turned to watch Pfc. John E. Clark of Windsor, Vt., and Katz, the International Brigade veteran, carry the wounded Leitner across on a litter. Out of the corner of his eye, Janis spotted a movement in the bushes on the bank. A Jap with a light machine-gun had parted the bushes and was taking aim at the litter-bearers and their burden. Janis raised his M1 and fired two shots. The Jap squealed and slumped over his gun.

"I just wanted to make sure I got him," said Janis, explaining the extra shot. His score for the day was seven Japs.

Meanwhile the BAR men covering the withdrawal were busy. Japs seemed to pop up all over the riverbank. Pvt. Bob Cole of Englewood, Calif., got six of them, and T-5 Clyde Shields of Egg Harbor, Wis., saw two roll down the bank in his sights.

At 0930 hours the last man withdrew. The sweating mortarmen were ripping open their 113th shell case when the cease-fire order came. Lt. Weston trudged wearily into the unit CP, head bent as he worked the bolt on his carbine.

One of his men watched him with obvious admiration. "You know," he said, "the Fightin' Preacher got at least two Japs before we withdrew. I thought he was going to apologize again. Instead, all he said was that he could have got another Jap if his bolt hadn't jammed."

★ ★ ★ ★ ★

Always outnumbered, devastated by disease and hunger, the Marauders achieved their goal and caused havoc behind enemy lines. They harassed supply and communication lines and cut off the Japanese rear at Maingkwan. In March they severed Japanese supply lines in Hukawng Valley. On May 17, they helped Chinese troops to capture Myitkina airfield in a climactic battle. The Marauders were consolidated with the 475th Infantry on August 10, 1944. On June 21, 1954, the 475th was redesignated the 75th Infantry. It is from the redesignation of Merrill's Marauders into the 75th Infantry Regiment that the modern-day 75th Ranger Regiment traces its current unit designation.

Lovely Americans

ROBERT SHAPLEN

> I have returned. By the grace of Almighty God, our forces stand
> again on Philippine soil.
> —General Douglas MacArthur,
> October 20, 1944, Palo, Philippines

The liberation of Paris in the summer of 1944 was one of the greatest mo-
ments of the Second World War. Andy Rooney, writing for *Stars and Stripes* at
the time, described it as one of the happiest days in the history of the world.
In the Pacific, there was another scene of jubilation as the Americans under
General Douglas A. MacArthur returned to liberate the Philippines from
Japanese occupation. In one of his greatest moments, MacArthur with Filipino President Sergio Osmena at his side, waded ashore at Palo, Leyte on
October 20, 1994 within hours of the initial landings. After a brief inspection
of the damage wrought by the bombardment, he went quickly to a radio
arranged by signalmen. In a voice deep with emotion, MacArthur began to
speak: "TO THE PEOPLE OF THE PHILIPPINES: I have returned. By the
grace of Almighty God our forces stand again on Philippine soil."

It was the beginning of the end of a brutal Japanese occupation.
The Japanese military had stripped the country of food and materials to
supply their war effort, conscripted slave laborers, forced thousands of
women to work as "comfort girls" at Japanese brothels, and tortured and
killed thousands in an effort to end the resistance movement that had
been fighting since the war began. With American help, the time had
come to liberate themselves from Japanese rule. As American forces
moved into Leyte the people came forward to meet them and offer assis-
tance. Robert Shaplen landed on October 20th with American forces and
was present for the liberation of Tacloban, the first major town to be freed
from Japanese control. His report reminds us of the great joy that arrived

with American soldiers in Europe and Asia as ordinary people cast off their bonds of tyranny.

$$\star \quad \star \quad \star \quad \star \quad \star$$

For nearly two and a half years the American troops in General Douglas MacArthur's Southwest Pacific Command fought in some of the world's most uncivilized territory. As they made their way along the New Guinea coast and invaded New Britain, the Admiralty Islands, Biak, Morotai, and other places with strange names, they experienced none of the satisfaction of the Allied troops in Europe, who have been marching through town after town on triumphant crusades of liberation. The only towns the men in the Pacific saw were the native *kampongs* and the only welcome they received from the not visibly overjoyed inhabitants was an unintelligible chatter. With the invasion of the Philippines, MacArthur's men finally got their reward. Ever since Bataan, as the world knew, MacArthur had had one aspiration: to return to the Islands. For him the invasion of Leyte was a personal triumph, the end of a long, complicated battle. But for the men, weary of jungles, it was something more; it was like coming out of darkness into the light.

I landed on Leyte the morning of October 20th as a correspondent attached to the Seventh Regiment of the First Cavalry Division, which was dismounted when it left the United States, soon after Pearl Harbor, with the objective, even then, of helping recapture the Philippines. Under cover of violent naval gunfire, capped by a cascade of rockets that literally tore our landing beach apart, we got ashore successfully, with less opposition than we had expected. A few bomb-happy Japanese snipers were still in the trees and a few others were still in the concrete pillboxes along the shore, but these were quickly disposed of. The snipers were picked off their perches by sharpshooters with carbines and Garands and the pillboxes were dynamited. Three divisions to the south of us, particularly the Twenty-fourth Division, on our left flank, ran into much heavier opposition. We were able to push rapidly north toward the town of Tacloban, four miles from our landing point. It turned out that the troops of the notorious Sixteenth Imperial Japanese Division, whom our division had expected to encounter in the Tacloban area, had been moved south just before the invasion. In the village of San José, some four hundred yards from where we landed, we found several Japanese automobiles, a large quantity of Japanese beer (bottled in Manila), and some new guns the enemy had not taken the time to destroy in his flight. San José was deserted. All but a few of the houses, which had been bombed for days from the air before the landing and shelled for hours from the sea that morning, were rubble, and even those that were standing looked as if they were ready to fall down. The cavalrymen didn't stay in San José very long. They pushed on toward the Barayan River, a narrow stream a little less than a mile ahead. Here the Japs had, conveniently, left a bridge intact, so the cavalry kept moving. By dusk we had reached what was supposed to be our second-day objective, a road junction a mile or so from Tacloban. Here we established a perimeter defense for the night, and here began the magnificent reception we got in the Philippines. This, it seemed to me, was what all the men had been waiting for during the long, malarial months in the jungles.

Hundreds of soldiers will always remember the white-clad figure of the Filipino who came walking toward us (running was more like it), wheeling a bicycle, at four o'clock that afternoon. It had been raining and the road was too slippery to ride on. The advance troops spied him several hundred yards ahead through the trees and held their fire when they saw him waving frantically, taking off and putting on his broad-brimmed hat again and again. As he approached, his face appeared to be composed entirely of smile. It was impossible to understand what he was saying, but it was easy to see that he was filled with an almost hysterical happiness. He grabbed the hand of every soldier he could reach and shook it ecstatically. When he had quieted down, we were able, with the help of one of the Filipino soldiers with us, to learn that his name was Isaios Budlong and that he had formerly been a telegraph operator in Tacloban. To him went the honor of being the first liberated Filipino. He had left the town that morning and made his way through whatever was left of the Japanese lines to reach us.

Having liberated Budlong, the troops began digging foxholes and setting up mortars and machine guns in preparation for a possible Jap counterattack. As they dug in, more Filipinos came running down the two roads leading to the junction. In half an hour there were a hundred of them milling around us. There were men, one of whom brought a large box of Japanese hard crackers and gave it to Lieutenant Colonel Robert P. Kirk, our squadron commander; and there were young girls, mothers carrying crying infants in their arms, and old women, their faces wrinkled, their skin hanging loosely. One old woman stood at the side of the road, her hands outstretched. Like Budlong, she reached out at the soldiers near her, but whereas his hands had darted eagerly, hers moved through the air with a gentle, swinging motion, touching a man only now and then, as a woman would fondle a piece of silk. She looked as if she were dreaming and couldn't believe her dream, and she had as beatific a smile on her worn, brown face as I have ever seen.

Most of the men and women who came toward us were in rags. After a few minutes, those of them that lived nearby ran home to change into the clothes they had been saving for the day of liberation. Before it was dark, they were back again, the girls in bright cotton dresses, the men in white or blue trousers and shirts. The young men were exuberant. They wanted, even before food—which they obviously needed badly—guns, so that they could join in the fight against the Japs. Most of them spoke English, but haltingly. A twenty-one-year-old lad named Guillermo Peñaranda asked us, "Where is our president?" We were glad to be able to tell him that President Sergio Osmeña was with General MacArthur and would be in Tacloban in a day or two. Restituta Jarohohon, a pretty twenty-year-old girl with her first child in her arms, shook hands with everyone and said, "We are very glad to meet you." The Filipinos told us that the Japanese had fled into the hills beyond Tacloban. Despite the artillery and mortar fire from the beach behind us, and the mosquitoes that swarmed into our fox-holes, we slept peacefully that night.

In the morning, we went on north toward Tacloban. On the outskirts, we ran into some opposition. Two hundred Japs were well entrenched on a low hill on the southeast side. It took us three hours to clean them out with artillery and mortar fire. While we were stalled, the Filipinos once again came to us before we could get to them. A long-legged, loosely put-together figure who looked as if he had been drawn by Thomas Benton came running up the road to Colonel Walter E. Finnegan, our regimental commander, and said that he was Governor Bernardo Torres. He wore lavender pants, a yellow shirt, and a broad yellow hat. He told us that he had been the Governor of Leyte Province before the Japs came to Tacloban, in May, 1942, and that the Japs had kept him on as Governor until they had become dissatisfied with him in that job. Then they had appointed him Director of Agriculture for the Philippines and put him in charge of food production for the Visayan island group, of which Leyte is one. Torres seemed more than eager to tell us what he could about the Japs—where they were and what they had done to the civilians of the town. He said that the hated Kempeitai, the Jap military police, had had a large force in Tacloban and had maltreated the natives.

The case of Torres is a queer one and a good example of the ticklish question: when is a collaborationist not a collaborationist? Torres was so eager to tell everything he knew that he was suspect. Three days later, when Colonel Ruperto Kangleon, the guerrilla chief on Leyte, was made military governor of the island, one of his first actions was to have Torres put in jail, together with about two hundred other suspected collaborationists. Kangleon had for nearly three years led an armed revolt in the hills, and his forces had killed thirty-eight hundred Japanese soldiers since February. This was a case of a bitter, fighting opponent of the Japs showing his contempt for a man who had stayed behind and tried to compromise. Yet there may well be something to be said for Torres, and if there is, it will be said at the trial that he and others like him will get before the Philippine and American authorities. Townspeople whose loyalty to the Americans cannot be doubted thought highly of Torres and trusted him. He got for them what little food the Japs did not steal and maintained as amicable relations as possible with an entrenched enemy through the difficult months. He was no Pétain, like the Japanese puppet Governor Pastor Salazar, but he was not a Tito, like Kangleon, either.

While we were talking to Torres in front of the command post, we could hear shots in the center of the town. From the windows of the houses, Jap sharpshooters were trying to pick off the Americans in the streets. Before the war, Tacloban was a town of eighteen thousand. It had a movie theatre, an ice plant, an athletic field, several restaurants, and a sizable business district near the wharves. The Japs had occupied practically all the business buildings and the best dwellings, and when several other correspondents and I reached the town, the remains of their paraphernalia of war were scattered everywhere.

We correspondents walked into town behind the troops and were directed to the two-story house of Mayor Vicente Quintero, a small, bespectacled man, who was looking very happy. He set up some Jap beer for us and also brought out a bottle of whiskey he said he had been saving for the great day. His home had beautiful, polished floors of narra and molave, Philippine hardwoods. Quintero has been Mayor for twelve years. "We are very glad to see you," he said. "It has been a long time. Things have been very hard under the Japanese." Until three months before, he said, most families had managed to get enough rice and *camotes*, or yams. Since then, the Japanese had pressed more and more Filipinos into the labor battalions, and there had been few left to work the fields. The Japanese had needed the additional forced labor for a series of airstrips they were feverishly building on the island. Children as young as ten, as well as old men and women, had been conscripted, Quintero told us. As we left his house, toward evening, we encountered fifty Formosans, used by the Japs as laborers, who had been taken prisoner by our forces and were being brought through town to division headquarters. They looked scared and frazzled as they stumbled by, their thin arms upraised.

That night I slept, along with many of the cavalrymen, on the floor of the Leyte Intermediate School for Girls. In the morning I walked to the market place, where there was to be a meeting of the citizens at ten o'clock. There I met young Bob Price, the son of Tacloban's most celebrated citizen, Walter Price, an American. The elder Price went to the Philippines as an infantry captain in the Spanish-American War and stayed there when the war was over, married a Filipino, and raised a family of seventeen. Price was the founder and owner of the Leyte Transportation Company, and probably the wealthiest man on the island, and he and his family lived in a luxurious concrete house that has six bathrooms. He is now a prisoner of the Japanese in Manila. Bob and his brother Joe, who were beaten and imprisoned three times—once for seventy-seven days, on a charge of working with the guerrillas—were allowed to remain in Tacloban. They both look more like Filipinos than Americans.

The ten-o'clock meeting was the principal event of the liberation of Tacloban. One purpose of the gathering was to welcome the American troops and another was to recruit native labor to work for the Philippine Civil Affairs Unit, an organization set up in Australia a year ago to control civilian affairs on the Islands when we got there. The meeting was opened by Caesar Sotto, a former Davao assemblyman and Labor Commissioner of Leyte Province, who had been forced by the Japs to recruit the workers for the airstrips. Sotto was dressed in an immaculate white suit. He mounted a platform that had been set up in the center of the market place and, in a brief speech in Visayan, introduced Saturino Gonzales, a member of the Provincial Board, who spoke in English. "The Americans have arrived to redeem us from slavery," Gonzales said. "We had to obey the Japanese to save our necks, but there was never any doubt, as you know, what our feelings were beneath. I ask you to consider now what the policies of the American government were like before the Japanese came and how they are to be compared to the Japanese administration. You will now understand the famous democratic ways of the United States."

Sotto spoke again, and a man next to me in the crowd explained that he was comparing the food policies of the Japanese and Americans as an argument to round up labor volunteers. As Sotto waved a K-ration container to emphasize his point, the crowd roared, in English, "Long live the Americans! Lovely Americans!" Mr. Sotto went on to say that ten thousand tons of rice would be brought in shortly by the Americans and that

President Osmeña was already on Leyte. The rice and their president being the two things the Filipinos most wanted, this statement brought forth further cries of "Lovely Americans!"

The next speaker was Captain Abner Pickering, one of the American Civil Affairs officers. Pickering has been in the Philippines off and on for twenty-five years and before the war was in business in Manila. "My friends," he said, in English, after the applause died down, "when I landed in Leyte the day before yesterday, it was the first time in three years that I had been in the Philippines. The Japanese will never come back to Tacloban. It took us several years to get organized, to get the ships, to get the bases for us to return, but now we're here to stay. The Philippines are yours. Your Commonwealth Government will be set up under your own president, President Osmeña. We are going to see that you get food and clothing. We want you to be patient. We need labor. You will get paid for the work you do in Philippine currency and with it you will be able to buy the rice and the other products we will bring. But, by God, you'll do it as free men!" It is doubtful whether most of the audience understood everything Captain Pickering said. Whether they did or not, the important fact to them was that here, on the platform in front of them, an American was talking; that was enough. When he finished, the applause lasted several minutes.

Vicente Delacruz, ex-Governor of Leyte Province and the last speaker, touched upon more spiritual matters. "We all need to be rebaptized in our churches," he said. "The first sin was committed by Adam and Eve. The second sin was committed by Germany and Japan. When the Japanese were here, our months were talking for them but our hearts were one-hundred-percent American. For the Americans we will work not three, not four days a week but three hundred and sixty-five days a year, and we will work for nothing." Captain Pickering waved a hand in protest, but the gesture was ignored. "Lovely Americans!" the crowd shouted. "We will work, we will work!"

★   ★   ★   ★   ★

The battle to free the Philippines was not without the cost of thousands of American and Filipino lives as fighting enveloped Leyte and Luzon. Over 15,000 Americans were killed or wounded in the taking of Leyte alone. In Luzon, the Japanese went on a killing spree as they fought tenaciously to hold onto Manila. Tens of thousands of civilians were killed and the city destroyed. General Tomoyuki Yamashita, who commanded Japanese forces in the Philippines, would be tried and executed after the war for war crimes committed during this time.

Inchon

MATTHEW BUNKER RIDGWAY

Adversity reveals the genius of a general; good fortune conceals it.
—Horace, *Satires*, 25 B.C.

Those who have not taken part in war can hardly imagine its terrors or know the comradeship that can only be forged by dangers shared with friends. For the young of every generation, war seems like a huge adventure. When you hear the stories from a veteran, however, their experiences bring with them caution and warning. My best friend's father had served in Korea as an automatic rifleman. He told us what it was like to be huddled in a foxhole, far out in front of the American line as a listening post. They heard in the pitch-black darkness as North Korean soldiers moved inexorably past them. Opening fire or calling for help would only mean certain death once their position was discovered. They spent the night in that hole praying for the light of day, praying they might be spared.

The Korean War came as a surprise to the western powers on June 25, 1950. In the predawn hours of June 25, 1950 North Korea struck across the 38th parallel with a thunderous artillery barrage and 135,000 troops. Advised and equipped by the Soviets with 150 T-34s and huge reserves of manpower, their surprise attack was a devastating success. At least two-thirds of the Korean Army, a paper force of 38,000, were off duty at the time, leaving the country open to attack. North Korea attacked at such key locations as Kaesong, Chunchon, Uijongbu, and Ongjin. Within days the outnumbered and outgunned South Korean forces were in full retreat. Seoul was captured by the North Koreans on the afternoon of June 28, but the North Koreans had not accomplished their goal of a quick surrender by the Rhee government and the disintegration of the South Korean Army.

By August the South Korean forces and the U.S. Eighth Army, which had arrived to help South Korea resist the Communist invasion, were driven into a small area in the southeast corner of the Korean peninsula around the city of Pusan. The situation was dire; Seoul had fallen to the North Koreans weeks earlier. By September only the area around Pusan remained in U.N. control. Yet in the face of defeat General MacArthur saw a path to victory. Famous for his maxim of "hit 'em where they ain't," he planned an amphibious invasion of the port town of Inchon on the western shore of the Korean peninsula. Striking there would cut off the North Korean armies from supply and allow a rapid advance to recapture Seoul.

General Matthew B. Ridgway, who would become Commander in Chief of the Far East Command in April of 1951, discussed the brilliance of MacArthur's planning in his history of the Korean War, published in 1967. He takes us into the planning of strategy at the highest levels and sheds light on one of MacArthur's greatest achievements.

★ ★ ★ ★ ★

The Inchon landing, Operation Chromite, the daring 5000-to-1 shot that restored the initiative to our forces in Korea and kept them from being pushed into the sea, was a typical MacArthur operation, from inception to execution. Almost before the rest of us fully comprehended that our nation was at war, MacArthur had begun to plan the amphibious enveloping movement, so characteristic of all his Pacific strategy, that would hit the enemy where he least looked for a blow, would sever his supply lines, and trap him between anvil and hammer. While others thought of a way to withdraw our forces safely, MacArthur planned for victory.

He did not, at first, have many on his side. I know that I was not alone in doubting the feasibility of his plan as it was outlined to the Joint Chiefs of Staff. There were some who were not reconciled until the success of the move was beyond denying. But General MacArthur was not merely a military genius. He was a brilliant advocate who could argue his points with so much persuasiveness that men determined to stand up against him were won to enthusiastic support.

Even while our bloodied and outnumbered forces were withdrawing into the Pusan perimeter, and while MacArthur was urging that more and more manpower and supplies be given him, there were sober and reasoned voices at home that warned against committing too much of our diminished military strength to an action that might prove only the opening skirmish in a war that would soon extend to Europe and quickly engage the whole world. We had other positions far more vital and more defensible than Korea to protect in other theaters and we had almost no force to spare as it was. In the Far East we had our major field command, the Eighth Army, an occupation force that had had practically no assigned responsibility for Korea. To accomplish its mission of occupation and internal security, it was dispersed throughout Japan and had access to few training areas where its units might keep themselves combat-ready. Indeed, training of these troops for combat-readiness had long since been reduced to second priority.

Despite MacArthur's warning that the danger in the Far East was real he had seen his command steadily whittled down. Every one of the Eighth Army's four infantry divisions (including one called the 1st Cavalry Division) was below its authorized makeshift strength of 12,500, a figure itself dangerously below the full wartime complement of 18,900. Every division was short 1500 rifles and all its 90-mm. antitank guns, missing three infantry battalions out of nine, lacking one firing battery out of every three in the divisional artillery, and all regimental tank companies. Only the 1st Cavalry Division had retained its organic medium tank battalion. There were no corps headquarters and no vital corps units such as medium and heavy artillery, engineer and communications troops.

The naval and air forces had been shortchanged too, the naval forces being below strength in combat ships, in amphibious craft of every type and in minesweepers and minesweeping equipment. The Air Force at the start had no jet fighters at all and too few combat and troop-carrying planes while its visual and photographic reconnaissance, as has already been noted, was severely handicapped by lack of trained personnel.

But it was not just in the Far East that our military might was threadbare. At home we had the skeletonized 3rd Division, sliced to its bare bones by the economizers, plus the 82nd Airborne Division, making up our entire General Reserve.

This was the state in which demobilization had left us. More than that, it had put us into a position where we had nowhere to reach for trained manpower but into the reserve, the just-discharged veterans of World War II, most of them newly settled into the good jobs and homes they had dreamed of through years of combat, and all of them understandably dismayed at having to go back, after having once made their contribution of toil, blood, and sweat, and make it all over again under the worst possible circumstances. The administration was reluctant to reactivate these men too. Yet where else was it to find what it needed? To draft many thousands of youngsters and make them combat-ready would take a year. And the battle was so urgent now that troops had to be dispatched by air. Nothing would do but to put the ex-soldiers back into boots.

It was into this atmosphere that MacArthur's hurried requests for larger and larger commitments were flung. He had first asked for authority to commit a Regimental Combat Team, then had estimated two full-strength divisions were needed. On July 7, he asked for four to four and a half full-strength divisions supported by an Airborne Regimental Combat Team and an armored group of four medium tank battalions. Two days later, he radioed the Joint Chiefs of Staff that he needed without delay an additional "field army of at least four divisions with all component services." He was, understandably, impatient with his superiors in the Pentagon and they, also understandably, were hesitant to commit all our current military muscle, and more that we had not yet developed, to a theater we had not selected, and perhaps a very secondary one at that.

There was doubt too whether the Far East requests for ordnance were not far out of line, and fear that we might be expending matériel already on hand and wasting our military substance beyond our ability to replace it in less than one to two years. It was not entirely clear, either, that Mr. Truman's policies—his urgent desire to do everything possible to avoid provoking a third world war in our lamentable state of unreadiness—were completely understood in Tokyo. It was decided therefore that the President's special representative, Averell Harriman, should travel to Tokyo to consult with General MacArthur. General Larry Norstad and I were ordered to go with him.

When we left Washington, there was a strong feeling in the Pentagon—a feeling that I shared—against granting MacArthur's request for the 3rd Division. It was tragically understrength, completely unready for combat, and its removal would reduce the General Reserve to a single major unit, the 82nd Airborne Division. As for dispatching the 82nd, or defusing it for the sake of supplying MacArthur with the airborne Regimental Combat Team he was requesting, I was prepared to dig my heels in against that. But I reckoned, as all of us did, without MacArthur's persuasiveness, his self-confidence, his eloquence, or his consummate skill in presenting a daring military plan.

The conference, which took place in Tokyo from August 6 to 8, was a personal triumph for MacArthur. Only Mr. Harriman, Generals Norstad and Almond, and I were with MacArthur when he, in a two-and-a-half-hour presentation, outlined his master plan for Korea and his needs for fulfilling it. When he had finished he had won us all over to his views. I know that after this brilliant exposition, and after I had studied the plans for Operation Chromite, the Inchon landing, my own doubts were largely dissolved. On the return flight, Mr. Harriman, General Norstad, and I agreed that we were prepared to support MacArthur's requests when we got home, for the alternatives seemed dangerous in the extreme.

MacArthur had argued the need primarily for speedy victory in South Korea before the winter set in and scored a victory of its own. Non-battle casualties in a bitter Korean winter, he had urged, might exceed the expected battle casualties of a short campaign. By mid-November, he warned us, the snow and bitter winds would be upon us. Meanwhile, he was losing a thousand men a day and replacements were not even holding his forces even. Delay in achieving victory would also increase the danger of open intervention by Chinese and Soviet forces, he argued. But to achieve the destruction of enemy forces in South Korea, the offensive would have to be launched September 25—with adequate forces so that the operation would have every chance of success. Otherwise, with the enemy dug into his positions, and his armies reinforced, we faced the prospect of a far more difficult and costly operation at a time less favorable to us.

This summation, of course, does not do justice to the painstakingly detailed and persuasive arguments our Far East Commander presented.

Throughout this conference and the hour I had spent beside General MacArthur at the luncheon table the preceding day, his recognition of authority superior to him, of his channels of command, and of his sphere of responsibility was clear and unmistakable, and his loyalty to constituted authority was manifest.

I was so impressed in this respect that, at the first opportunity following this conference, when I was alone with Mr. Harriman and General Norstad, I said so in substantially the same language. They both stated their agreement.

Mr. Harriman added a conclusion of his own, that "political and personal considerations should be put to one side and our Government deal with General MacArthur on the lofty level of the great national asset which he is."

We all went home ready to argue for the prompt fulfillment of MacArthur's request, for the immediate release to him of the 3rd Division (its bones fleshed out to some extent by the inclusion of the 65th Infantry Regiment from Puerto Rico, plus a battalion from the 33rd Infantry Regiment then in Panama).

My notes of that Tokyo Conference, notes of which no copy was ever made and which are still in my possession, indicate that the talk was far-ranging and frank, covering not only the immediate situation in Korea but many of the Commander's private plans for meeting contingencies that fortunately never arose. He was especially ardent about Formosa. Were the Red Chinese so foolish as to launch an assault on that island he would, he promised, hasten down there, assume command, and "deliver such a crushing defeat it would be one of the decisive battles of the world—a disaster so great it would rock Asia, and perhaps turn back Communism." As for the possibility that the Red Chinese might commit themselves to such folly, he was doubtful. But, he said, "I pray nightly that they will—would get down on my knees." Whether this vision of himself as the swordsman who would slay the Communist dragon was what prompted his eventual reckless drive to the borders of Manchuria no one of course can now divine. But I suspect that it did add luster to his dream of victory.

At that time, however, I was particularly impressed, as I have said earlier, with MacArthur's recognition of authority superior to his own. His presentation did not reveal the slightest lack of loyalty to authority. Not a single portent then appeared of that clash of wills, bordering closely on insubordination, that would lead to this gallant old soldier's abrupt dismissal. He was confident, optimistic, proud, eloquent, and utterly without fear—yet he was completely a soldier, seemingly ready to implement, without cavil or complaint, whatever decisions his superiors communicated to him.

As for the Inchon, the brilliance of this plan, the logic of its conception, and the extreme care with which the finest detail had been dealt with persuaded me quickly to support it. But this was not my decision to make; and before the operation could be approved there were doubting Thomases on the JCS who had to be won over.

The doubts of the plan's success were well-founded, for a combination of perfect timing, perfect luck, precise coordination, complete surprise, and extreme gallantry were all needed to spell victory here. It would have been difficult to find, on the entire tortuous Korean coastline, a spot more difficult to assault. Inchon's natural defenses rendered it nearly immune to hostile approach by sea. The thirty-foot tides, receding, left a tight and twisting channel through mile-wide mudflats that seemed ideally fashioned to ground our LSTs and turn them into artillery targets. What seemed to me an impregnable small island dominated the channel. And the channel itself, the only approach to the port, had surely been mined, as the island was most certainly fortified. In addition, the operation was timed for the typhoon season and there was at least an even chance that a howling storm might scatter our amphibious forces and lay them all open to destruction.

It is no wonder then that the Thomases continued to doubt. Veterans like Rear Admiral James H. Doyle, and Major General Oliver P. Smith, both experienced in the amphibious operations of World War II, failed to warm up to the idea. A number of alternate plans were put forward, including a landing at Wonsan on the east coast or, well to the south of Inchon, at Kumsan, where the pressure might be more quickly felt by the enemy on the Pusan front. But MacArthur would have none of these, although he was later to be grateful that his staff had prepared a detailed plan for the Wonsan landing. Only Inchon would do, for only a landing at Inchon offered the opportunity for the climactic stroke needed if the enemy was to be destroyed before winter—a slashing of the enemy's main artery of supply and communications and an opportunity for a junction with the forces breaking out of the Pusan perimeter, to crush the enemy's forces in between.

To examine into the feasibility of this plan, which had so far been presented only in concept, the JCS, in the middle of August, sent Admiral Forrest P. Sherman, Chief of Naval Operations, and General J. Lawton Collins, Army Chief of Staff, to meet with MacArthur and his staff in Tokyo. All key officers were present at the meeting, including Admiral Doyle and General Smith. General MacArthur outdid himself, not only in presenting the arguments in favor of Operation Chromite (in addition to the military advantages, success at Inchon would, he pointed out, enable the South Koreans to harvest their rice crop and would provide the valuable psychological lift of liberating the new nation's capital city) but especially in conveying his own supreme confidence in early victory. Admiral Doyle, near the end of the conference, volunteered the remark that the operation was at least "not impossible." But Admiral C. Turner Joy found his own misgivings erased. Even Admiral Sherman, the most skeptical of all, was, according to Joy, "almost persuaded." It took the Commander in Chief another day, and a long private discussion with Sherman, to complete the persuasion. "I wish," said Sherman after his private session with MacArthur, "I had that man's confidence."

Confidence, of course, was not quite enough. Now the concurrence of the administration, the permission to strip our General Reserve bare and risk all on one daring throw of the dice, had to be won. All the pros and cons were solemnly weighed: There would be but two hours of high tide on September 15 (the date selected for the landing) before the landing craft would be left powerless on the mud; the 1st Provisional

Marine Brigade would have to be withdrawn from the desperate Pusan beachhead to fill out the 1st Marine Division; there was a shortage of shipping; the envelopment would be so deep and so far to the north that it might not provide early relief to the southern front; a typhoon might be in the making—but *surprise*, the indispensable element in every operation of this sort, was almost certain. The North Koreans would never expect the Americans to lend themselves to such an "impossible and insane" undertaking. (It is ironical that MacArthur would himself, before the year was out, discount the chances of the Chinese commander's committing sizable forces across the Yalu—because "no commander in his right senses" would do that.)

Louis Johnson, Secretary of Defense, quickly approved the MacArthur plan. Operation Chromite, the 5000-to-1 gamble, was cleared for execution. Even while the beleaguered GIs in the Pusan perimeter were staving off disaster by a hairsbreadth every hour, the Theater Commander began to make ready the move that would completely rout the enemy, and assure our hold on Korea. It was a maneuver not unlike James Wolfe's assault on Quebec in 1759, an attack at the point where the enemy "knew" no attack could possibly come.

The first step in Operation Chromite was to scout the harbor islands, which commanded the straitened channel. A young Navy lieutenant, Eugene Clark, was put ashore near Inchon on the night of September 1 and worked two weeks, largely under cover of darkness, to locate gun emplacements and to measure the height of the seawall. So successful were his efforts that he actually turned on a light in a lighthouse to guide the first assault ships into Inchon harbor before dawn on September 15.

The action opened at dawn with a heavy bombardment by American destroyers, whose skippers gallantly steamed up the channel under the very muzzles of enemy cannons, and by British and American cruisers. The first task was to neutralize Wolmi-do, the little island that sat right athwart the channel, with all channel traffic within point-blank range of its guns. The island however was not nearly so strongly fortified as had been feared and its guns were quickly silenced by the naval bombardment. Marine Corsair planes strafed the island beaches and at half-past six the 3rd Battalion of the 5th Marines stormed ashore, scattering the dazed defenders and securing the island within forty-five minutes. Artillery was positioned on the island then to support the assault upon the seawall. In places the Marines used ladders to scale the wall, which stood four feet above the prows of the LSTs. Elsewhere the LSTs simply rammed holes in the wall, or Marines opened holes with dynamite, through which the assault troops poured. They had only too little daylight to work in. By dark the advance elements of the 1st Marine Division were securely dug in on their beachhead ready to repel counterattacks. But so complete and so devastating had been the surprise and so sudden the victory, that the counterattack never came. The next day, after a sharp tank battle, Kimpo Airfield, Seoul's airport, had been secured, and a day later the 7th Infantry Division landed unopposed at Inchon and sped inland to sever the main escape routes of the NKPA still fighting along the Naktong.

The battle to retake Seoul, however, was bitter. Although, as he had reported, MacArthur had the city safe "in friendly hands" by the twenty-fifth, the Marines still fought from house to house, from barricade to barricade, against enemy machine guns, antitank cannon, and sniper fire until the twenty-eighth, when the last North Korean was flushed out of his flaming refuge and smoke rose from every quarter.

For boldness in concept, for competence in professional planning, and for courage, dash, and skill in execution, this operation ranks high in military annals. Like every great military victory, the Inchon triumph brought sudden new problems—problems that had not been sufficiently reckoned with ahead of time. Before a major operation of this sort, it is customary to assemble all key commanders and staff officers and "war-game" the action on a map. Each commander is then called upon to outline his plan for meeting every possible situation, from complete failure to stunning victory. This time, there had been insufficient planning for the stunning victory, if indeed there had been any planning at all. The United Nations Command paid dearly for this failure. Because of it, large numbers of the North Korean People's Army escaped to fight again—either as organized units in the north or in large-scale guerilla actions behind our lines in the south.

Washington too had been hesitant in laying out a detailed course of action for exploitation of a victory, deferring decisions pending the resolution of some of the major mysteries—what would the Chinese reaction to the victory be? How would Russia respond?

It was generally assumed by most of the staff planners, and by General Walker himself, that the X Corps, then under direct control of Tokyo, would, when firmly established ashore, pass to the control of Eighth Army so that it could be moved and supplied more efficiently. But MacArthur insisted on keeping the X Corps under his own control, and the feeling that the Eighth Army was being slighted again in favor of MacArthur's "pets" grew stronger still. While there was never any open expression of jealousy or unwillingness to cooperate, there was no mistaking the fact that the atmosphere of mutual trust so necessary to smooth cooperation was lacking.

A more subtle result of the Inchon triumph was the development of an almost superstitious regard for General MacArthur's infallibility. Even his superiors, it seemed, began to doubt if they should question *any* of MacArthur's decisions and as a result he was deprived of the advantage of forthright and informed criticism, such as every commander should have—particularly when he is trying to "run a war" from 700 miles away. A good many military leaders have recognized that it takes a special kind of moral courage (rarer I think than physical courage) to stand up to your military superior and tell him you think his plan is wrong. That is the time, as General George C. Marshall used to say, when you "lay your commission on the line." But every military leader, from the lowest to the highest, owes it to the men whose lives are at his disposal to speak out clearly when he feels that a serious mistake is about to be made.

Some few small voices were raised against MacArthur's new decision—a plan for an amphibious landing at Wonsan, on the east coast, another end-run in the Inchon style and in the MacArthur tradition. Yet no one vigorously protested, even though some of the drawbacks to the plan were obvious and overriding. But this maneuver was the apparent reason why MacArthur wanted the X Corps to remain under GHQ direction. This made sense of a sort, although the plan itself had very serious flaws.

To accomplish the Wonsan landing, it was necessary to outload most of the X Corps at Inchon and Pusan (the 1st Marine Division pulling out though Inchon and the 7th Division traveling overland by rail and road to Pusan) taxing the rail lines and the inadequate facilities of these two ports, at a most critical time and severely interrupting the flow of supplies which the Eighth Army soon would sorely miss. (With the withdrawal clogging roads and rails, even artillery ammunition had to be brought to Seoul by air.)

Whatever the arguments in favor of another Inchon-type assault on Wonsan, they did not outweigh the importance of closing the trap quickly on the fleeing North Koreans. There was a good highway and a rail line—bombed and battered, it is true—overland from Seoul to Wonsan, through one of the relatively level stretches of the peninsula. The forces put ashore at Inchon could have moved with reasonable swiftness up this road, north and east to Wonsan, to link up with forces driving straight up the east coast. This would then have closed the gate on the rapidly fleeing enemy and have left him no time to regroup and refresh his forces.

Serious planning for exploiting the Inchon victory, however, did not begin until September 26, two days before fighting ceased in the streets of Seoul. At that time MacArthur asked for a plan to "destroy North Korean forces in another amphibious envelopment—coordinated with overland pursuit." Two plans were put forward. In one, the Eighth Army would drive north and northwest toward Pyongyang, the enemy capital, while an amphibious assault would seize the capital port, Chinampo, on the Yellow Sea. In the other plan, the Eighth Army would strike north and northeast along the Seoul-Wonsan corridor, while Wonsan would be the object of a similar amphibious assault. General Walker, assuming the X Corps would be under his command, favored sending that force immediately overland to Wonsan. But this was not to be.

There was some talk, too, of cutting across the peninsula at the waist or narrow point, to put the UN forces astride the country from Pyongyang to Wonsan. This, in theory, seemed practical enough. But a quick study of the terrain—the indescribably rugged and narrow passes, the countless twists and turns and tunnels in the rail lines (which our own airmen had worked over unceasingly)—would have given a logistics expert nightmares. If there was any good argument in favor of keeping the X Corps under the direct command of GHQ it was the extreme difficulty of trying to feed its stomachs and its guns and its gasoline engines, with all supply matters under the control of a commander on the other side of a steep and almost trackless mountain range.

No one denied the need for a port like Wonsan through which the huge tonnages of food, ammunition, and gasoline could be carried to feed the combat armies who would be operating to the west and north. The real question was simply, should Wonsan be approached overland or by sea? General MacArthur decided in favor of the assault by sea. The naval authorities on the spot and the division commanders involved all opposed the amphibious envelopment but none strongly raised his voice, simply because at that time no one was questioning the judgment or prescience of the man who had just worked a military miracle. Had he suggested that one battalion walk on water to reach the port, there might have been someone ready to give it a try.

The plan for crossing the 38th parallel to destroy all the hostile forces on the peninsula had of course required prior approval from Washington, for the implications of such a crossing were manifold. Red China had been threatening by radio almost daily that it would come into the war if North Korea were invaded; and there was some feeling that the

Soviet Union might also feel called upon to step in once the symbolic deadline had been crossed. It was clear enough, however, that if the NKPA were not destroyed quickly and if it were allowed to crawl back into a sanctuary and licks its wounds, another invasion might soon follow. So after some deliberation the Truman administration approved a JCS recommendation that MacArthur be authorized to operate in North Korea. There was one condition attached to this authority, and consciousness of this condition may just possibly have influenced MacArthur in his otherwise inexplicable refusal ultimately to admit that the Chinese had entered the war in force. For his authority to conduct operations north of the border, radioed to him on September 27, was contingent upon the proviso that "there has been no entry into North Korea by major Soviet or Chinese Communist Forces, no announcement of intended entry, nor a threat to counter our operations militarily in Korea." Beyond that, Secretary of Defense Marshall told MacArthur: "We want you to feel unhampered tactically and strategically to proceed north of the 38th parallel."

Complete victory seemed now in view—a golden apple that would handsomely symbolize the crowning effort of a brilliant military career. Once in reach of this prize, MacArthur would not allow himself to be delayed or admonished. Instead he plunged northward in pursuit of a vanishing enemy, and changed his plans from week to week to accelerate the advance, without regard for dark hints of possible disaster.

★ ★ ★ ★ ★

Seoul was recaptured as North Korean forces, cut off from supply, staggered back toward the 38th parallel. The Chinese intervened in the fighting on October 25, 1950 with 270,000 men, forcing the U.N. forces out of North Korea. MacArthur was recalled by President Truman on April 11, 1951. General Ridgway would lead U.N. forces until a ceasefire agreement was reached on July 27, 1953 that reestablished North and South Korea in the proximity of the 38th parallel.

A Reporter's Journal from Hell: The Ia Drang Valley

JOE GALLOWAY

> We few, we happy few, we band of brothers;
> For he to-day that sheds his blood with me
> Shall be my brother.
>> —Shakespeare, *Henry V*, Act IV, Scene 3

The Ia Drang Valley is located in the central highlands of southern Vietnam near the Cambodian border. It was there in November of 1965 the first major battle occurred between the newly-arrived U.S. Army and the communist People's Army of Vietnam. Ho Chi Minh and the leaders of North Vietnam sent three regular army regiments into the south to escalate the war against the southern Republic of Vietnam and their American allies. Infiltrating southern Vietnam from the Ho Chi Minh trail through Laos and Cambodia, the North Vietnamese put the Special Forces camp at Plei Mei under siege and were engaged by units of the American First Air Cavalry division for the first time. The objective for the North Vietnamese generals was to draw the Americans and their helicopters into battle, to study their tactics, and find a way to overcome them.

    The Air Cavalry was a concept authorized by President Kennedy along with the U.S. Special Forces (Green Berets) as a means of reorganizing the army to fight brushfire wars on the world's frontiers against Communism. The use of helicopters would allow rapid movement of large numbers of men and materiel over impassable terrain directly into action, creating a truly three-dimensional battlefield for the enemy. It was a kind of warfare never seen before. The combination of rapid mobility, artillery, and air support would enable the army to isolate and destroy enemy units.

215

The American objective was clear — to find the enemy and destroy him. As the North Vietnamese retreated from their siege of Plei Mei, the Americans captured documents and maps that identified Ia Drang Valley as a staging area for units moving through Cambodia. The assignment to search the valley fell to Lieutenant Colonel Hal Moore, a West Point graduate who had seen action in Korea as a company commander, and the 450 men of the 1st Battalion, 7th Cavalry of the First Air Cavalry Division. A day before the mission, Hal Moore and Sgt. Major Basil Plumley visited Man Yang pass along Highway 19 between An Khe and Pleiku. Eleven years earlier, France's elite Mobile 100 had been ambushed there by Viet Minh guerrillas and virtually annihilated. It was a reminder not to underestimate their new adversary.

On November 14, the 1st Battalion and B Company, 2nd Battalion, 7th Cavalry were air-lifted to the foot of a mountain named Chu Pong into a jungle clearing named LZ X-Ray. Without knowing it, they had deployed within a short distance of three enemy regiments of North Vietnamese and a battalion of Viet Cong. Within thirty minutes of landing the Americans found themselves surrounded and under attack by thousands of enemy soldiers. If the North Vietnamese could deny the Americans reinforcement and supply from their landing field they would be overrun and annihilated. Thus began a three-day engagement in a desperate battle of defense against a tough, well-led, and disciplined enemy on his home territory.

Joseph Galloway was a young reporter working for UPI in 1965. Following his leads about the 1st Cavalry's mission to X-Ray he managed to hitch a ride to the battlefield on the evening of November 14. He would be the only reporter to cover the events of the next three days, a battle in which he would put down his camera and pick up a rifle to defend his life and the lives of the men at his side. He recounted his experiences at the Ia Drang in a revised journal in 2002 entitled *A Reporter's Journal from Hell.*

★   ★   ★   ★   ★

It had been a bloody, furious battle all afternoon at XRay. Hal Moore and his men clung desperately to a football-sized clearing at the foot of the Chu Pong Massif, a high mountain mass than ran into Cambodia, five miles distant. Moore's battalion had suffered dozens of men killed and scores wounded. Among the dead: a tall, rangy captain named Tom Metsker, a graduate of The Citadel Class of '71 and Moore's S-2 or battalion intelligence officer. He had been wounded in the shoulder in the opening minutes of the battle and, later, had been sent to a helicopter for medical evacuation. Already aboard the chopper, Tom noticed a stretcher party bringing a much more seriously wounded officer, Capt. Ray LeFebvre, to the crowded helicopter. Tom got off to give his place to Ray, and as he stood in the open door a sniper shot him in the back. He fell into the chopper and was dead when it reached Pleiku/Camp Holloway. I mention this because 33 years later I would marry Tom Metsker's daughter, Karen, and today I am helping raise Tom's three grandchildren.

I was aboard a Huey helicopter piloted by Maj. Bruce Crandall. His call sign was Ancient Serpent 6—and friends sometimes referred to him as Old Snakeshit. This was his last flight of a long, dangerous day. He had had one helicopter shot full of holes and was working on his second bird. It was loaded with crates of ammo and grenades and five-gallon clear plastic bladders of water. I sat on a crate of grenades, peering out into the darkness. As we drew near the landing zone I could see blinking lights moving in a stream down the slopes of the mountain. For a moment I thought I was seeing muzzle flashes, but Matt Dillon shouted that they were tiny lamps that the enemy soldiers had to light their way in difficult terrain. A lot more enemy were on their way to the fight!

The two choppers roared in to land in the tall elephant grass. We jumped off, turned and began throwing ammo boxes and water bladders out. Emptied, both choppers lifted off as we lay prone in the tall grass. The darkness was almost total. Artillery rounds sailed over and exploded in the distance all around us. A voice came out of that darkness: Follow me and I'll take you to the command post . . . and watch where you step! There are bodies all over the place and they are all ours. In a couple minutes I was getting a short briefing from Lt. Col. Moore who welcomed me with a firm handshake. He told me we were surrounded by the enemy; there had been hard fighting all afternoon and more was coming soon. Then he turned to talk to Dillon, heard about those lights on the mountain and quickly ordered him to help the artillery liaison guy bring fire down on them to make their journey to war even more treacherous. I sat with my back against a small tree close by, rifle across my lap, waiting for what was to come. I felt good. I now had a front row seat at a major battle, something I had been looking to find these last eight months. It was Sunday, November 14, 1965.

That feeling of euphoria lasted until just after first light the next morning. Lt. Col. Moore had a platoon cut off and surrounded by enemy. They had been out there all afternoon and night and much of his energy and planning was devoted to getting them back into the perimeter. He had been planning another assault in that direction when all hell broke loose. An enemy battalion launched an all-out assault on the southeast side of the perimeter, a thin line of shallow foxholes dug in the tall grass by the 100 men of Charlie Company, 1st Battalion. A storm of small arms and machine gun fire and B40 rocket grenades swept over Charlie Company and straight through the command post which was no more than 50 yards behind them. A hail of bullets cracked and snapped all around us. I was flat on my belly, wishing I had spent the night digging a hole in that rock-hard ground. Wishing I could get even lower. About then I felt a thump in my ribs and carefully turned my head to see what it was. What it was was a size 12 combat boot on the foot of Sgt. Maj. Basil L. Plumley, a bear of a man who hailed from West Virginia. He was a veteran's veteran. Had fought in World War II where he made all four combat parachute jumps of the 82nd Airborne Division—Sicily, Salerno, Normandy and Remagen, the Bridge Too Far. One combat jump in Korea with the 187th Regimental Combat Team. He was now working on his third war, his third award of the Combat Infantryman's Badge—an honor the Army accorded to no more than 270 individuals in total. A very impressive dude, he was and is. The sergeant major bent at the waist and shouted over the incredible din of battle— "You can't take no pictures laying down there on the ground, Sonny." I thought to myself he's right. I also thought fleetingly that we might all die here in this place—and if I am going to die I would just as soon take mine standing up beside a man like this. Like a fool, I got up. I followed the sergeant major over to the makeshift aid station where Doc Carrera and Sgt. Tommie Keeton were tending the wounded. Plumley hollered at them: Gentlemen, prepare to defend yourselves! As he pulled out his .45 pistol and jacked a round into the chamber.

Over on the perimeter the enemy had overrun two of Capt. Bob Edwards' three rifle platoons. The captain himself was slumped in his foxhole bleeding from a bad wound. Within the space of two hours Charlie Company, which began the day with a strength of about 100 men, would lose 42 men killed and 20 wounded.

During this fighting two events occurred which are burned into my memory. First, I was over near the clearing shooting a few pictures when I caught movement out of the corner of my eye. A tall, lanky GI jumped out of one of the mortar pits about 30 yards away and ran, zig-zagging under fire, across that corner of the clearing. He jumped under the bush I was crouching behind and shouted: Joe. Joe Galloway! Don't you know me man? I'm Vince Cantu from Refugio! In the middle of the worst day of the worst battle of the Vietnam War a guy who graduated with me from Refugio High School, Class of '59, was grabbing and hugging me. "You got to get down, Joe. There are guys dying all around us. This is dangerous shit." Vince and I talked a little bit. He told me his term of service would be up in two weeks, if he survived this day and the next and the next. "I'll be home in Refugio for Christmas," he said. I asked him to go by and say hello to my mom and dad—but not to get too explicit with the details of where and under what circumstances we had met. Vince made it out, made it home, and in my late mother's photo albums is a snapshot of Vince and his young daughter sitting in their living room. Vince is a supervisor at the Houston Metro bus service, thinking about retiring soon and starting up a new version of a rock band he had when we were teen-agers down home. The Rockin' Dominoes. We are still best friends.

The second event came after I had moved back to the command post, located behind a huge termite mound, a key terrain feature in this part of the Highlands. These things were big as a small car, hard as concrete and provided good cover for both us and the enemy. I had just leaned back when suddenly I could hear Moore shouting loudly: "Charlie, call that SOB off of us. CALL HIM OFF!" I turned to my left and could see two F-100 Supersabre jets, one behind the other, headed straight for us. The first had just released two cans of napalm. The second was about to the do the same. Lt. Charlie Hastings, the Air Force forward observer, was screaming into his mike: Pull up! Pull up! The second plane pulled up. That left the two cans of napalm loblollying end over end toward us. Gregg Dillon buried his face in my shoulder. Later he would tell me he had heard if napalm was coming in you should protect your eyes. The two cans went right over our heads and impacted no more than 20 yards from us, the jellied gasoline spreading out and flaming up going away from us. That 20 yards saved our lives, but through the blazing fire I could see two men, two Americans, dancing in that fire. I jumped to my feet. So did medic Tommy Burlile. Burlile was shot in the head by a sniper before he could reach the scene. I charged on in and someone was yelling, "Get this man's feet!" I reached down and grabbed the ankles of a horribly burned soldier. They crumbled and the skin and flesh, now cooked, rubbed off. I could feel his bare ankle bones in the palms of my hands. We carried him to the aid station. Later I would learn that his name was Jimmy D. Nakayama of Rigby, Idaho. His wife Trudie had given birth to their first child, a daughter she named Nikki, on November 7. Jimmy died in an Army hospital two days later, on November 17. For a lot of years I looked for Jimmy's wife and daughter. Last month, after the movie *We Were Soldiers* was released I received a letter from Jimmy's widow. Last week a letter came from his daughter Nikki, now 36 years old and the mother of two young sons. No single day has passed since that long-ago November day that I have not thought about Jimmy Nakayama, the young woman who loved him, and the daughter who would never know a father's love.

You cannot always remain a witness, above and removed from the story you are covering. There are some events which demand your participation. The battle of Landing Zone XRay was one such event in my life. I will not here recount every event of that battle which continued until the afternoon of November 16—and was then followed by an even more horrific battle called Landing Zone Albany which virtually destroyed a sister battalion, the 2nd Battalion 7th Cavalry. At LZ XRay 80 men died and 124 were wounded, many of them terribly. At LZ Albany 155 Americans were killed and another 121 wounded, most of them in the space of six hours time. Four days—234 Americans killed. Perhaps as many as 2,000 North Vietnamese soldiers of the 33rd, 320th and 66th Regiments also died there, by our hand.

It was a watershed event in the American war in Vietnam. At that point 1,100 Americans had died in Vietnam. Before the war ended a total of 58,200 made the supreme sacrifice for our country.

I left XRay the way I had arrived, aboard a Huey helicopter flown by Bruce Crandall, Ancient Serpent 6. But none of us who survived left there the same man he was when he arrived. We had been drenched in blood and horror. I had heard the command "Fix Bayonets!" and seen men use those bayonets on other men. I had carried both the wounded and dead, hauled ammo and water, and, yes, on occasion I put down my cameras and picked up my rifle and used it.

When it was done I flew back to Camp Holloway, hitched a ride to the MACV compound and got on that creaky military phone system and called UPI Saigon. Bureau chief Bryce Miller answered and I fed him my notebooks, names and hometowns, and told him an envelope of film was on the way. When I was done he said: "Have you heard about Dickie Chappelle?" I said no; what? Dickie was a good friend. She had given me some good advice about what we were doing: "The first rule for a war correspondent is you must LIVE to get out and tell the story." I had somehow, against all odds, just done that. Miller then said: "Dickie was killed a few days ago on a Marine operation near Chu Lai. Someone stepped on a booby-trapped mortar shell and she bled to death." I put down the phone and walked outside and sat down on the wooden steps of the Officers Club, put my face in my hands and wept for my old friend, and all my new friends who had died in these terrible November days. The UPI boss, Ernie Hoberecht, wrote me a letter of congratulations on my reporting of the battle and raised my salary from $135 a week to $150 a week. Unheard of. I told my mother about that raise and her response was: "Joe, that's blood money." I thought that perhaps she was right, but it sure wasn't much money for so much blood. The war would drag on for ten long years and many old and new friends would die before it ended.

I soldiered on for UPI until the fall of 1966 and left, swearing I would never return to Vietnam. UPI sent me back in 1971, 1973 and again in 1975 for the end of it. Since the end of the war I have gone back four more times doing research on the book, helping make an ABC documentary ("They Were Young and Brave," Day One, aired January 1994 and again in the summer of 1994), and one recent trip with my best friend, Lt. Gen. (ret) Hal Moore to walk the old French battlefield at Dienbienphu. On the 1993 documentary trip Hal Moore and I and half a dozen other American veterans of the battle went back to XRay and Albany in company with half a dozen North Vietnamese generals and colonels who had fought against us there. Together we walked those old battlefields and agreed that those events of November, 1965, had been pivotal in all our lives. We have broken bread with them in their homes in Hanoi. It's hard to explain to someone who hasn't lived it, but in a strange sort of way we are blood brothers. There is no hatred; only a shared relief that at least some of us survived to carry the memories of those who died, and bear witness to the horror of this war and all wars.

★   ★   ★   ★   ★

The U.S. Army had two things the French Mobile 100 did not: artillery and air support. Col. Hal Moore would make effective use of both to defend landing zone X-Ray, along with the courage and loyalty of the men under his command. The fighting in Ia Drang Valley in 1965, however, would determine the future of the war in Vietnam. The thirty-four day campaign in the Ia Drang cost the 7th Cavalry 305 killed in action versus an estimated 3,500 enemy dead. The North Vietnamese generals looked at the twelve to-one casualty ratio and decided it was a war of attrition they could win over the years. The American people would lose heart, as the French before them, when their casualties mounted and the war would continue.

Secretary of Defense McNamara visited Ambassador Lodge and General Westmoreland in Saigon, who asked for massive reinforcements soon after the battle at X-Ray. He then met with General Harry Kinnard and Col. Moore, who warned him that the North Vietnamese were well disciplined and prepared to fight a long war. He would write a secret memo to President Johnson outlining the choices for the future—a diplomatic compromise and withdrawal from Vietnam, or the massive escalation of American forces as requested by General Westmoreland. He warned that there was no guarantee of success, and a likelihood of a stalemate by 1967 with much higher stakes. In December, President Johnson would approve the escalation of ground forces committed to the struggle in South Vietnam. His rules of engagement, however, forbade missions into Cambodia and Laos, ensuring the enemy a safe haven.

Col. Moore would serve a further six months in Vietnam commanding the third brigade of the 1st Air Cavalry. He would retire from the Army in 1977 with the rank of Lt. General. Joseph Galloway would serve sixteen months in Vietnam working for UPI and return three more times before the fall of South Vietnam in 1975. He would later cover the 1991 Gulf War on assignment from General H. Norman Schwarzkopf, with the 24 Infantry Division (mechanized) in western Iraq. He is now a senior writer for U.S. News. In 1990 both Moore and Galloway would meet Vietnamese Senior General Vo Nguyen Giap on a documentary trip to Vietnam. In 1993 they would revisit the X-Ray battlefield accompanied by former officers of the North Vietnamese Army who had opposed them, including Lt. General Nguyen Huu An, who commanded PVAN forces at the battle in 1965.

If I Die in a Combat Zone

TIM O'BRIEN

It doesn't take a hero to order men into battle. It takes a hero to
be one of those men who goes into battle.
                            —Gen. H. Norman Schwarzkopf

Tim O'Brien did not want to be a soldier. In 1968 he graduated with a
degree in political science from Macalester College and a draft notice calling him for military service. O'Brien considered Vietnam an unjust war,
yet he would not shame his family and friends by refusing to go. His edu-
cation, he reasoned, would surely be put to good use in the army behind a
typewriter. Within a year, however, Tim had traded the peaceful farmlands
of his small-town Minnesota home for the minefields of Son My district
of South Vietnam, serving as a radio operator in an infantry platoon.

O'Brien's tour of duty lasted from 1969–1970. Upon returning
home, he went on to graduate school at Harvard. As with all men who lived
through war, Tim tried to make sense of what he had been through. In a
style evocative of writers such as Hemingway, Whitman, and Crane, he
wrote a memoir of his tour of duty entitled *If I Die in a Combat Zone, Box Me
Up and Send Me Home.* The *New York Times* declared his work, "a personal
document of aching clarity . . . a beautiful, painful book." His writing stands
as a voice for the men who are citizen soldiers, called by their country in
times of need to pick up a rifle and take their place in the front lines. Along
with his memoir, and two later works of thinly-veiled fiction: *The Things
They Carried* (nominated for a Pulitzer Prize), and *In the Lake of the Woods*, his
works remain some of the best writing about the Vietnam war. In the chapter "Wise Endurance" O'Brien contemplates the meaning of courage.

★   ★   ★   ★   ★

Captain Johansen watched the soldiers raise their bottles of beer to their mouths, drinking to the end of the day, another sunrise and finally another red line at the edge of the sky where the sun was disappearing. Johansen was separated from his soldiers by a deadfall canyon of character and temperament. They were there and he was here. He was quite alone, resting against his poncho and pack, his face at rest, his eyes relaxed against the coming of dark. He had no companions. He was about a week away from leaving command of Alpha Company, and a fine eight-hour job was ready for him in the rear.

Captain Johansen had watched the men for an hour. They had dug foxholes, shallow slices out of the hard clay; then they'd squirted mosquito repellent over themselves, spread their sleeping gear near their holes, and now they were drinking beer. The soldiers were happy. No enemy, no blood for over a week, nothing but night, then day.

"I'd rather be brave," he suddenly said to me. "I'd rather be brave than almost anything. How does that strike you?"

"It's nothing to laugh at, sir."

"What about yourself?"

"Sometimes I look back at those days around My Lai, sir, and I wish I would have acted better, more bravely. I did my best, though. But I'll think about it."

A month before, on a blistering day, Johansen had charged a Viet Cong soldier. He'd killed him at chest-to-chest range, more or less, first throwing a grenade, then running flat out across a paddy, up to the Viet Cong's ditch, then shooting him to death. With the steady, blood-headed intensity of Sir Lancelot, Captain Johansen was brave. It was strange that he thought about it at all.

But I thought about it. Arizona, the dead kid I always remember first, died on the same day that Johansen's Viet Cong died. Arizona bulled out across a flat piece of land, just like the captain, and I only remember his long limp body in the grass. It's the charge, the light brigade with only one man, that is the first thing to think about when thinking about courage. People who do it are remembered as brave, win or lose. They are heroes forever. It seems like courage, the charge.

When I was a kid in eight grade and not at all concerned about being brave except as a way to seem to other people, usually a pretty girl, I was pushed out of line while we were waiting for the school bus. The kid who did it was big. He had a flat-top haircut and freckles and a grin that meant he could massacre me if it came to that. Being big with words, I told him to go piss on the principal's desk, and he started shoving, the stiff-finger-on-the-chest technique, backing me up with little spurts of the wrist. Honor was clearly at stake. I was in the right and he was the kind of human being I detest most, a perfect bully. So I shoved back, and there was a little scuffle, then the bus came. Before I got off—rather, just as I was stepping out in front of my house—he hollered out for everyone to hear that there would be a fight the next Monday. It was Friday. I had three nights to ponder the prospect. There was no doubt about the outcome. There wasn't a chance. On Monday I went to the bus, being inconspicuous but not too inconspicuous; getting beat was a trifle better than hiding. I hoped he'd forgotten. Finally he fought me, and we danced around on the ice in front of the bicycle rack. I bobbed like hell, and the enemy fell twice, not that I ever hit him, and by all accounts it ended in a draw.

But at a place east of My Lai, within smell of the South China Sea, bullets seemed aimed straight at you.

Isolated, a stretch of meadow, the sound going into the air, through the air, right at your head, you writhe like a man suddenly waking in the middle of a heart transplant, the old heart out, the new one poised somewhere unseen in the enemy's hands. The pain, even with the ether or sodium chloride, explodes in the empty cavity, and the terror is in waiting for the cavity to be filled, for life to start pumping and throbbing again.

You whimper, low or screeching, and it doesn't start anywhere. The throat does the pleading for you, taking the heart's place, the soul gone. Numbness. Dumbness. No thoughts.

I was not at My Lai when the massacre occurred. I was in the paddies and sleeping in the clay, with Johansen and Arizona and Alpha Company, a year and more later. But if a man can squirm in a meadow, he can shoot children. Neither are examples of courage.

"You're a sensitive guy," Johansen said. "Go get me a beer from one of those soldiers, will you?" I fetched a beer and sat with the captain. "You don't have to carry the radio for me, you know. It's a good shot, the antenna sticking up. You've done a good job, don't get me wrong, I knew you'd do a good job first time I saw you. But it's easy to get shot walking with me. Officers are favorite targets. The radio antenna's a good target you know. VC knows damn well there's an officer around, so they shoot at it. And . . . well, you're a sensitive guy, like I said. Some guys are just numb to death."

"I'd just as soon go on," I said.

Johansen told me not to forget to call situation reports back to headquarters. He went off and checked the positions.

Courage is nothing to laugh at, not if it is proper courage and exercised by men who know what they do is proper. Proper courage is wise courage. It's acting wisely, acting wisely when fear would have a man act otherwise. It is the endurance of the soul in spite of fear—wisely. Plato, I recalled, wrote something like that. In the dialogue called *Laches*:

> Socrates: And now, Laches, do you try and tell me in like manner, What is that common quality which is called courage, and which includes all the various uses of the term when applied both to pleasure and pain, and in all the cases to which I was just referring?
> Laches: I should say that courage is a sort of endurance of the soul, if I am to speak of the universal nature which pervades them all.
> Socrates: But that is what we must do if we are to answer our own question. And yet I cannot say that every kind of endurance is, in my opinion, to be deemed courage. Hear my reason. I am sure, Laches, that you would consider courage to be a very noble quality.
> Laches: Most noble, certainly.
> Socrates: And you would say that a wise endurance is also good and noble?
> Laches: Very noble.
> Socrates: But what would you say of a foolish endurance? Is not that, on the other hand, to be regarded as evil and hurtful?
> Laches: True. . . .
> Socrates: Then, according to you, only the wise endurance is courage?
> Laches: It seems so.

What, then, under the dispassionate moon of Vietnam, in the birdless, insectless, silence—what, then, is wise endurance? Despising bullyism as I did, thinking the war wrong from the beginning—even in tenth grade, writing a term paper on a war I never believed I would have to fight—I had endured. I'd stayed on through basic training, watching the fat kid named Kline shivering in fear, thrusting my blade into the rubber tires at the bayonet range, scoring expert with the M-16. I'd endured through advanced infantry training, with the rest of the draftees. I'd planned to run away, to slip across the border in the dead of night. I'd planned for two months, drawing maps and researching at the Fort Lewis library, learning all the terrible details about plane fares to Sweden, muffling my voice over the telephone, making a lie to my parents to get them to send my passport and health record. I'd almost not endured.

But was the endurance, the final midnight walk over the tarred runway at Fort Lewis and up into the plane, was it wise? There is the phrase: courage of conviction. Doubtless, I thought, conviction can be right or wrong. But I had reasons to oppose the war in Vietnam. The reasons could be murmured like the Psalms on a cold-moon Vietnam night: Kill and fight only for certain causes; certain causes somehow involve self-evident truths; Hitler's blitzkrieg, the attack on Pearl Harbor, these were somehow self-evident grounds for using force, just as bullyism will, in the end, call for force; but the war in Vietnam drifted in and out of human lives, taking them or sparing them like a headless, berserk taxi hack, without evident cause, a war fought for uncertain reasons.

The conviction seemed right. And, if right, was my apparent courage in enduring merely a well-disguised cowardice? When my father wrote that at least his son was discovering how much he could take and still go on, was he ignoring his son's failure to utter a dramatic and certain and courageous no to the war? Was his son a fool? A sheep being stripped of wool that is his by right?

One day Alpha Company was strung out in a long line, walking from one village near Pinkville to another. Some boys were herding cows in a free-fire zone. They were not supposed to be there: legal targets for our machine guns and M-16's. We fired at them, cows and boys together, the whole company, or nearly all of it, like target practice at Fort Lewis. The boys escaped, but one cow stood its ground. Bullets struck its flanks, exploding globs of flesh, boring into its belly. The cow stood parallel to the soldiers, a wonderful profile. It looked away, in a single direction, and it did not move. I did not shoot, but I did endure, without protest, except to ask the man in front of me why he was shooting and smiling.

Alpha Company had a bad time near the My Lai's. Mines were the worst, every size and kind of mine. Toepoppers, Bouncing Betties, booby-trapped artillery and mortar rounds and hand grenades. Slocum, Smith, Easton, Dunn, Chip, Tom—all those soldiers walked on and on and on, enduring the terror, waiting, and the mines finally got them. Were they wise to keep walking? The alternative, looking back and listening to the radio and seeing Captain Johansen finish his rounds and return to his poncho, the alternative, I thought, was to sit on a single splotch of earth and silently wait for the war to end.

"Will you be glad to get to the rear, sir?"

"Sure," he said, grinning and with a shrug. "I'll miss the company. But I don't suppose I'll miss the war much."

"I don't know how you can be so dispassionate. God, I'd be hiding in my foxhole, a mile into the ground, just waiting for a chopper to take me out of here."

Captain Johansen rolled up in a poncho; he lay on his side and seemed to go to sleep.

Whatever it is, soldiering in a war is something that makes a fellow think about courage, makes a man wonder what it is and if he has it. Some say Ernest Hemingway was obsessed by the need to show bravery in battle. It started, they say, somewhere in World War I and ended when he passed his final test in Idaho. If the man was obsessed with the notion of courage, that was a fault. But, reading Hemingway's war journalism and his war stories, you get the sense that he was simply *concerned* about bravery, hence about cowardice, and that seems a virtue, a sublime and profound concern that few men have. For courage, according to Plato, is one of the four parts of virtue. It is there with temperance, justice, and wisdom, and all parts are necessary to make the sublime human being. In fact, Plato says, men without courage are men without temperance, justice, or wisdom, just as without wisdom men are not truly courageous. Men must *know* what they do is courageous, they must *know* it is right, and that kind of knowledge is wisdom and nothing else. Which is why I know few brave men. Either they are stupid and do not know what is right. Or they know what is right and cannot bring themselves to do it. Or they know what is right and do it, but do not feel and understand the fear that must be overcome. It takes a special man.

Courage is more than the charge.

More than dying or suffering the loss of a love in silence or being gallant.

It is temperament and, more, wisdom. Was the cow, standing immobile and passive, more courageous than the Vietnamese boys who ran like rabbits from Alpha Company's barrage? Hardly. Cows are very stupid.

Most soldiers in Alpha Company did not think about human courage. There were malingerers in Alpha Company. Men who cared little about bravery. "Shit, man, the trick of being in the Nam is gettin' *out* of the Nam. And I don't mean gettin' out in a plastic body bag. I mean gettin' out alive, so my girl can grab me so I'll know it." The malingerers manufactured some of the best, most persuasive ailments ever, some good enough to fool a skeptical high school nurse.

When we walked through the sultry villes and sluggish, sullen land called Pinkville, the mass of men in Alpha Company talked little about dying. To talk about it was bad luck, the ultimate self-fulfilling prophecy.

Death was taboo. The word for getting killed was "wasted." When you hit a Bouncing Betty and it blows you to bits, you get wasted. Fear was taboo. It could be mentioned, of course, but it had to be accompanied with a shrug and a grin and obvious resignation. All this took the meaning out of courage. We could not gaze straight at fear and dying, not, at least, while out in the field, and so there was no way to face the question.

"You don't talk about being a hero, with a star pinned on your shirt and feeling all puffed up." The soldier couldn't understand when I asked him about the day he ran from his foxhole, through enemy fire, to wrap useless cloth around a dying soldier's chest. "I reacted, I guess. I just did it."

"Did it seem the right thing to do?"

"No," Doc said. "Not right, not wrong either."

"Did you think you might be shot?"

"Yes. I guess I did. Maybe not. When someone hollers for the medic, if you're a medic you run toward the shout. That's it, I guess."

"But isn't there the feeling you might *die?*"

Doc had his legs crossed and was leaning over a can of C rations. He seemed intent on them. "No. I won't die over here." He laughed. "Maybe I'll never die. I just wondered why I didn't feel anything hit me. Something should have hit me, there was so much firing. I sort of ran over, waiting for a kind of blast or punch in the back. My back always feels most exposed."

Before the war, my favorite heroes had been make-believe men. Alan Ladd of *Shane*, Captain Vere, Humphrey Bogart as the proprietor of Café d'Americain, Frederic Henry. Especially Frederic Henry. Henry was able to leave war, being good and brave enough at it, for real love, and although he missed the men of war, he did not miss the fear and killing. And Henry, like all my heroes, was not obsessed by courage; he knew it was only one part of virtue, that love and justice were other parts.

To a man, my heroes before going to Vietnam were hard and realistic. To a man, they were removed from other men, able to climb above and gaze down at other men. Bogie in his office, looking down at roulette wheels and travelers. Vere, elevated; the *Star*, searching justice. Shane, loving the boy, detesting violence, looking down and saying goodbye aboard that stocky horse.

To a man, my heroes were wise. Perhaps Vere was an exception. But when he allowed Billy Budd to die, he was at least seeking justice, tormented by a need for wisdom, even omniscience. But certainly Shane and Bogart and Henry had learned much and knew much, having gone through their special agonies.

And each was courageous. Bogie. How could a man leave Ingrid Bergman, send her away, even for the most noble of causes? Shane, facing his villain. Vere, sending a stuttering, blond, purely innocent youth to the gallows. And especially Frederic Henry. Talking with his love, Catherine Barkley:

"You're brave."

"No," she said. "But I would like to be."

"I'm not," I said. "I know where I stand. I've been out long enough to know. I'm like a ball-player that bats two hundred and thirty and knows he's no better."

"What is a ball-player that bats two hundred and thirty? It's awfully impressive."

"It's not. It means a mediocre hitter in baseball."

"But still a hitter," she prodded me.

"I guess we're both conceited," I said. "But you are brave."

Henry, and the rest of my heroes, had been out long enough to know; experienced and wise. Batting two hundred and thirty? Realistic, able to speak the truth. Conceited? Never. And, most strikingly, each of the heroes *thought* about courage, *cared* about being brave, at least enough to talk about it and wonder to others about it.

But in Vietnam, out in the villages of My Lai and My Khe, where the question of courage is critical, no once except Captain Johansen seemed to care. Not the malingerers, certainly. Not Arizona, the kid who was shot in the chest in his private charge. Not the Doc. So, when the time in my life came to replace fictional heroes with real ones, the candidates were sparse, and it was to be the captain or no one.

Looking at him, only a shadow rolled in a poncho, lying on his side asleep, I wondered what it was about him that made him a real hero.

He was blond. Heroes somehow are blond in the ideal. He had driven racing automobiles as a civilian and had a red slab of scarred flesh as his prize. He had medals. One was for killing the Viet Cong, a Silver Star. He was like Vere, Bogie, Shane, and Frederic Henry, companionless among herds of other men, men lesser than he, but still sad and haunted that he was not perfect. At least, so it appeared. Perhaps other men, some of the troopers he led who were not so brave, died when he did not and should have, by a hero's standard.

Like my fictional prewar heroes, Captain Johansen's courage was a model. And just as I could never match Alan Ladd's prowess, nor Captain

Vere's intensity of conviction, nor Robert Jordan's resolution to confront his own certain death (in Jordan's place, I would have climbed back on my horse, bad leg and all, and galloped away till I bled to death in the saddle), I could not match my captain. Still, I found a living hero, and it was good to learn that human beings sometimes embody valor, that they do not always dissolve at the end of a book or movie reel.

I thought about courage off and on for the rest of my tour in Vietnam. When I compared subsequent company commanders to Johansen, it was clear that he alone cared enough about being brave to think about it and try to do it. Captain Smith admitted that he was a coward, using just that word. Captain Forsythe strutted and pretended, but he failed.

On the outside, things did not change much after Captain Johansen. We lost about the same number of men. We fought about the same number of battles, always small little skirmishes.

But losing him was like the Trojans losing Hector. He gave some amount of reason to fight. Certainly there were never any political reasons. The war, like Hector's own war, was silly and stupid. Troy was besieged for the sake of a pretty woman. And Helen, for God's sake, was a woman most of the grubby, warted Trojans could never have. Vietnam was under siege in pursuit of a pretty, tantalizing, promiscuous, particularly American brand of government and style. And most of Alpha Company would have preferred a likable whore to self-determination. So Captain Johansen helped to mitigate and melt the silliness, showing the grace and poise a man can have under the worst of circumstances, a wrong war. We clung to him.

Even forgetting the captain, looking at myself and the days I writhed insensible under bullets and the other days when I did okay, somehow shooting back or talking coherently into the radio or simply watching without embarrassment how the fighting went, some of the futility and stupidity disappeared. The idea is manliness, crudely idealized. You liken dead friends to the pure vision of the eternal dead soldier. You liken living friends to the mass of dusty troops who have swarmed the world forever. And you try to find a hero.

It is more difficult, however, to think of yourself in those ways. As the eternal Hector, dying gallantly. It is impossible. That's the problem. Knowing yourself, you can't make it real for yourself. It's said when you learn you're not much of a hero.

Grace under pressure, Hemingway would say. That is how you recognize a brave man. But somehow grace under pressure is insufficient. It's too easy to affect grace, and it's too hard to see through it. I remembered the taut-faced GI's who gracefully buckled, copping out so smoothly, with such poise, that no one ever knew. The malingerers were adept: "I know we're in a tight spot, sir. I wouldn't go back to the rear, you know me. But—" then a straight-faced, solid, eye-to-eye lie. Grace under pressure means you can confront things gracefully or squeeze out of them gracefully. But to make those two things equal with the easy word "grace" is wrong. Grace under pressure is not courage.

Or the other cliché: A coward dies a thousand deaths but a brave man only once. That seems wrong, too. Is a man once and for always a coward? Once and for always a hero?

It is more likely that men act cowardly and, at other times, act with courage, each in different measure, each with varying consistency. The men who do well on the average, perhaps with one moment of glory, those men are brave.

And those who are neither cowards nor heroes, those men sweating beads of pearly fear, failing and whimpering and trying again—the mass of men in Alpha Company—even they may be redeemable. The easy aphorisms hold no hope for the middle man, the man who wants to try but has already died more than once, squirming under the bullets, going through the act of death and coming through embarrassingly alive. The bullets stop. As in slow motion, physical things gleam. Noise dissolves. You tentatively peek up, wondering if it is the end. Then you look at the other men, reading your own caved-in belly deep in their eyes. The fright dies the same way novocaine wears off in the dentist's chair. You promise, almost moving your lips, to do better next time; that by itself is a kind of courage.

★ ★ ★ ★ ★

Tim O'Brien left Harvard to become a newspaper reporter and to write fiction. He now serves as a visiting professor and endowed chair at Southwest Texas State University where he teaches creative writing.

Crusade

RICK ATKINSON

In thy faint slumbers I by thee have watch'd
And heard thee murmur tales of iron wars . . . .
—Shakespeare, *Henry IV*

73 Easting is a map reference in the western desert of Iraq. It was at this desolate place of shifting sands the first major encounter between the U.S. 2nd Armored Cavalry and the elite Iraqi Republican Guard took place. On the night of February 23 and 24, in accordance with General Norman Schwarzkopf's plan for the ground assault called Operation Desert Sabre, VII Corps raced east from Saudi Arabia into Iraq in a maneuver later nicknamed the "Hail Mary." In the center of the advance were the men and tanks of the U.S. 3rd Armored Division and the 2nd Cavalry Regiment supported by the 1st Infantry Division. The corps had two goals: to cut off Iraqi retreat from Kuwait, and to destroy five Republican Guard divisions near the Iraq-Kuwait border that might attack the Arab and Marine Corps units moving into Kuwait to the south.

Reaching 70 Easting at 16:22, the 2nd Cavalry's Eagle Troop's 2nd Squadron knocked out a screen of eight Iraqi T-72 tanks. Beyond, they could see T-72s in prepared positions at 73 Easting. This was the Iraqi Brigade Assembly Area. Fearing the loss of surprise, Eagle Troop's Captain H. R. McMaster decided not to wait for the heavier units to come forward, pass through his lines and engage the Iraqis. McMaster ordered Eagle Troop to advance and engage the Iraqi tanks. The enemy vehicles were deployed in Soviet style defensive positions. The American forces advanced out of a sandstorm achieving surprise. Historian Rick Atkinson describes the battle from his book *Crusade*.

★   ★   ★   ★   ★

Riyadh

The Iraqi army, having demonstrated little aptitude for the simpler requisites of warfare, now faced the most difficult of military maneuvers: a withdrawal under fire. No tougher test of generalship could confront a commander than the exigency of conducting a coherent retreat. Even great battle captains, of which Iraq was singularly bereft, often found themselves overmatched by simultaneously trying to organize an effective rear guard capable of slowing enemy pursuit, evacuate the wounded and, if possible, the dead, and rally dispirited and humiliated soldiers, whose every step in retrograde was a reminder of defeat.

Rare was the army that could retire gracefully from the field. Perhaps the most celebrated retreat was that of Xenophon, the Athenian warrior, who after the battle of Cunaxa in 401 b.c.—not far from present-day Baghdad—led the Ten Thousand on a five-month *anabasis* (upcountry march) along the Tigris, fighting off Persian cavalry, hostile tribesmen, and winter hardships to reach safety on the Black Sea. A successful withdrawal usually required not only pluck by the vanquished, but also miscalculation or ineptitude by the victor. Some 340,000 British and Allied soldiers escaped from Dunkirk in 1940 after Hitler halted his Fourth Army tanks at the Aa Canal, foolishly relying on Hermann Goering's boast that the Luftwaffe would destroy the trapped force. ("It is always good to let a broken army return home to show the civilian population what a beating they have had," the Führer later explained.)

Even orderly retreats often were costly. After the Allies breached the Gustav Line in May 1944, the Germans maintained reasonable discipline while pulling out of Italy but still sustained seventy thousand casualties. Six years later, when Chinese soldiers poured into North Korea from Manchuria, the U.S. Army's 2nd Division braved a murderous gauntlet during the withdrawal from Chongchon River at a cost of three thousand dead and wounded. During the same sad week, troops from X Corps and the 1st Marine Division endured an even worse ordeal while retreating from Chosin Reservoir in temperatures so bitterly cold that mortar tubes cracked and blood plasma froze solid.

When a commander failed to prevent retreat from becoming rout, the results could be even more horrific—witness the Prussians' loss of 140,000 men while being chased by Napoleon across half of Europe after Jena and Auerstädt in 1806; or Bonaparte's own headlong dash from Russia six years later; or the Union Army's flight from First Bull Run in 1861, when a tidy withdrawal became a stampede "miles long and a hundred yards wide" all the way back to Washington.

Clearly the Iraqi retreat was no latter-day *anabasis*. In some respects it was grimmer than Bull Run or Chongchon River, since neither Irvin McDowell in northern Virginia nor MacArthur's commanders in Korea faced an enemy who owned the skies as well as the land. Lacking cover but for the fickle veil provided by bad weather, the Iraqis were forced to flee across open country patrolled by hundreds of allied bombers.

On Tuesday afternoon the Army's Tiger Brigade, leading the 2nd Marine Division, had rolled over Mutlaa Ridge to capture the high ground and highway interchanges bordering Al Jahra at the west end of Kuwait Bay. (Although CENTCOM's script had called for this key terrain to be captured by the Egyptians, Walt Boomer brushed the plan aside with a curt "Bullshit. *We* are going to take that junction.") At least fifty Iraqis were killed in bloody fighting around the Al Jahra police station. Allied armor now blocked the only overland escape route from Kuwait City, completing the encirclement of the capital begun earlier in the day with air strikes on the Highway of Death.

The Iraqis were not without a withdrawal plan, of sorts. Unfortunately for Baghdad, the scheme was known to the Americans.

For months Iraq had practiced admirable "emissions control," EMCON, the art of minimizing radio and other electronic signals to prevent the enemy from eavesdropping or homing in on the radiating source. Allied intelligence had concluded that willful violators of Iraqi COMSEC, communications security, might be executed. But the adroit use of military radio networks is a highly perishable skill unless it is routinely practiced. If EMCON helped preserve Iraqi security, it also stripped the army of proficiency in orchestrating military maneuvers—a self-inflicted wound known in the intelligence world as "EMCON suicide."

A vast array of allied antennae—aboard satellites, aircraft, and on the ground—strained to intercept any stray Iraqi signal. As the air war took its toll on the enemy command and communications network, some units had "come up" with occasional radio transmissions. The Americans hotly debated whether it was better to eavesdrop on such broadcasts or electronically jam them. (Among the U.S. jamming systems operating in northern Saudi Arabia was the so-called Sandcrab, a 5000-watt contraption with an antenna larger than a football field.) In some cases only the cryptographic data at the beginning of the message were jammed, confusing the Iraqis and causing them to broadcast uncoded, "in the clear."

The Republican Guard, however, had remained silent since September 15, communicating primarily by secure land lines. Using intelligence gathered by the National Security Agency and other sources, CENTCOM assembled a blueprint of the Iraqi communications architecture in the Kuwaiti theater. A day before the ground attack, the intelligence chief Jack Leide had decided that of fourteen "nodes"—suspected headquarters or antennae farms—ten would be destroyed by air strikes or long-range artillery. Four others, all in the northern sectors controlled by Republican Guard divisions, were left intact in the hope that the enemy would resort to radio communications.

The strategy worked. Once the allied attack forced the Iraqis to begin moving, stationary land lines became an impediment. Late on February 25, for the first time in five months, the Republican Guard came up on the air with an FM radio broadcast from the Tawalkana commander, directing his subordinates to begin forming a defensive line against the allied onslaught. As the division struggled to mount its defense, a transmission from Basrah early on the 26th—either from the Republican Guard commander or his chief of staff—warned the Tawalkana that they were violating COMSEC. The Tawalkana commander angrily replied that with the American attack well under way he had little security left to protect.

This squabble, monitored by the National Security Agency and relayed to Riyadh, was followed six hours later by other intercepted messages. Another Republican Guard division—subsequently recognized as the Hammurabi—was informed by Guard headquarters in Basrah that heavy equipment transporters (HETs) had been dispatched to haul their T-72 tanks northward; heavy-duty tractors also had been sent to pull out the division's artillery. The Madinah Division, in turn, was instructed to burn unneeded equipment and move west by southwest into blocking positions.

This knowledge was most helpful to the allies. Leide carried the translated intercepts to Schwarzkopf in the war room, where, in combination with JSTARS radar images of enemy vehicles being repositioned, they gave a clear picture of enemy intentions. The Tawalkana commander, not without courage, was trying to cobble together a defensive line with three of his own brigades plus a pair plucked from other divisions. His command-and-control appeared so shaky, however, that he was trying to direct individual battalions rather than work through his brigade subordinates.

"The Tawalkana is the sacrificial lamb at this point," Leide's deputy, Colonel Chuck Thomas, told Schwarzkopf. "They're going to delay us as long as they can." The Madinah would form another screen line while the Hammurabi and any forces that had escaped from southern

Kuwait pulled back to the Basrah pocket, a strategy Iraqi commanders had used in the war against Iran.

The Defense Intelligence Agency now assessed twenty-six of forty-three Iraqi divisions in the Kuwaiti theater as "combat ineffective." More than thirty thousand prisoners had been captured. Iraqi tactical reserves west of the Wadi al Batin were collapsing under pressure from the British. Colin Powell, who before G-Day had estimated that the ground attack would take two weeks at most, now believed the end was in sight after three days. "Norm," the chairman told Schwarzkopf, "this is going so well that it won't take much longer."

Schwarzkopf still had one armored division that had not been committed to the fray, the 1st Cavalry. Waller and Steve Arnold had pressed without success to get the division released in order, as Arnold put it, "to reinforce success, to make the attack on the Republican Guard overwhelming." For two days the CINC resisted. "What the hell do I do if the Iraqis focus their counterattack on the Egyptians?" he asked. "What if we're running off to the north, having no trouble, while they're beating up on the Egyptians? If that happens, I've got a problem."

Now, however, the threat of counterattack had dissipated. The Egyptians had finally reached their objective—the Al Abraq military barracks in western Kuwait—and turned east toward Ali As Salem Air Base. John Tilelli, the 1st Cavalry commander, believed that Iraqi defenses were weak enough to permit an attack straight up the Wadi al Batin. Schwarzkopf again demurred, but agreed to let the division pull back from its feint up the wadi, swing west through the breach opened by the Big Red One, and race north to join VII Corp—a 200-mile trek. That would give Franks five divisions—including the British—and the cavalry regiment.

Franks again phoned Yeosock, who repeated Schwarzkopf's displeasure with VII Corp's pace. "Do you think I should talk to the CINC myself?" Franks asked. "Yeah," Yeosock agreed, "sounds like a good idea. Why don't you call him?"

At 4 p.m. on Tuesday, clutching a stubby grease pencil used to mark his rain-streaked map, Franks called the war room by satellite phone from his forward command post. Struggling to make himself heard over the wind and the boom of artillery fire, he explained to Schwarzkopf the disposition of his divisions. The 2nd Cavalry had already found the Tawalkana screen line; soon they would give way to Rhame's 1st Division. But Franks also worried about a bypassed brigade of enemy troops on his right flank. When he suggested sending some forces south to clean out the pockets—a proposal initially recommended by Yeosock—Schwarzkopf interjected, "Fred, for Christ's sake, don't turn south! Turn east. Go after 'em!'"

Franks quickly agreed. "We know where the enemy is," he told the CINC. "We think we have a seam down there and we're going to push the Big Red One through it. Tomorrow I'll have three divisions massed against the Republican Guard. I figure it will take us forty-eight hours or so, with those three divisions intact, to get through them. I don't think they see us coming. We're going to surprise them."

Schwarzkopf, perhaps reluctant to rattle the corps commander in the middle of a fight, made no mention to Franks of his anger. "Fine. Press the fight, Fred," he said. "Keep the pressure on." Schwarzkopf told Franks of the radio intercepts, quickly recounting the squabble between the Tawalkana commander and Republican Guard headquarters. HETs, the CINC added, apparently had been sent to extract the Hammurabi. Heavy fog was predicted for Wednesday morning, so a night attack seemed advisable. "You'll have good shooting tonight," the CINC said. "Don't let them break contact. Keep 'em on the run."

Franks signed off, his exhaustion temporarily masked by a fresh surge of adrenaline. At 5:30 he flew back to the corps headquarters and briefed his staff. "We're going to drive the corps hard for the next twenty-four to thirty-six hours, day and night, to overcome all resistance and to prevent the enemy from withdrawing," Franks warned. "We'll synchronize our fight, as we always have, but we'll have to crank up the heat. The way home is through the Republican Guard."

73 Easting, Iraq

The eight thousand soldiers of the 2nd Cavalry, leading VII Corps across Iraq much as the regiment once led Patton's Third Army across Europe, had been on the move since shortly after 6 a.m. Colonel Don Holder for the first time brought all three maneuver squadrons abreast. He carefully controlled their progress by means of north-south grid lines called eastings. (The 81 Easting was one kilometer east of the 80, and so on.) Franks had ordered the regiment forward to the 60 Easting, approximately twenty-five miles from the Kuwaiti border. Hesitant to embroil his cavalry in a slugging match before Rhame arrived with the 1st Division's three hundred tanks, the corps commander advised Holder to probe only with his scouts. Holder interpreted this order broadly; rather than expose the lightly armed scouts, he instead moved forward the entire regiment—including his 125 MIAIS. "We're all scouts," he told his staff.

That the Tawalkana lurked near the 70 Easting had been suspected since Monday afternoon. The suspicion was confirmed at 7:15 a.m. Tuesday when an OH-58 helicopter crew spotted an Iraqi T-72 tank, a sure sign of the Republican Guard. An hour later cavalrymen destroyed two enemy personnel carriers with TOW and mortar fire; a captured Iraqi captain, schooled at Fort Benning and fluent in English, provided further intelligence. Several other skirmishes erupted across the regimental front as the cavalry bumped into pickets deployed five to seven miles west of the main enemy line. An Iron Troop platoon routed five Bedouin with camels after noticing army boots beneath the men's robes and grenade launchers protruding from the animals' packs. "The regiment," Holder reported to Franks, "has found the security zone of the Tawalkana Division."

Franks ordered the cavalry to edge forward to the 70 Easting. The intensifying *shamal*, which was bedeviling other American units across southeastern Iraq and Kuwait, now grounded Holder's helicopters. Instead of being able to look at least ten miles deep, the regiment found visibility limited to the reach of their thermal sights. As the afternoon slipped by, Holder inched his squadrons forward past the 62 Easting, then 63, 64, 65.

Sitting in the rear of his command track, Holder turned to the regimental operations officer, Major Doug Lute. "If the enemy is getting out of Kuwait," he asked, "why die for it?" Franks had demanded caution; the cavalry had accomplished its mission by fixing the enemy's location. Artillery and Air Force bombers were ready to pounce. Rhame would soon arrive with the Big Red One. "We don't want to bloody ourselves if we don't have to," Holder added. "I'm not going to impale this regiment for the sake of body counts or glory."

By 4 p.m.—about the time Franks called Schwarzkopf to clarify his plan—the howling westerly wind had lessened slightly, although visibility with the naked eye was still less than half a mile. Flat and barren, the terrain in many places rippled just enough to hide enemy armor until the Americans had closed within a thousand yards or so—less than half the distance at which U.S. tank and Bradley gunners preferred to shoot.

The three cavalry troops on Holder's left flank—Ghost, Eagle, and Iron—each mustered approximately 140 soldiers mounting twelve Bradleys and nine M1A1S. By chance, all three were commanded by West Point classmates of Gerald Davie, whose unfortunate troop in the 7th Cavalry was fighting battalions from both the Tawalkana and his own 3rd Armored Division farther north. Eagle Troop, under Captain H. R. McMaster, Jr., had just passed the 67 Easting when machine gun fire poured from a cluster of buildings behind a sand berm. (The compound proved to be the headquarters for the enemy's armor training area, the Iraqi equivalent of the U.S. Army's National Training Center in California.) As several Bradleys returned the fire with their 25mm cannons, McMaster wheeled his nine MIAIS on line and ordered a simultaneous volley of tank rounds and TOW missiles. Cinderblock walls exploded, roofs collapsed, flames danced from the shattered buildings.

Taking the point with his tanks in a wedge and the Bradleys tucked behind to protect the flanks and rear, McMaster swung north past the burning outpost. At 4:18 p.m. the troop crested a low hill. "Contact!" his gunner yelled. "Tanks, direct front!" McMaster dropped down inside the hatch to peer through his own sights. At least eight T-72s lay behind shallow dirt fortifications in a "reverse slope" ambush, hoping to surprise the Americans as they came over the rise with their turrets silhouetted against the sky. "Fire, fire sabot!" McMaster ordered.

With a deep roar the round burst from the muzzle at one mile per second. The barrel jerked back in violent recoil and the Abrams's front wheels lifted three inches off the ground. The first enemy tank, seen as a small rectangle in the thermal sights, blew up as the round struck just above the turret ring. McMaster's loader slammed another shell into the breech. "Up!" he barked. Again flame licked from the muzzle and a second T-72 exploded, the turret ripping free of the hull in a fountain of orange fire. A pair of enemy sabot rounds burrowed harmlessly into the sand on either side of McMaster's Abrams. Ricocheting bullets struck sparks off the hull. McMaster's gunner fired for the third time; a third tank, only four hundred meters away, blew up.

Eagle Troop now creaked down the slope at twenty miles an hour. Game but overwhelmed, the Iraqi tankers fired wildly, then sat paralyzed while their automatic loaders—which required ten seconds between shots, an eternity in armored combat—slowly pushed home another round. (The tubes of reloading T-72s raised up slightly before dipping toward the ground, a sure sign that the enemy crew was momentarily helpless.) Iraqi commanders strained desperately to see through the smoke and haze. American intelligence had expected at least some of the enemy tanks to be outfitted with Belgian thermal sights. In this brigade of the Tawalkana, however, gunners possessed only ordinary telescopic lenses, a fatal disadvantage. Here the blind fought the sighted.

Within four minutes all of the T-72s and several BMPs in the first line of defense were in flames. Bradley gunners "scratched the backs" of the MIAIS, killing enemy infantrymen who hid or feigned death until the American tanks rolled past and then tried to shoot them in the rear grill with RPGs. Smoke boiled from the shattered Iraqi hulls, where the charred bodies of crewmen lay draped over their hatch rims. Ammunition cooked off in spectacular orange pinwheels. The stench of burning hair and flesh drifted across the desert.

A mile beyond the first line lay a second tier of seventeen T-72s parked across a three-mile front. McMaster, reminded on the radio by his executive officer that the 70 Easting was the regimental limit of advance, plunged ahead. "I can't stop," he replied. "We're still in contact. Tell them I'm sorry." Once again the Iraqis stood their ground and fought as the Americans charged forward; once again the enemy line disintegrated.

At 4:40 p.m. McMaster halted Eagle Troop on the 74 Easting, forming a defensive circle not unlike a wagon train. A hundred crackling fires cut through the afternoon gloom. Mortar crews set up their tubes and dumped shells—set to detonate twenty feet above the ground—on enemy infantrymen fleeing among the dunes to the east. Eagle would be credited with the destruction of twenty-eight tanks, sixteen personnel carriers, and thirty-nine trucks—with no American losses. The entire fight had lasted twenty-three minutes.

On Eagle's right flank Iron Troop paused at the 68 Easting as small arms fire poured from the same buildings McMaster had just passed on the north. The cinder-block compound again shuddered under a volley of American tank and cannon fire, this time from the south. Iron's scouts now spotted several vaguely rectangular shapes two miles down range. Edging forward, Captain Daniel B. Miller saw the unmistakable silhouette of Iraqi tanks. Positioned behind a network of L-shaped berms, the enemy turrets slowly swung toward the oncoming Americans. "Action front, action front," Miller warned. "Follow me." With two Bradley platoons positioned on each flank, Iron's tanks attacked in a flying wedge.

The enemy line quickly crumpled and collapsed. Miller pushed his scouts forward five hundred yards, just beyond the 70 Easting. Soon a second formation of enemy tanks—apparently counterattacking from the southeast—moved into range. Gunfire again erupted. One TOW appeared to skip across the hull of a T-72, hitting another in the turret. Iron Troop's 4th Platoon swung to the south and caught the enemy in a crossfire.

As the second Iraqi echelon dissolved, Iron took its only casualties of the fight. A 1st Platoon Bradley, commanded by Sergeant First Class Ron Mullinix and temporarily disarmed by an electrical malfunction, headed for the protection of an empty tank revetment. Mullinix spotted a small globe of fire streaking across the desert from the south: an errant TOW from Killer Troop, which had mistaken the Bradley for an Iraqi armored vehicle. The missile struck the Bradley turret, ricocheted, and ripped off the driver's hatch. Shrapnel spattered Mullinix in the legs and peppered the back of his driver, Private First Class Gregory Scott.

Fire swept through the Bradley, melting the radio and igniting the machine gun ammunition box. Coaxial rounds sprayed the turret. The gunner, Sergeant Kirk Alcorn, had been flung from his hatch by the blast. His face burned and eyelids seared shut, Alcorn crawled across the TOW launcher and leaped to the ground. Scott rolled screaming across the desert, his back and arms afire. Mullinix hobbled over to help beat out the flames and rip off the driver's burning flak jacket. The three wounded soldiers, all of whom would survive, were bundled into the rear of another Bradley to await a medic.

The third and final act in the Battle of 73 Easting unfolded to the north, where Ghost Troop anchored the regimental left flank. Unlike the relatively brief fights in the Eagle and Iron sectors this one lasted several hours.

On learning of Eagle's contact on his right, Captain Joseph F. Sartiano, Jr., had pushed his two Bradley platoons to the flanks and moved Ghost's eight tanks forward in the center. "Troop on line," he ordered. "Tanks lead." Having requested and received permission to move past the 70 Easting in order to see beyond a rise in the desert pan, Ghost crept forward on a three-mile front.

Sartiano's gunner, a twenty-year-old corporal from Arizona named Frank Wood, pressed his forehead against the vinyl headrest on his thermal sight. He could see a curious lump directly ahead, but it emitted no telltale heat signature. When Wood depressed the button that activated his laser range finder, crimson numerals flashed in the viewpiece: 587 meters. Switching to his day scope—a ten-power telescopic lens—Wood found the same amorphous mass through the veil of swirling sand. "Hey, sir, what's this?" he called. "Take a look." Sartiano, wearing goggles and a bandana knotted across his mouth and nose, dropped down from the open hatch and squinted into his own eyepiece on the right side of the tank.

At that moment Wood saw movement. Eight or nine soldiers swam into view, gathered near an armored personnel carrier. "Holy shit! Troops!" he yelled. "These guys don't have their hands up!" Wood fired a machine gun burst as the Iraqis scrambled toward the rear ramp of the BMP. Bodies jerked grotesquely when the bullets struck home. Men slumped to the ground, struggled to their knees, and pitched forward again. One slug caught an Iraqi in the back of the skull, blowing his head open. As Sartiano turned his attention to the rest of the troop, Wood destroyed the BMP with a tank round.

The Iraqi tanks and other vehicles, Sartiano realized, had been sitting still with their engines off, reducing their heat signature. Almost the entire troop had begun firing at the same time. For the first fifteen minutes the radio burst with excited chatter: "Engaged and destroyed one enemy tank!" "Engaging two vehicles." "Enemy tank destroyed."

As in the south, the Tawalkana had established a defensive line. Tanks and personnel carriers were parked behind sand mounds—"kill-me berms"—that obscured the Iraqis' vision, restricted the free play of their turrets, and offered little protection against TOWs or tank rounds. Rather than push through the line as Eagle had done, Ghost remained along the 73 Easting—firing, repositioning laterally, firing again.

Using tactics developed in countless gunnery sessions and exercises, the American crews methodically selected their targets, shooting those at closest range first before working deeper into the enemy ranks. Gunners on the flanks fired at targets "from the outside in"; gunners in the middle fired "from the inside out." Bradley sights were more powerful than those on the MIAI, and the turret—or doghouse—was a foot higher than the Abrams turret, giving the Bradley crew slightly better visibility and allowing them to use tracer rounds to pinpoint targets for the tankers.

The Tawalkana fought back, though ineffectually. Bullets pinged off the American tanks, and a few mortar rounds detonated overhead, shredding the duffel bags and water cans lashed to the Abrams and Bradley hulls. Sartiano spotted several beautiful blue bursts as Sagger missiles streaked harmlessly overhead.

A few minutes into the fight, Iraqi gunners found their mark for the first and only time. On Sartiano's left flank, where 1st Platoon was firing at enemy infantry and personnel carriers, a 73mm round from a BMP grazed the front slope of Ghost I–6. "What was that?" shouted the Bradley gunner, Sergeant Nels A. Moller. Those were his last words. A second round struck beneath the TOW launcher, killing Moller and wounding a soldier in the back before blowing through the rear ramp. The driver and Bradley commander leaped from the burning vehicle. Other cavalrymen pried at the jammed ramp with a crowbar before hoisting the wounded crewmen out through the cargo hatch on top. (Hours later, when Hawk Troop moved forward to relieve Ghost, the lead tank mistook I–6 for an enemy vehicle; a 120mm round destroyed what was left of the smoldering Bradley, where Moller's body still lay.)

The Tawalkana defensive line was no more. For the next three hours, however, enemy tanks, personnel carriers, and trucks poured into Ghost's kill sack. At 5:40 p.m. an Iraqi company counterattacked from the northeast. Bradleys from 1st Platoon destroyed four enemy vehicles with TOWs at twelve hundred meters, blunting the charge. Iraqi infantry scrambled from the rear of their personnel carriers only to be cut down with machine gun and cannon fire. Eleven more tanks and BMPs blew up as the Americans called in artillery strikes and lobbed more than two hundred mortar rounds at the enemy.

Sartiano, pleading for air support, shifted several tanks to reinforce 1st Platoon on the left. Together they shattered another company-sized counterattack from the northeast. The American gunners watched and waited in ambush, chain-smoking cigarettes between firefights. Shortly after 8 p.m. a third enemy force of sixteen vehicles appeared from the southeast. With Iraqi engines running hot and the weather improving, the enemy was now plainly visible to Sartiano's gunners at ranges of four thousand yards or more. Some were destroyed with long-range tank or TOW shots. A few ambitious Bradley gunners fired at targets beyond the 3700-meter TOW range, causing the missiles to "squelch" by snapping their control wires.

Most of the killing along the 73 Easting was the handiwork of direct fire, but not all. The 210th Field Artillery Brigade had fully expected to be left behind as the cavalry squadrons thundered across Iraq. Instead, the deliberate advance ordered by Franks and effected by Holder and other commanders permitted the guns to keep pace. Now the corps commander's determination to concentrate his combat power paid dividends. From 5:30 to 9 p.m. two thousand howitzer rounds and a dozen MLRS rockets dumped 130,000 bomblets in front of Ghost, Eagle, and Iron, terrorizing the enemy and ripping up Iraqi supply trains.

Adding to the mayhem was a procession of Air Force bombers. While an OA-10 spotter plane circled overhead to mark targets with white phosphorous rockets, F-16s and A-10s attacked with bombs and cannon fire. Sartiano would long believe the Air Force had abandoned him in his hour of need, but in fact ten Falcons and six Warthogs decimated Iraqi artillery and armored forces east of the front line. Several Apaches, airborne again as the *shamal* waned, destroyed an artillery battery with Hellfires and ripped up a convoy fleeing northeast on a two-lane highway near the Kuwaiti border.

At 10 p.m. the battlefield fell silent but for the crackle of flames and the periodic boom of burning ammunition. In four hours Holder's three cavalry troops had fired three hundred TOWs and tank rounds, plus seven thousand cannon and machine gun rounds. More than two hundred

Iraqi armored and wheeled vehicles were destroyed. Nearly all of one Tawalkana brigade and elements of the 12th Armored Division had been obliterated. Because troops on the regimental right had encountered no T-72s, Holder was able to assure Franks that the cavalry had found a gap in the enemy defenses to the south. Into that breach the corps commander could now steer the Big Red One, which began filtering through the 2nd Cavalry before midnight.

Other battles would be more destructive than 73 Easting. Other units would fight with the same proficiency demonstrated by Holder's dragoons. Yet in this first major engagement against the Republican Guard, the U.S. Army demonstrated in a few hours the consequences of twenty years' toil since Vietnam. Here could be seen, with almost flawless precision, the lethality of modern American weapons; the hegemony afforded by AirLand Battle doctrine, with its brutal ballet of armor, artillery, and air power; and, not least, the élan of the American soldier, who fought with a competence worthy of his forefathers on more celebrated battlefields in more celebrated wars.

Here the terrible truth of this war was wholly revealed: the enemy never had a chance.

★   ★   ★   ★   ★

American technology and firepower devastated the enemy force McMaster's unit charged, and destroyed the Iraqi tanks at 73 Easting at close range. Unlike previous engagements, the destruction of the first Iraqi tanks did not result in the wholesale surrender of Iraqi soldiers. The Iraqis stood their ground while their tanks and armored personnel carriers of the Tawakalna Division attempted to maneuver and fight. Eagle Troop destroyed more than 20 tanks and other armored vehicles, a number of trucks and bunkers, and took large numbers of prisoners with no losses to themselves. In 20 minutes, Eagle Troop had advanced in constant heavy contact with Iraqi armor from 67 Easting to 74 Easting. Their success was followed up by the 1st Infantry Division who carried on the attack to take Objective Norfolk the following morning and by the 3rd AD to the north who engaged and destroyed the remaining elements of the two Iraqi divisions.

Black Hawk Down

MARK BOWDEN

> There is many a boy here today who looks on war as all glory,
> but boys, it is all hell.
> —Gen. William Tecumseh Sherman

In 1991, Somalia was ravaged by a state of civil war between five rival factions. The conflict destroyed much of the agriculture of the region and the population faced starvation. The world community began sending food and humanitarian aid to ease the suffering. Warring factions seized most of the shipments and used them to feed their soldiers and trade for weapons. The United Nations began Operation Provide Relief in August of 1992 followed by the American-led Operation Restore Hope in December the same year to provide military protection for relief workers and supplies.

In March 1993, all the political factions of Somalia had signed an agreement to restore order to the country, including the commencement of disarmament. This led to violence in June when gunmen from General Mohammed Farrah Aidid's powerful faction ambushed and killed twenty-four Pakistani soldiers. The next day the U.N. Security Council passed a resolution calling for the arrest of those responsible for the attack. The American mission shifted from providing security for U.N. workers to locating and capturing General Aidid and his clan's leadership.

On October 3, 1993 the Americans received intelligence that Aidid's top advisors were meeting at a location in downtown Mogidishu. Task Force Ranger, a U.S. Special Operations force of Rangers, Delta Force, and helicopters from the 160th "Night Stalkers" Regiment were rallied for a daylight mission to capture them. The plan called for an airborne assault on the target building with an evacuation by a second ground force in a convoy of jeeps and trucks. Sgt. Matt Eversmann was a squad leader in the Rangers assigned to provide cover for the Delta Force operators as they assaulted the target building. Mark Bowden described the action in his book *Black Hawk Down* as the men prepared for the mission in the moments before liftoff. His writing captures the anticipation of young men, confident in their training and comrades, facing battle for the first time.

★   ★   ★   ★   ★

At liftoff, Matt Eversmann said a Hail Mary. He was curled into a seat between two helicopter crew chiefs, the knees of his long legs up to his shoulders. Before him, jammed on both sides of the Black Hawk helicopter, was his "chalk," twelve young men in flak vests over tan desert camouflage fatigues.

He knew their faces so well they were like brothers. The older guys on this crew, like Eversmann, a staff sergeant with five years in at age twenty-six, had lived and trained together for years. Some had come up together through basic training, jump school, and Ranger school. They had traveled the world, to Korea, Thailand, Central America . . . they knew each other better than most brothers did. They'd been drunk together, gotten into fights, slept on forest floors, jumped out of airplanes, climbed mountains, shot down foaming rivers with their hearts in their throats, baked and frozen and starved together, passed countless bored hours, teased one another endlessly about girlfriends or lack of same, driven out in the middle of the night from Fort Benning to retrieve each other from some diner or strip club out on Victory Drive after getting drunk and falling asleep or pissing off some barkeep. Through all those things, they had been training for a moment like this. It was the first time the lanky sergeant had been put in charge, and he was nervous about it.

Pray for us sinners, now, and at the hour of our death, amen.

It was midafternoon, October 3, 1993. Eversmann's Chalk Four was part of a force of U.S. Army Rangers and Delta Force operators who were about to drop in uninvited on a gathering of Habr Gidr clan leaders in the heart of Mogadishu, Somalia. This ragged clan, led by warlord Mohamed Farrah Aidid, had picked a fight with the United States of America, and it was, without a doubt, going down. Today's targets were two of Aidid's lieutenants. They would be arrested and imprisoned with a growing number of the belligerent clan's bosses on an island off the southern Somali coast city of Kismayo. Chalk Four's piece of this snatch-and-grab was simple. Each of the four Ranger chalks had a corner of the block around the target house. Eversmann's would rope down to the northwest corner and set up a blocking position. With Rangers on all four corners, no one would enter the zone where Delta was working, and no one would leave.

They had done this dozens of times without difficulty, in practice and on the task force's six previous missions. The pattern was clear in Eversmann's mind. He knew which way to move when he hit the ground, where his soldiers would be. Those out of the left side of the bird would assemble on the left side of the street. Those out of the right side would assemble right. Then they would peel off in both directions, with the medics and the youngest guys in the middle. Private First Class Todd Blackburn was the baby on Eversmann's bird, a kid fresh out of Florida high school who had not yet even been to Ranger school. He'd need watching. Sergeant Scott Galentine was older but also inexperienced here in Mog. He was a replacement, just in from Benning. The burden of responsibility for these young Rangers weighed heavily on Eversmann. This time out they were *his*.

As chalk leader, he was handed headphones when he took his front seat. They were bulky and had a mouthpiece and were connected by a long black cord to a plug on the ceiling. He took his helmet off and settled the phones over his ears.

One of the crew chiefs tapped his shoulder.

"Matt, be sure you remember to take those off before you leave," he said, pointing to the cord.

Then they had stewed on the hot tarmac for what seemed an hour, breathing the pungent diesel fumes and oozing sweat under their body armor and gear, fingering their weapons anxiously, every man figuring this mission would probably be scratched before they got off the ground. That's how it usually went. There were twenty false alarms for every real mission. Back when they'd arrived in Mog five weeks earlier, they were so flush with excitement that cheers went up from Black Hawk to Black Hawk every time they boarded the birds. Now spin-ups like this were routine and usually amounted to nothing.

Waiting for the code word for launch, which today was "Irene," they were a formidable sum of men and machines. There were four of the amazing AH-6 Little Birds, two-seat bubble-front attack helicopters that could fly just about anywhere. The Little Birds were loaded with rockets this time, a first. Two would make the initial sweep over the target and two more would help with rear security. There were four MH-6 Little Birds with benches mounted on both sides for delivering the spearhead of the assault force, Delta's C Squadron, one of three operational elements in the army's top secret commando unit. Following this strike force were eight of the elongated troop-carrying Black Hawks: two carrying Delta assaulters and their ground command, four for delivering the Rangers (Company B, 3rd Battalion of the army's 75th Infantry, the Ranger Regiment out of Fort Benning, Georgia), one carrying a crack CSAR (Combat Search and Rescue) team, and one to fly the two mission commanders—Lieutenant Colonel Tom Matthews, who was coordinating the pilots of the 160th SOAR (Special Operations Aviation Regiment out of Fort Campbell, Kentucky); and Delta Lieutenant Colonel Gary Harrell, who had responsibility for the men on the ground. The ground convoy, which was lined up and idling out by the front gate, consisted of nine wide-body Humvees and three five-ton trucks. The trucks would be used to haul the prisoners and assault forces out. The Humvees were filled with Rangers, Delta operators, and four members of SEAL (Sea, Air, Land) Team Six, part of the navy's special forces branch. Counting the three surveillance birds and the spy plane high overhead, there were nineteen aircraft, twelve vehicles, and about 160 men. It was an eager armada on a taut rope.

There were signs this one would go. The commander of Task Force Ranger, Major General William F. Garrison, had come out to see them off. He had never done that before. A tall, slender, gray-haired man in desert fatigues with half an unlit cigar jutting from the corner of his mouth, Garrison had walked from chopper to chopper and then stooped down by each Humvee.

"Be careful," he said in his Texas drawl.

Then he'd move on to the next man.

"Good luck."

Then the next.

"Be careful."

The swell of all those revving engines made the earth tremble and their pulses race. It was stirring to be part of it, the cocked fist of America's military might. Woe to whatever stood in their way. Bristling with grenades and ammo, gripping the steel of their automatic weapons, their hearts pounding under their flak vests, they waited with a heady mix of hope and dread. They ran through last-minute mental checklists, saying prayers, triple-checking weapons, rehearsing their precise tactical choreography, performing little rituals . . . whatever it was that prepared them for battle. They all knew this mission might get hairy. It was an audacious daylight thrust into the "Black Sea," the very heart of Habr Gidr territory in central Mogadishu and warlord Aidid's stronghold. Their target was a three-story house of whitewashed stone with a flat roof, a modern modular home in one of the city's few remaining clusters of intact large buildings, surrounded by blocks and blocks of tin-roofed dwellings of muddy stone. Hundreds of thousands of clan members lived in this labyrinth of irregular dirt streets and cactus-lined paths. There were no decent maps. Pure Indian country.

The men had watched the rockets being loaded on the AH-6s. Garrison hadn't done that on any of their earlier missions. It meant they were expecting trouble. The men had girded themselves with extra ammo, stuffing magazines and grenades into every available pocket and pouch of their load-bearing harnesses, leaving behind canteens, bayonets, night-vision goggles, and any other gear they felt would be deadweight on a fast daylight raid. The prospect of getting into a scrape didn't worry them. Not at all. They welcomed it. They were predators, heavy metal avengers, unstoppable, *invincible*. The feeling was, after six weeks of diddling around they were finally going in to kick some serious Somali ass.

It was 3:32 P.M. when the chalk leader inside the lead Black Hawk, *Super Six Four*, heard over the intercom the soft voice of the pilot, Chief Warrant Officer Mike Durant, clearly pleased.

Durant announced, "Fuckin' *Irene*."

And the armada launched, lifting off from the shabby airport by the sea into an embracing blue vista of sky and Indian Ocean. They eased out across a littered strip of white sand and moved low and fast over running breakers that formed faint crests parallel to the shore. In close formation they banked and flew down the coastline southwest. From each bird the booted legs of the eager soldiers dangled from the benches and open doors.

Unrolling toward a hazy desert horizon, Mogadishu in midafternoon sun was so bright it was as if the aperture on the world's lens was stuck one click wide. From a distance the ancient port city had an auburn hue, with its streets of ocher sand and its rooftops of Spanish tile and rusted tin. The only tall structures still standing after years of civil war were the ornate white towers of mosques—Islam being the only thing all Somalia held sacred. There were many scrub trees, the tallest just over the low rooftops, and between them high stone walls with pale traces of yellow and pink and gray, fading remnants of pre-civil war civility. Set there along the coast, framed to the west by desert and the east by gleaming teal ocean, it might have been some sleepy Mediterranean resort.

As the helicopter force swept in over it, gliding back in from the ocean and then banking right and sprinting northeast along the city's western edge, Mogadishu spread beneath them in its awful reality, a catastrophe, the world capital of things-gone-completely-to-hell. It was as if the city had been ravaged by some fatal urban disease. The few paved avenues were crumbling and littered with mountains of trash, debris, and the rusted hulks of burned-out vehicles. Those walls and buildings that had not been reduced to heaps of gray rubble were pockmarked with bullet scars. Telephone poles leaned at ominous angles like voodoo totems topped by stiff sprays of dreadlocks—the stubs of their severed wires (long since stripped for sale on the thriving black market). Public spaces displayed the hulking stone platforms that once held statuary from the heroic old days of dictator Mohamed Siad Barre, the national memory stripped bare not out of revolutionary fervor, but to sell the bronze and copper for scrap. The few proud old government and university buildings that still stood were inhabited now by refugees. Everything of value had been looted, right down to metal window frames, doorknobs, and hinges. At night, campfires glowed from third- and fourth-story windows of the old Polytechnic Institute. Every open space was clotted with the dense makeshift villages of the disinherited, round stick huts covered with layers of rags and shacks made of scavenged scraps of wood and patches of rusted tin. From above they looked like an advanced stage of some festering urban rot.

In his bird, *Super Six Seven*, Eversmann rehearsed the plan in his mind. By the time they reached the street, the D-boys would already be taking down the target house, rounding up Somali prisoners and shooting anyone foolish enough to fight back. Word was there were two big boys in this house, men whom the task force had identified as "Tier One Personalities," Aidid's top men. As the D-boys did their work and the Rangers kept the curious at bay, the ground convoy of trucks and Humvees would roll in through the city, right up to the target house. The prisoners would be herded into the trucks. The assault team and blocking force would jump in behind them and they would all drive back to finish out a nice Sunday afternoon on the beach. It would take about an hour.

To make room for the Rangers in the Black Hawks, the seats in back had been removed. The men who were not in the doorways were squatting on ammo cans or seated on the flak-proof Kevlar panels laid out on the floor. They all wore desert camouflage fatigues, with Kevlar vests and helmets and about fifty pounds of equipment and ammo strapped to their load-bearing harnesses, which fit on over the vests. All had goggles and thick leather gloves. Those layers of gear made even the slightest of them look bulky, robotic, and intimidating. Stripped down to their dirt-brown T-shirts and shorts, which is how they spent most of their time in the hangar, most looked like the pimply teenagers they were (average age nineteen). They were immensely proud of their Ranger status. It spared them most of the numbing noncombat-related routine that drove many an army enlistee nuts. The Rangers trained for war full-time. They were fitter, faster, and first—"Rangers lead the way!" was their motto. Each had volunteered at least three times to get where they were, for the army, for airborne, and for the Rangers. They were the cream, the most highly motivated young soldiers of their generation, selected to fit the army's ideal—they were all male and, revealingly, nearly all white (there were only two blacks among the 140-man company). Some were professional soldiers, like Lieutenant Larry Perino, a 1990 West Point graduate. Some were over-achievers in search of a different challenge, like Specialist John Waddell on Chalk Two, who had enlisted after finishing high school in Natchez, Mississippi, with a 4.0 GPA. Some were daredevils in search of a physical challenge. Others were self-improvers, young men who had found themselves adrift after high school, or in trouble with drugs, booze, the law, or all three. They were harder-edged than most young men of their generation who, on this Sunday in early autumn, were weeks into their fall college semester. Most of these Rangers had been kicked around some, had tasted failure. But there were no goof-offs. Every man had worked to be here, probably harder than he'd ever worked in his life. Those with troubled pasts had taken harsh measure of themselves. Beneath their best hard-ass act, most were achingly earnest, patriotic, and idealistic. They had literally taken the army up on its offer to "Be All You Can Be."

They held themselves to a higher standard than normal soldiers. With their buff bodies, distinct crew cuts—sides and back of the head completely shaved—and their grunted *Hoo-ah* greeting, they saw themselves as the army at its gung ho best. Many, if they could make it, aspired to join Special Forces, maybe even get picked to try out for Delta, the hale, secret supersoldiers now leading this force in. Only the very best of them would be invited to try out, and only one of every ten invited would make it through selection. In this ancient male hierarchy, the Rangers were a few steps up the ladder, but the D-boys owned the uppermost rung.

Rangers knew the surest path to that height was combat experience. So far, Mog had been mostly a tease. War was always about to happen. *About to happen.* Even the missions, exciting as they'd been, had fallen short. The Somalis—whom they called "Skinnies" or "Sammies"—had taken a few wild shots at them, enough to get the Rangers' blood up and unleash a hellish torrent of return fire, but nothing that qualified as a genuine balls-out firefight.

Which is what they wanted. All of these guys. If there were any hesitant thoughts, they were buttoned tight. A lot of these men had started as afraid of war as anyone, but the fear had been drummed out. Especially in Ranger training. About a fourth of those who volunteered washed out, enough so that those who emerged with their Ranger tab at the end were riding the headiest wave of accomplishment in their young lives. The weak had been weeded out. The strong had stepped up. Then came weeks, months, years of constant training. The *Hoo-ahs* couldn't wait to go to war. They were an all-star football team that had endured bruising, exhausting, dangerous practice sessions twelve hours a day, seven days a week—for *years*—without ever getting to play a game.

They yearned for battle. They passed around the dog-eared paperback memoirs of soldiers from past conflicts, many written by former Rangers, and savored the affectionate, comradely tone of their stories, feeling bad for the poor suckers who bought it or got crippled or maimed but identifying with the righteous men who survived the experience whole. They studied the old photos, which were the same from every war, young men looking dirty and tired, half dressed in army combat fatigues, dogtags hanging around their skinny necks, posing with arms draped over each other's shoulders in exotic lands. They could see themselves in those snapshots, surrounded by *their* buddies, fighting *their* war. It was THE test, the only one that counted.

Sergeant Mike Goodale had tried to explain this to his mother one time, on leave in Illinois. His mom was a nurse, incredulous at his bravado.

"Why would anybody *want* to go to war?" she asked.

Goodale told her it would be like, as a nurse, after all her training, never getting the chance to work in a hospital. It would be like that.

"You want to find out if you can really do the job," he explained.

Like those guys in books. They'd been tested and proven. It was another generation of Rangers' turn now. Their turn.

It didn't matter that none of the men in these helicopters knew enough to write a high school paper about Somalia. They took the army's line without hesitation. Warlords had so ravaged the nation battling among themselves that their people were starving to death. When the world sent food, the evil warlords hoarded it and killed those who tried to stop them. So the civilized world had decided to lower the hammer, invite the baddest boys on the planet over to clean things up. 'Nuff said. Little the Rangers had seen since arriving at the end of August had altered that perception. Mogadishu was like the postapocalyptic world of Mel Gibson's *Mad Max* movies, a world ruled by roving gangs of armed thugs. They were here to rout the worst of the warlords and restore sanity and civilization.

Eversmann had always just enjoyed being a Ranger. He wasn't sure how he felt about being in charge, even if it was just temporary. He'd won the distinction by default. His platoon sergeant had been summoned home by an illness in his family, and then the guy who replaced him had keeled over with an epileptic seizure. He, too, had been sent home. Eversmann was the senior man in line. He accepted the task hesitantly. That morning at Mass in the mess he'd prayed about it.

Airborne now at last, Eversmann swelled with energy and pride as he looked out over the full armada. It was a state-of-the-art military force. Already circling high above the target was the slickest intelligence support America had to offer, including satellites, a high-flying P3 Orion spy plane, and three OH-58 observation helicopters, which looked like the bubble-front Little Bird choppers with a five-foot bulbous polyp growing out of the top. The observation birds were equipped with video cameras and radio equipment that would relay the action live to General Garrison and the other senior officers in the Joint Operations Center (JOC) back at the beach. Moviemakers and popular authors might strain to imagine the peak capabilities of the U.S. military, but here was the real thing about to strike. It was a well-oiled, fully equipped, late-twentieth-century fighting machine. America's best were going to war, and Sergeant Matt Eversmann was among them.

★　★　★　★　★

During the attack on the target building, a Black Hawk was shot down by a rocket-propelled grenade. American forces came under heavy attack by Aidid's militia as they tried to evacuate the target area by convoy and secure the first crash site. A second helicopter piloted by Mike Durant was then shot down and overrun by the enemy. Two Delta Force snipers, Sgt. First Class Randy Shughart and Master Sgt. Gary Gordon, gave their lives trying to protect Durant after being inserted by helicopter before American forces could reach them. Each would receive the Medal of Honor. The Rangers and other units with them were trapped overnight in enemy-held territory until they evacuated with the help of the 10th Mountain Division, and Malaysian and Pakistani U.N. troops with armored vehicles. Mike Durant was captured but was later returned to American forces. In all, eighteen Americans were killed in action with another seventy-nine wounded. It is estimated that the Somalis suffered over a thousand casualties. Although the mission was ultimately a success, American forces left Somalia only days later. The U.N. abandoned the country in 1995. General Aidid declared himself president, but the world community did not recognize his government as legitimate. He died in August, 1996 from a wound he suffered while fighting other factions. His son, Hussein Mohamed Farrah, a naturalized American citizen, was chosen by his father's clan to become the new president.

Among Warriors in Iraq

MIKE TUCKER

Hemingway's dead-solid right about war—it's a street fight. War is a street fight, simply on another level. And the same rule applies: Put the other guy down so he stays down. If we lose the street fight in Iraq, all the glad-handing and politicking and money we've spent here won't amount to dust in the wind.

—Specialist Sylas Carter, U.S. Combat Infantryman, Mosul, Northern Iraq

Eight months after George W. Bush proclaimed major combat in Iraq over in 2003, author Mike Tucker found himself right in the thick of it—dirty, profane, violent, lethal, and daily major combat—with some of America's most highly trained and accomplished soldiers. Tucker's book, *Among Warriors in Iraq*, is a street-level view of the struggles of maintaining control in the anarchy that pervaded Iraq after Coalition forces declared victory. Tucker traveled with Special Forces groups in both Mosul and Fallujah, cities whose citizens were not convinced the war was over, and who were willing to do anything to ensure that the struggle would continue. Here is his frank and uncensored account, seen through the resilient eyes of the soldiers willing to pay the ultimate price for victory.

Mike Tucker is a Marine infantry veteran with a Special Operations background, and an author. He broke Burmese Army lines in 2002 with Karen guerrillas, and has investigated war crimes in Burma and northern Iraq. In 2003, he journeyed throughout Iraqi Kurdistan, interviewing Kurds from all walks of life. Later, he joined U.S. Army snipers, scouts, light infantry, paratroopers, and Special Forces commandos for nineteen weeks on raids and patrols in northern and western Iraq. He remained in Iraq for fourteen months.

The following selection from *Among Warriors in Iraq* details the mission American forces undertook to bring peace to that troubled land. The men and women he encountered were dedicated to the cause of securing a lasting peace for the Iraqi people.

★ ★ ★ ★ ★

War is a journey into the unknown, with death on your back and a woman on your mind. At war in Iraq on January 9, 2004, we rode to raid on Xenophon's trail, deep in southwest Asia. It was dawn and gray and cold in the western Iraqi desert just east of the Euphrates River. We were lead gun truck, on point for a ten-truck raiding party, a hawk's flight from the sands where Xenophon's Greek light infantrymen prevailed over Persian cavalry four centuries before Christ walked the earth.

I was with hard-core light infantry, 10th Mountain warriors with the spirit and heart and wit of the Karen guerrilla fighters I'd patrolled with behind Burmese Army lines in July 2002. I'd fought with the Karen on December 13, 1992, when we'd together raided a Burmese Army slave labor party near Shotoh Mountain, across the Salween River from northwestern Thailand. Ten years later, after five years of living in Thailand and an MA degree on the GI Bill, I was fortunate to link up with Karen National Liberation Army guerrilla fighters behind Burmese Army lines and patrol on long-range reconnaissance in Karen highlands. Like the Karen, the men of 10th Mountain Division in Fallujah were combat veterans, eyes hardened by sun and wind and rain and war. Xenophon the Athenian likely commanded a few like 10th Mountain in these sands.

We fire rifles and the Greeks threw spears, but victory still goes to the commander with the most guts and guile and the fighter with the most heart. These are men who have sharpened the tip of the spear and held point and, therefore, know a wee bit about winning a street fight, once they're in it. One such man was Sergeant Shawn Hall of Buffalo, New York.

Hall, a fire team leader from 1st Platoon, Attack Company 1-32, had talked at length about the guerrilla war in Iraq the night before with his comrades of 10th Mountain in a concrete bungalow crammed with olive-green cots and flickering lights and clips loaded with live rounds. Guitars screamed from Specialist Peter "Wildman" Marston's small portable stereo, rifles and machine guns hanging off the walls. Wildman hailed from the forests and fields shadowed by stone cliffs deep in New Hampshire.

The next morning, Wildman stood tall on the Ma Deuce, a .50-caliber machine gun mounted on a thick steel pole, gripping its triggers. Fallujah was far to our three o'clock as we rolled on desert trails, minarets and clusters of date palms and mud huts some three thousand meters northwest, easy. There were donkeys and sheep on the southern horizon, moving slowly in the brightening dawn. Wildman was at our twelve o'clock, to my immediate right. Hall sat on my left, the stock of his M.203 assault rifle/grenade launcher jammed in his right shoulder. He asked me to scan the desert from our nine to twelve. I raised my scopes.

After nineteen weeks of raids, patrols, and desert reconnaissance in Iraq, I flew in the darkness north for Mosul on Valentine's Day 2004. I prayed a Hail Mary as we took off in Sinatra's wee dark hours of the morning from Baghdad, all tactical lights off, a blacked-out plane on a black moonless night, and unstrapped my Kukri knife. I carried a Kukri in Fallujah. A Kukri is the fighting knife for the Ghurka light infantry of the British Army, a heavy-bladed knife; mine was a gift from an American warrior in Mosul. On four occasions in Iraq, I was handed a 9mm Beretta sidearm and told, "Do not hesitate to use it." I knew what would be the consequence of capture by the insurgents: beheading. No one ever gave me combatant status in Iraq, but no one ever told me not to carry my Kukri fighting knife, either. On several occasions, the Kukri proved crucial, in truth. Every combat commander I had the good fortune to see action with told me, "Stay close to my men, move when they move, never get in front of my men, and always tell us when you see enemy." I wanted to see the insurgency killed, not negotiated with, and I listened closely to the men I saw action with accordingly.

In the mid-morning of Valentine's Day, I thanked the lovely U.S. Army nurses at the Mosul airfield for their delicious coffee, linked up with Kurdish translators, and made my way back to Dahuk, an ancient Kurdish mountain town.

Dahuk was my base when I traveled throughout Iraqi Kurdistan, interviewing Kurds from all walks of life, from July 18 to September 25, 2003, before linking up with U.S. Army snipers, scouts, light infantrymen, paratroopers, and U.S. Army Special Forces commandos in Mosul and Fallujah. I am a former Marine infantryman, and despite my prior service on active duty in a special operations capable unit and my work as an author and war correspondent, 1st Marine Division Public Affairs Office had denied me embedded journalist status in November 2002 and again in March 2003. From Bangkok in April 2003, with my combat narrative *The Long Patrol* behind me, I reckoned that Bob Kerrey, former U.S. Senator and a

Congressional Medal of Honor recipient for his actions as a U.S. Navy SEAL in Vietnam, might be able to help me get into Iraq. He knew well of my long-range reconnaissance behind Burmese Army lines for *The Long Patrol*. I reckoned that he'd find me qualified for Iraq. Fortunately, I was right: Bob wrote me letters of introduction to the Kurdish leadership in late June 2003.

I had no quarrel with President Bush's decision to lead America and the Coalition to war. America, along with other Western powers, was responsible for keeping Saddam's regime in power for decades. I believed we were, therefore, entirely responsible for taking it down. Like Captain Mark Zawachewsky of 1st Battalion-505th Parachute Infantry Regiment, 82nd Airborne Division, an Afghan and Iraq veteran, I felt that America, more than other Western nations, "had a moral responsibility to end Saddam's regime."

As Zawachewsky said in Fallujah on February 4, 2004, "We supported this regime, we armed it, and we didn't end it in '91. When you kill a cobra, chop off its head. This is unfinished business. We make a huge mistake, backing dictatorships for short-term geopolitical strategy, without reflecting on the long-term consequences. We had a moral responsibility to end Saddam's regime. I didn't see a need for the United States to go hunting for reasons to take down Saddam. There is never a wrong reason to end a dictatorship, particularly one as brutal as Saddam's was. And Uday and Qusay will not take power."

A few weeks earlier, a brother U.S. Army officer, Captain Terrence Caliguire, echoed his comrade when he told me in Fallujah on January 16, "There's an old saying in the army: never choose the easy wrong over the hard right. It was the right call to make and it was a very tough call. But President Bush did the right thing. We are in a just and noble cause here, and we must end it right. We must not cut and run. We ended a brutal and vile dictatorship. And at least three hundred thousand mass graves in the deserts of Iraq cry for justice."

I entered northern Iraq on July 18, 2003. Among Kurdish guerrilla fighters and farmers and artists, I documented previously unreported war crimes, such as the Gizi massacre. When I linked up with the Screaming Eagles in northern Iraq, through the Kurds, I handed war crimes reports of the Gizi massacre and Soriya massacre to 101st Division headquarters on September 27, 2003, as well as to the unit I was attached to as an embedded writer, 3rd Battalion-502nd Infantry Regiment.

From Mosul, I rallied to the 82nd Airborne, 10th Mountain, and Big Red One in Fallujah. In Dahuk, on Valentine's Day 2004, I reunited with

Kurdish military intelligence and peshmerga commanders, laid down my Kukri knife and war gear, and dusted off my books. The Kurds embraced me, slapping me on the back and offering tea and cigarettes all afternoon, and asked loads of questions about Mosul and the Saddam loyalist Sheikh Gazi Al Bowisa, the terrorist Zarqawi, and Al Quaeda in Fallujah. We ate hot, fresh bread and beef kebab and drank steaming, dark, sweet Ceylon tea. Dinner over, more smokes were passed around and more tea was served.

After farewells were made and the stars rose high in the western sky, I walked up a mountain trail in the clear cold night and watched Dahuk erupt in a sea of lights bordering the high rocky mountains to the north.

On the southern reaches of Dahuk, the ruins of the Kurdish village of Nazarkhay lie south of a former Ba'athist prison, stones piled and scattered amidst high wild grass in a wide valley. Nazarkhay was destroyed by Ba'athist secret police and Iraqi Army troops in the reign of terror Saddam unleashed against the Kurds in 1987 and 1988, Al Anfal. The ruins lay east of my quarters on the KDP peshmerga base. Training for reconnaissance, raids, and patrols with Coalition forces in the late summer of 2003, farmers and shepherds would wave to me and shout Kurdish greetings, and I'd wave back and run on past the mounds of stones in the yellow-green grasses and golden fields of wheat.

Hall scoped the desert south of Fallujah, dust boiling up behind us as our raiding party slowed over massive ruts in the hard-packed sand, and spoke in a hard, low-toned voice, never losing his fields of fire, eyes on the desert south of us.

"Guerrilla warriors win guerrilla wars. And we are guerrilla warriors, Mr. Tucker, we damn sure are. But to win this war, we've gotta' fight as guerrilla warriors. The more we raid and patrol and seize the initiative, the closer we'll come to winning this war. Closer to Fallujah, keep your scopes up. Scope the mosques. Heads-up on mosques for snipers."

"Roger that," I said, and Hall nodded, shouldering his M.203. The truck jolted, breaking left slightly. Wildman, a distinguished scholar of hard rock like many of his comrades in 1st Platoon, Attack Company, shifted the barrel southwest as he gazed out over the far rock-strewn sands and scattered date palms.

We were deep in desert that had seen Persian lances answered by Greek spears and swords in that long ago, east of the wide brown waters of the Euphrates and west of the Tigris River's dark blue-green currents winding through the heart of ancient Mesopotamia. It was a bright, cold winter morning, and we rode on rutted and bumpy desert jeep trails, sea-gulls and ospreys and starlings swooping over us and gliding west toward the Euphrates.

The sun was behind us. The wind lashed at the American raiders in the back of the truck who were clad in desert camouflage fatigues, Kevlar helmets latched on their heads, flak jackets wrapped around their torsos.

Wildman, a big, barrel-chested man, swung the machine gun back to twelve o'clock, bending his knees as the truck lurched and rocked over the desert trail west. "Goddamn it's cold!" he yelled, and we laughed, grinning, dust drifting up behind us. High above us, flocks of seagulls headed for the Euphrates.

As he scanned the sandy, rolling slopes south of us, Hall kept his eyes on his fields of fire. A shepherd waved to us from perhaps two hundred meters south. I waved back as we rolled on. And Wildman leaned back and lifted his head and hollered, "Judas Priest! AC/DC! Metallica! Old School Warriors rock!"

Sergeant First Class Steve Huber from Hawaii, a career soldier, laughed and said in his gravelly, exuberant voice, "Old school heavy metal, Mr. Tucker, ancient warrior style, climb to glory! This is 10th Mountain. You're riding with Attack Company, 1st Platoon. Lieutenant Chesty and the Old School Warriors. Slay the fuckin' dragon, baby! Eighteen summers in the army, I've got now. My nineteenth will be in Iraq. Fuckin'-a guerrilla fighters!"

There were brave men at war in Iraq, brave and witty and kind and generous, and I was blessed to be among them. If I had ten thousand words, I could not do justice to their honor, commitment, and courage. Crossing the desert on that bitter cold January dawn near Fallujah were Marston and Huber and Hall. They kept eyes on the sands and far palm-shaded fields, clips jacked in, weapons locked and loaded. And they cursed the wind and the cold and Al Quaeda as they scanned the desert that stretched west to the Euphrates.

Dust clouded the trucks behind us. Hall winced, the cold winter wind burning his face. Huber, the tough, big-hearted platoon sergeant from Hawaii, shouted, "Beware the devil, because that bastard is in Fallujah. Death to Al Quaeda!"

And the Wildman laughed and hollered into the brightening Iraqi skies, "Goddamn Al Quaeda to hell, and all Bin Laden's motherfuckers!" In turn Hall screamed, "Hell yes Wildman!" and we hailed the Wildman's exhortations. Our truck rocked on over the rugged trail. Huber shouldered his rifle, eyeing the desert.

Wildman stood fast on the Ma Deuce, steady, .50-caliber linked bullets falling from the machine gun into an ammo can in the bed of the truck, the linked live rounds swaying as we rode to raid, wind ripping down cold on us from out of the north.

Minarets of distant mosques in Fallujah loomed up on the western horizon like lighthouses on a far shore. I scoped the minarets for snipers and saw birds circling the tan stone towers. Hall nodded and kept his eyes on the desert south of us.

I left Fallujah on February 6, 2004, swooped to Coalition Provisional Authority in Baghdad, and a few days later, had the good fortune to interview Lieutenant General Ricardo Sanchez, commanding general of the Coalition Joint Task Force-7.

A cheerful, down-to-earth Texan, Sanchez has thick black hair, piercing coal-black eyes, and is built solid like a middleweight prizefighter. When he listens to you, he leans forward slightly, giving you his full attention. An amiable, good-hearted gentleman, I'd first met him on a January 21, 2004, raid in Fallujah led by First Lieutenant Chad Jenkins of Dublin, Ohio, and Sergeant First Class Vernon Pollard of Hobbs, New Mexico, and our comrades in 10th Mountain. I nicknamed the general "Sun Tzu," after the legendary Chinese general, poet, and author of *Art of War*. Like Sun Tzu, Sanchez never hesitated to unleash lightning raids on his enemies.

We were now ten months beyond President Bush's May 1, 2003, declaration that "major combat" had ended in Iraq. Having seen combat throughout Iraq, knowing that there is no such thing as a small firefight, and knowing that Al Quaeda had succeeded in linking up with Iraqi insurgents in western Iraq, I knew that our men and women were still very much at war in Iraq.

All combat is major. Kurdish Democratic Party Military Intelligence had warned me, before I left Dahuk in late September 2003, that their intelligence network throughout Iraq was reporting greatly increased contacts between former Ba'athist intelligence, military, and political leaders in Iraq—contacts to Al Quaeda in western Iraq and to Iraqi insurgents in western and northern Iraq. Western Iraq, of course, was never cleared, held, and secured in the initial March to April 2003 actions of the Iraq War.

One ancient law of war is you must never relinquish the initiative, once seized. Yet President Bush had violated that ancient law of war in Iraq, refusing to order the Coalition to strike and kill all former elements of the Iraqi Army and Saddam's regime. Still, I remember thinking as I waited to talk with Sanchez, the men I'd seen action with in Iraq were damned glad to have ended Saddam's regime.

Sanchez greeted me in Baghdad on Lincoln's birthday, February 12, 2004, and we shook hands. I set my coffee down and fished out my notebook from a bellows pocket. He leaned back on a black leather couch, a black leather shoulder holster rigged over his desert fatigues, M-9 Beretta 9mm sidearm holstered, clip jacked in, and four clips set in leather pouches on his rig.

"Lieutenant General Sanchez," I said, "Private First Class Steve Newport from Idaho, a combat infantryman from the 101st, said the following on November 1, 2003, in Mosul: 'When my grandchildren ask me what I did in the great war to defeat Saddam, I'll tell them that I was there, with my brothers, on the front lines. And we slept in bomb factories. And we fought in the sand and wind and rain. And we freed Iraq from a brutal dictatorship. When we talk to Iraqis on the street, on patrol—really, Americans have no idea how vicious Saddam was, how brutal he was. I know why I'm here. I know why we came. And we will see it through, to the end. We must win this war.'

"Sir, I heard similar remarks from many of our warriors in Iraq. What are your own thoughts, on PFC Newport's reflections on the war in Iraq?"

"I'm proud to lead men like PFC Newport," he said without hesitation, sitting bolt upright now, his face hard. "To know that our soldiers are inspired to carry on, to fight the fight, and believe in our cause here. Saddam was a very brutal dictator, as PFC Newport says. And Saddam is not coming back. Ba'athism is not coming back. The message I've been giving the troops is that this war has been a noble endeavor. Truly, a magnificent endeavor. The fact that a dictatorship in Iraq is gone is a great thing. We broke the chains. We liberated Iraq. Saddam's Ba'athist dictatorship had suppressed Iraqis for thirty-five years. Horrifying oppression. Saddam used weapons of mass destruction against his own people," he said, squinting.

"And it's an honor to lead young warriors like PFC Newport," Sanchez continued, speaking very softly now, eyes blazing. "Everything he said is right on the mark—our soldiers and all our servicemen and women have sacrificed greatly in this war. They slugged it out, just as he says, 'in the sand and wind and rain.' Valiant, determined warriors. They are the future of our nation's army, and they are the backbone of our country."

"Roger that," I said, and he nodded. I sipped from my coffee and he drank from a liter bottle of water. He set the bottle down and leaned back, spreading one arm over the back of the couch.

"General, Captain Caliguire—"

"Didn't he get a nickname?" Sanchez broke in, grinning merrily now, his black eyebrows raised.

"Hell yes! Vegas, sir. You must never sit down at a card table with Vegas. His favorite saying is, 'If I were a gambling man, and I am!' A great combat commander from Task Force 1Panther in Fallujah. Captain Caliguire said the toughest thing he has had to do in Iraq is talk to his men about carrying on after the loss of Staff Sergeant Paul J. Johnson, a very-well-respected paratrooper and solid NCO. Staff Sergeant Johnson was from Calumet, Michigan, sir. Captain Caliguire talked about the burden of command. One thing the captain said that has stayed with me is, 'Staff Sergeant Johnson would've wanted us to carry on and crush the insurgents.' You've had to deal with that same reality of war, of losing good men and women in Iraq," and Sanchez looked down, squinting some more. After a spell he glanced up quickly.

"When all the parades are over, it is inevitable that you'll lose a soldier," he said softly, and his voice was deeper now. He shook his head slowly, wincing. There was no weariness about him, just the gritty toughness of a soldier who has spent his life serving America in war and peace and has seen his comrades fall. A reflective look came over him, his eyes bright. I was reminded of General Douglas MacArthur's warrior creed: "Duty. Honor. Country." The general sat back in Baghdad and folded his arms.

"War is a rough trade, and it's hard to carry on sometimes," he said softly. "Our fighting men and women, who are putting it on the line night and day, both here and in Afghanistan and in so many other battlefields right now, must know that if they die in this war, it is because of a struggle that was worthy, not because of a failure of leadership. The question I ask myself as a commander, as a leader, is 'Am I leading men and women into battle because of a struggle that is worthy?' If we as leaders cannot answer that question, then we have a tremendous burden to bear. We must be able to answer that question with a just answer, we must go into combat for a struggle that is worthy. I have no doubt our cause is just here and this struggle is a worthy one," Sanchez said, eyes intense. "Did you see *Saving Private Ryan?*" he asked quickly.

I told the general that I'd seen that movie, directed by Steven Spielberg—perhaps the best film on men and war, and certainly one of the most moving. Mr. Spielberg's father had fought in Burma in WWII, and there is a strong, deep spirit of homage in the film for American warriors of his father's generation.

"And you recall the scene in the church?" Sanchez asked.

"The Ranger captain talks about losing his men and dealing with their deaths. Tom Hanks played the captain," I said, and he nodded, lines deep in his forehead.

"Exactly. Speilberg really got it right, there. Speilberg saw right to the heart of it. It's a powerful scene and it is very real, strikes a chord with anyone who has ever led men in combat. Spielberg really gets to the heart of the burden of command. It never leaves you. It's something you live with, something you wrestle with, something you accept. That scene is far more eloquent than anything I could say—really. It's very moving, profoundly moving. This is a worthy endeavor in Iraq and no matter what price we pay, it is worth the price to defeat tyranny and terrorism in Iraq. Every single soldier I've met in Iraq—I've never heard a complaint about fighting this war. Every soldier I've met who has been wounded, the first thing they say to me is 'Sir, how do I get back to my buddies?' That is a testament to their fighting spirit and their faith in their comrades," he said, leaning forward slightly.

"America has kind of lost touch with our military, due to the all-volunteer army, navy, and air force. The Marines, of course, have always been an all-volunteer force, with the exception of a few years during the Vietnam War. There's a gap there, between our military and our society. What the American people must know is that American sons and daughters are making a huge difference in Iraq. They are making history, and I am proud to have the privilege of commanding them. It is an extraordinary honor."

★   ★   ★   ★   ★

On January 30, 2006 the Iraqis held a very successful nationwide election—a solid milestone on their road to true independence and recovery. Mike Tucker went on to cover the war in Afghanistan, embedded with paratroopers and Special Forces.